THE LIFE AND
LETTERS OF
KENNETH ESCOTT KIRK
Bishop of Oxford 1937-1954

By the same author

AN INTRODUCTION TO CANON LAW IN THE CHURCH OF ENGLAND. Being the Lichfield Cathedral Divinity Lectures for 1956. (H. & S.)

CANONIZATION AND AUTHORITY IN THE WESTERN CHURCH. (O.U.P.)

N. P. WILLIAMS. (S.P.C.K.)

With W. Holtzmann: PAPAL DECRETALS RELATING TO THE DIOCESE OF LINCOLN IN THE TWELFTH CENTURY. (Lincoln Record Society)

Editor: BEAUTY AND BANDS by K. E. Kirk. (H. & S.)

THE LIFE AND
LETTERS OF
KENNETH ESCOTT KIRK

Bishop of Oxford 1937-1954

by

Eric Waldram Kemp

Fellow and Chaplain of Exeter College, Oxford,
Canon and Prebendary of Caistor in Lincoln Cathedral

LONDON
HODDER AND STOUGHTON

Printed in Great Britain for
Hodder and Stoughton Limited by
The Camelot Press Limited
London and Southampton

CONTENTS

CONTENTS

INTRODUCTION

THERE are those who hold that no biography should be written until at least fifty years after the death of the subject, and the present author, having now written two modern biographies, has much sympathy with that point of view. No biography of a person who has recently died can have the historical objectivity of a later work, nor can it tell the full story about some controversial matters. All the evidence will not be available and there are personal feelings to be considered. On the other hand it is important that as much evidence as possible should be gathered while memories are fresh and there are still alive those who were involved in the events to be described. The present biography is, therefore, a collection of evidence drawn from such sources and from documents which Dr. Kirk left behind at his home and in the diocesan archives which have been examined by the kind permission of his successor. It should be emphasized that very little of the Bishop's personal writing has survived—very few personal letters, and that one or two people who perhaps knew him better than anyone else pre-deceased him. The task of revealing the inner man has therefore been difficult and only patient of limited success. The biographer's personal knowledge of his subject consists of having as an undergraduate served on the Committee of the Oxford University Church Union under Dr. Kirk's chairmanship, of having attended his lectures, of later having served him as Secretary of the Diocesan Ordination Candidates Fund and as Commissary for Religious Communities, and for the last year of the Bishop's life having been his son-in-law. Throughout the book the attempt has been made to present affairs and problems as Dr. Kirk saw them. No doubt, in places, this has resulted in a partial and one-sided account which the biographies of other churchmen yet to be written will correct. It is hoped that this book may be accepted as a fair and balanced portrait of a great theologian and pastoral bishop, but it should also be regarded as a provisional contribution to that impartial history of the Church of England in the first half of the twentieth century which no doubt will be written some two or three generations hence.

It remains to express thanks to those who have helped in the preparation of this book. The number is too large for all to receive individual mention. Among some who are no longer alive Bishops G. K. A. Bell and G. B. Allen, F. P. Harton, Dean of Wells, and Mr. S. H. Wood gave help of special value. Among the living thanks are due to the Bishops of Exeter, Oxford, Buckingham, and Reading, Bishops Rawlinson and Parham, the Abbot of Nashdom, the Very Rev. H. W. Blackburne, the Rev. Dr. P. T. B. Clayton, the Principals of Cuddesdon and St. Stephen's House, the Rev. Dr. S. C. Carpenter, Canon J. McLeod Campbell, the Rev. F. B. Girling, the Rev. O. Oberlin-Harris, the officers of the Student Christian Movement. The Rev. A. Clementson and his sisters, Lt.-Col. I. Leslie-Melville, Dr. J. R. H. Weaver, Captain J. H. Wood, Mr. R. C. Freeman, Sir Offley Wakeman, Sir Robert Martin, Mr. L. W. Henry, Mr. Leonard Cutts, the Misses Stratton and many others who have contributed reminiscences or answered questions. It would, of course, have been quite impossible to write this book at all without the constant help of Dr. Kirk's family, his children, his sister and her husband, and Miss Carter, now Mrs. Roberts.

I have to thank the Church Union and the Society of SS. Peter and Paul for permission to quote from the Reports of the Anglo-Catholic Congresses; the S.P.C.K. for quotations from *Essays Catholic and Critical*, and *The Coherence of Christian Doctrine*; the S.C.M. Press for quotations from *A Study of Silent Minds* and the *Story of the Student Christian Movement*; the Oxford University Press for quotations from *The Menace to Faith*; Messrs. Longmans, Green and Co. Ltd., for quotations from *Some Principles of Moral Theology, Conscience and its Problems*, and *The Vision of God*; Messrs. Macmillan for quotations from *The Church in the Furnace* and *The Official History of the Great War*; Messrs. Herbert Jenkins for a quotation from *The New Church in the New Age*.

Special thanks are due to the Rev. Francis Frost of the Séminaire des Facultés Catholiques in the University of Lille who has been working for some time on a study of Dr. Kirk's Moral Theology and who has placed his extensive bibliography at the disposal of the present writer.

I

THE BEGINNING

KENNETH ESCOTT KIRK was born at 8.15 a.m. on Sunday
February 21st, 1886, at 77 Watson Road, Broomhill, Sheffield.
He was baptized on March 17th at the Wesley Chapel, Fulwood
Road, Sheffield. On his father's side he was the grandson of the Rev.
John Kirk who was well-known in Nonconformist circles in the middle
of the last century as a preacher and writer. John Kirk had started life
as a Lincolnshire farm-labourer but had given such evidence of ability
of mind that the Wesleyans took him up and provided for an education which led eventually to the Methodist ministry. John Kirk
married Eliza Eastwood of Paull, but she died while most of her five or
six children were still young. He married again, a Miss Osborn, a
member of the prominent Sheffield family of steel manufacturers who
owned the Clyde Steel Works and traded under the name of Samuel
Osborn and Co. John Kirk himself died in 1875 leaving her with the
family of stepchildren to care for, of whom Kathleen and Frank Herbert were the youngest. Kathleen changed from the family Methodism
to join the Church of England in 1886, being prepared for confirmation by the celebrated Fr. Ommaney of St. Matthew's, Sheffield.
A few years later she felt a call to the Religious Life and in the
early nineties became a member of the Community of St. Peter at
Horbury.

Frank Kirk was born in 1856 and was educated at the Wesley
College, Sheffield. He had the reputation of being a promising
classic, but his father's death in 1875 dashed all hope of being able to
go to a university. His stepmother's family accepted responsibility
and put him into a bank. Later he joined the Clyde Steel Works as
a junior clerk and eventually rose to be secretary and director of
the company. He was an unusual man. To his business ability he
joined strong literary and dramatic interests. An obituary notice of
him says:

Though Mr. Kirk had many friends, comparatively few people were aware
of his enthusiasm for art, especially the literary branch. His love of the beautiful
was a very little known side of his character, but he had the literary passion,
and had he chosen to follow his bent seriously he might have emerged as a

writer of some distinction. Poems, unpublished, and rarely seen, and prose essays which had never seen the inside of a printer's shop were the products of a well-instructed mind, and they had the quiet piquancy which was bestowed by a lively sympathy and the talent of facile expression. Mr. Kirk read deeply and he was also a student of the drama.

Under his direction the family and some friends formed a small troupe of actors who gave performances for various charitable causes. He was an expert conjuror and delighted in the entertainment of his children and their friends. Kenneth inherited many of his father's qualities— a capacity for business, a quiet sense of humour, a love of literature and of the drama. He could also on occasion turn out an amusing specimen of light verse.

Frank Kirk married Miss Edith Escott, a member of an old farming family of Parracombe, Devon, among whom was the original of John Ridd in *Lorna Doone*. She and her sister Annie were two of the early generation of secondary school mistresses. Annie Escott, who never married, became a headmistress under the Council of the Girls' Public Day School Trust and in 1915 was elected President of the Incorporated Association of Headmistresses. Edith Escott shared her sister's interests and abilities but abandoned her career when she married. She did not feel herself sufficiently well qualified to return to school teaching after her children had grown up, and it is doubtful whether her health would have allowed it. Although she lived to be eighty-seven she was not physically strong but she maintained her intellectual interests to the end and spent her last years in Kenneth's household. She had two other children after Kenneth—a girl, Marjorie, born in 1888, and another boy, Leslie, born in 1890. It was Mrs. Kirk, with the help of her sister, who largely shaped the educational policy for all three children.

The connexion with the Clyde Steel Works did not mean that the family was well off. Indeed their circumstances were very narrow. Frank Kirk was a junior clerk at the time of his marriage and even as a director had only a small salary, not more than about £600 a year at most. All three children earned their education by winning scholarships and there was little to spare, but both parents were determined that all three of their children should have the best possible education, and in the event all three did go to Oxford. Kenneth, like the others, had to carve his own way and this affected both his intense scholarly ambition and his business sense. It did not in the least make him bitter or resentful, though it did make him thrifty to an almost exaggerated degree. He saw to it that his own children were brought up to be as careful of expense as he had had to be, and he was widely recognized as a business man of the highest competence.

The Kirk household was a very happy one, full of life, amusement and intellectual interests of all kinds, and with a firm basis of puritan piety. Among their friends were the children of the vicar of the neighbouring Anglican Church, the Rev. C. Clementson, and from an early stage in Kenneth's life there was a gradual move from Methodism to the Church of England. As we have seen Mr. Kirk's younger sister, Kathleen, had made the change in the year of Kenneth's birth. Mr. Kirk, himself, was greatly attracted by the liturgy of the Church of England and began to make a study of the Prayer Book. He did not, however, sever himself completely from Methodism and as late as 1905 he is found preaching to a Methodist afternoon Bible class. Eleven years later, at the time of his death, a Sheffield newspaper described him as "an adherent of the Conservative Party and a Churchman".

Kenneth appears to have been confirmed during Lent, 1899. At least he made his first Communion on Easter Day in that year. His brother and sister were both confirmed in 1905. The church which they originally attended, St. Thomas's, Crookes, was in the gift of alternate patrons, and when their friend Mr. Clementson left, a Low Church Patronage Trust appointed a vicar who made alterations in the services and furnishings of the church in a Low Church direction which the Kirks disliked and so they began to attend another church of a more congenial type.

He entered the Preparatory Department of Sheffield Royal Grammar School in September, 1894, and two years later won one of the Governors' open scholarships. His scholastic progress was such that in 1903 he was sent up to Oxford to try for scholarships at the University, and came away with a £60 Open Classical Exhibition at St. John's. Shortly afterwards he won the Sheffield Town Trust Scholarship and also became the first Sheffield boy on record to win the Akroyd Scholarship, described as 'the "blue Ribbon" of Yorkshire school competitions'.

Kenneth's ideas about his future were at this time very different from what they later became. He inherited to the full his father's love of literature and the drama, and he took a leading part in the production of plays not only in the family circle but also at school. He was a good actor and had a beautiful speaking voice. On the occasion of a visit to Sheffield by Mr. Frank Benson's touring company Kenneth sought an interview with Benson and expressed his determination to make the stage his career. Benson, however, told him to follow his own example and go to a University first. And so, in October, 1904 Kenneth Kirk went up to St. John's College, Oxford.

He held a Classical Exhibition and it was classics that he decided to read. In 1906 he took a First in Honour Classical Moderations and in the same year his College elected him a Casberd Scholar. Two years later he took a First in Greats. This last success was preceded by some hours of bitter anxiety. *The Morning Post* published on 28th July, 1908, an Oxford Greats Class List which had been sent to it on paper bearing the University Seal (*sic*) but which turned out to be completely bogus. In this list Kenneth was placed in the Fourth Class. He was away from home at the time and his family were much upset until he arrived with a telegram informing him that he had in fact been given a First.

At Oxford Kenneth entered into a variety of non-academic activities. He had since his seventeenth birthday been a member of the Engineer Volunteers and now he joined the University Rifles in which he reached the rank of sergeant. He was also an active member of his College Boat Club. In his Mods. Term he rowed in the Second Torpid and the following year in the First when the boat made six bumps each in under two minutes, and established a record. An entry in his father's diary for May, 1906, conjures up a picture familiar only in part to present day Oxford:

> Father, Mother and Auntie Bessie to Oxford for the Eights. They lodge with Mrs. Hoare in Little Clarendon Street; punting; watching the Races; Volunteer Reception and illuminated Promenade Concert in the Examination Schools, etc.

Outside his work for Schools the greatest influence on Kenneth's development during his time at Oxford seems to have been exercised by the Student Christian Movement. His connexion with it must have been formed within his first year at the University as he attended the Student Movement camp at Conishead in July, 1905. Readers who are familiar with the present state of religious societies at Oxford may need to be reminded that in those days there was the closest relationship between the Student Christian Movement and the Oxford Intercollegiate Christian Union (the O.I.C.C.U.). The beginnings of trouble which later led to separation were, however, already apparent. The prevailing intellectual atmosphere at Oxford, at least in the Greats School, was very secular in tone, and many young people of Christian upbringing had to struggle hard to keep their faith. They were helped by a number of men who, following the example of Charles Gore, were trying to bridge the gap between traditional Christian teaching and modern philosophy and criticism of the scriptures. It was over the question of Biblical criticism and its effect on certain doctrines, particularly the doctrine of the Atonement, that the split in University religious societies was eventually to come. The full story may be read in Dr. Tissington Tatlow's history of the Student Christian Movement.

Kenneth belonged to the O.I.C.C.U. and was active in persuading fellow undergraduates to go to the sermons which it arranged on Sunday evenings. He was not, however, associated with the narrower outlook of some of its members. A contemporary writes:

In 1905 the O.I.C.C.U. was in a relationship almost of rivalry with another society, the Oxford University Church Union (O.U.C.U.) which stood for definite Anglican churchmanship. The principal activity of the O.U.C.U. was to organise evening sermons at the University Church, St. Mary's, for undergraduates after Hall. Many of the greatest preachers of the Church of England were heard in these sermons. Every endeavour was made by senior religious leaders in the university to damp down any ill feeling or misplaced competition between the O.I.C.C.U. and the O.U.C.U. Many undergraduates belonged to both societies. As far as I remember Kirk belonged to both, and I clearly remember his telling me with manifest enthusiasm how in 1905 Father P. N. Waggett was the advertised preacher at the O.U.C.U.'s sermon on a particular Sunday when Dr. John R. Mott of the Student Christian Movement was holding a Mission arranged by the O.I.C.C.U. in the University Schools; and how Waggett ascended the pulpit and dismissed his hearers saying "I am not going to preach a sermon this evening because I want you all to go down the High to the Schools where you will hear a great servant of Christ, Dr. John Mott, proclaim the Gospel."

The same writer refers to the influence of Neville Talbot who was at the end of his undergraduate career and who "prevailed on a considerable number of younger dons and other clergy of the 'Catholic' school of Anglicanism to visit the Student Movement and see for themselves that it was possible to join with non-episcopalians in worship, prayer, and above all, in enthusiasm for foreign missions and 'Christian socialism', without in any way compromising their Catholic allegiance."

In his own College Kenneth belonged to an S.C.M. study group consisting of six or seven undergraduates who worked through the Epistle to the Ephesians. He was the youngest of the group, and another member of it has a vivid recollection of him sitting somewhat apart on a pouffe and being told by the others to shut up because of the questions he was raising about various points of doctrine, particularly the doctrine of Original Sin. Another study group to which he belonged was one started by E. J. Palmer of Balliol to study the lives of great missionaries. In this he met, besides Palmer himself, William Paton, J. McLeod Campbell and Colin Sharp who was later to be his brother-in-law. From 1905 onwards he was a regular attender at the Student Movement summer camps at Conishead and at Baslow.

A friend writes of him at this period:

When he came to Oxford he was evidently a confirmed member of the Church of England and he steadily moved in the direction of a firmly-based and intellectually established adherence to the historic and Catholic position of the Anglican Church. I think he was greatly influenced by an M.A. of St. John's named Heath who was somewhat of a mystery to the undergraduates. He was an older man, a coach or a professional man of some kind living in Oxford. Although not a member of the Senior Common Room he was frequently in college and regularly attended Holy Communion in the Chapel. He was a keen member of the University Volunteers, and under his influence Kenneth also became an active member of that military formation. Kenneth was a frequent communicant and attender at the voluntary services in the College Chapel as well as at the statutory services of matins which in those days were compulsory on a few mornings in each week. Kenneth's ecclesiastical position must have become increasingly 'High', I think, in those days. His Catholicism was a matter of conviction based on sound learning. He had a deep quiet sense of humour which made him gently (not scornfully) contemptuous of hasty and flamboyant opinions or utterances. He was, I think, a strong Liberal in politics.

It was probably in the summer of 1905, that Kenneth made his decision to take orders. He went to stay with the Clementsons who were now living at Bexhill. The Miss Clementsons remember him coming back from a long talk with Archdeacon Churton and saying that he had made up his mind to be ordained. Mention has been made of the prevailingly secular atmosphere in the Greats School at that time. The extent to which Kenneth was influenced by it is obscure. Certainly one of his undergraduate contemporaries regarded him as being dangerously 'liberal' or modernist, but his sister and brother-in-law emphasize rather that any serious and intellectually minded Christian had to face a radical re-examination of his premises and that Kenneth was no exception. Outstanding leaders of thought in Oxford, including some who were professing Christians, regarded theology as irrelevant to philosophy and secular learning, and spread their views powerfully at that time. Many years later Kenneth told the present writer that he had at one stage, no doubt while reading Greats, been worried about Christian belief and that he had found help in reading Newman's *Grammar of Assent*. The reader of Kenneth's *Some Principles of Moral Theology* will perhaps remember how prominent Newman's argument is in certain passages of that book. The same conversation also suggested that he might have been helped by Pascal. It is clear that in his own mind Kenneth reached a satisfactory solution of the conflict between traditional Christian belief and the new philosophical and critical studies. It was on the lines later to be known as Liberal Catholicism. The Bishop of Derby, Dr. Rawlinson, whose acquaintance with Kenneth dated from 1910, recalls that he was at that time what would be described as a 'practising Catholic' and was also a fairly radical New Testament critic.

The position which Kenneth eventually reached was a definitely theological one. He was always somewhat critical of the kind of attempted reconciliation of philosophy and theology pursued for example by William Temple, as his book *The Crisis of Christian Rationalism* (1936) shows. When he came to concentrate on the study of morals he took as his starting point a firm dogmatic basis, by contrast with the rationalist and philosophical studies which have been more usual in Anglican circles since the eighteenth century and which are essentially apologetic in their tone. While Kenneth would not have depreciated the importance of apologetic he seems to have been firmly convinced that argument alone would never make a man a Christian and that equal attention needed to be paid to the provision of guidance in the practical Christian life. Although this conviction was clearly deepened by his later experiences in London and as an Army chaplain there can be little doubt that it was formed in his undergraduate days.

After taking his degree in Greats Kenneth went on to the specialized study of theology. He was awarded a Liddon Theological Studentship and returned to Oxford for the Michaelmas Term, 1908. He tried unsuccessfully for a St. John's Fellowship by examination in September of that year, and a little later he was a candidate for the Chaplain-Fellowship at Exeter. Mr. C. T. Atkinson, who was a Fellow at the time, remembers that the Governing Body would have liked to elect him, but were anxious to have someone nearer to ordination to the priesthood, and so chose N. P. Williams, then a Prize Fellow of Magdalen, who was many years later to be Kenneth's colleague in the Chapter of Christ Church. Kenneth was back in Oxford for the Hilary

Term, 1909, and no doubt would have gone on either to take the Honour School of Theology or the B.D. had he not in March received an invitation to work for the Student Christian Movement in London. He was not to return to Oxford until ten years of varied and sometimes strange experience had passed.

II

THE STUDENT CHRISTIAN MOVEMENT

I

IN the early years of this century the presence in English Universities and Colleges and at the Inns of Court of considerable numbers of foreign students, particularly from India, began to attract the attention of those responsible for Christian work. In September, 1908, the Student Movement appointed a sub-committee to consider what it should do in this matter, and to encourage and unify work already begun among foreign students in the provincial towns. In London the London Intercollegiate Christian Union (L.I.C.C.U.), which was affiliated to the Student Movement, was preparing to appoint a Foreign Students Secretary who should be able to devote most of his time to this work. Early in 1909 Kenneth Kirk was invited to be the first holder of this post and he seems to have decided that the work was of sufficient importance to justify a break in his study of theology, at least for a period. He began his duties in April.

About the same time another branch of the Student Movement, the Student Missionary Volunteer Union (S.M.V.U.), appointed a committee under the chairmanship of J. McLeod Campbell to give attention to work among foreign students, and Kirk, who was a member of the committee, was asked to make a survey of the foreign student situation in the British Isles. This revealed the presence of about 1500 Oriental students in Great Britain. Dr. Tissington Tatlow writes:

The survey made by Kenneth Kirk was the basis of advice which the S.M.V.U.'s sub-committee embodied in a memorandum signed on its behalf by Campbell and Kirk; this guided the main lines of the policy of the Movement until the war brought new problems. The memorandum collected together information as to all the different kinds of work being done. It also stated clearly the objective of the Movement.

Our object may be stated as twofold: first of all, to win the friendship of Oriental students in our colleges; and secondly, to bring them in the end to the knowledge of Christ. We wish to make it clear that the first of these must be attained before we can hope to reach the second: but that we shall never be successful in either unless we keep definitely before ourselves the ideal of winning these our brothers for Christ.

Much stress was laid upon the indirect influence on the Oriental of the lives of those around him in relation to winning him. Personal friendship, the work of the Christian Unions and special Bible circles for Orientals were advocated. And the suggestion was made that where a Christian Union felt strong enough it should attempt to find good lodgings for Oriental students.[1]

The same writer also says: "The general work in London included meeting students at the docks on arrival, finding suitable lodgings, giving much personal assistance, such as getting papers signed for students entering the Inns of Court, providing special entertainments and introducing students into private houses."[2] This, then, was the kind of work that Kirk at first undertook.

Early in July, 1909, the country was shocked by the assassination of a distinguished Anglo-Indian official, Sir Curzon Wylie. The murderer was Madar Lal Dhingra, an Indian student in England, and this led to some discussion of Nationalist and revolutionary tendencies in the Indian community in England. The August number of *The Nineteenth Century* carried an article by a Mr. Edward Dicey, the general tenor of which was to urge the Inns of Court to be much more strict in calling Indian students to the Bar. Mr. Dicey suggested that differences in social habit prevented any effective mixing of Indian and English students and that the, in his view unavoidable, segregation of Indians facilitated the work of sedition. In the October number of the same periodical Kirk replied with an article called *Indian Students in England: another Point of View*. In this Kirk pointed out that Dicey was writing of only one section of the Indian student population—the law students —and that there were many others. He said:

An intimacy with many of these students which in more than one case has resulted in real friendship—friendship of a kind only possible between students, however different their courses of study—has convinced the writer that it is as difficult to make general statements about Indian students in England, which shall stand in any real relation to the facts, as about any other class whose association is due largely to artificial causes. A parallel case would be an attempt to describe the conditions, needs, and aspirations of let us say, the Rhodes scholars at Oxford. The basis of classification of the Indian students is little more than that of colour and isolation.

Kirk went on to argue that social intercourse between English and Indian students was far more possible than Dicey believed. He referred to the many people who had opened their houses to Indians and said

[1] Tissington Tatlow: *The Story of the Student Christian Movement of Great Britain and Ireland, 1933.* p. 555.
[2] *Ibid.* p. 555.

that in this way any Indian student could see much of the best sides
of English life and by degrees take a place in English society. He
concluded, however:

But this method is at best slow, and fails somewhat of the ideal. To revert to
the parallel of the University, it is as if the freshman should enter into the
society of the Senior Common Room and be received into the families of
professors and their wives, yet fail to touch all that part of University life
which consists in the interchange of confidence and friendship between young
men of the same age and standing. And what is lacking in the life of the
Indian in England is too often the friendship of English students. The impression left by Mr. Dicey's article is that such friendship is impossible. I have
tried to show that it is at least more possible than Mr. Dicey supposes. There are
difficulties on both sides. It is hard for the Indian to conquer the racial bashful-
ness with which he has learnt to approach the Englishman; and it is hard for the
English student so to widen his interests and ideals as to be able to share race
and colour. But in neither case is such a change of attitude impossible; and I
would conclude by putting on record the experience of many Englishmen of
the last forty years, and of a growing body of English students to-day that a
close and equal friendship with Indian students, if not at the outset easy, is
yet most certainly possible, and may perhaps, by breaking down in individual
cases the barrier of mutual misunderstanding, be a definite means of allaying
that racial suspicion to which the present sedition is so largely due.

This reluctance to generalize about human beings, and this insistence
on the problems of the individual indicate that Kirk's mind had already
taken that line which it was to develop during his experiences as an
Army chaplain, and which issued in his work for the revival of the
study of moral theology in the Church of England.

2

Kirk's work in London brought him into contact with University
College. At that time W. W. Seton, who was chairman of the committee of the London Intercollegiate Christian Union, was Secretary
of University College, and in 1908 was instrumental in opening a
residential hall for the College at Ealing. The College's charter did not
allow it as such to own the Hall, but Seton brought together a number
of professors and others as a Governing Body. He himself resided in
the Hall and was Bursar, but his idea was to have a young graduate as
Warden who should be capable of getting on well with the young
men and influencing them. The first Warden was Mr. S. H. Wood
who was also Secretary of the L.I.C.C.U. He left in 1910 and Kirk was
invited to take over from him as from September 1st. Kirk was also

appointed an Assistant in the Department of Philosophy at University College in the Session 1910-11 and continued in the Session 1911-12.

In preparation for his University work Kirk spent seven weeks of the summer of 1910 at the Sorbonne in Paris reading philosophy and theology, and this short period made a lasting impression on him. It was clear to his friends that his studies under French Catholic teachers influenced him very strongly and helped him to establish his mind about Christian belief and the nature of the Church.

Altogether Kirk spent about eighteen months at the Ealing Hall, and it was a period of immense activity. He continued his L.I.C.C.U. and Student Movement work, being deputy chairman of the Executive of the General College Department of the Movement and a member of the Bible Study Committee. He wrote for the S.C.M. Press a booklet on *The Christian Practice of Prayer*, and he was acknowledged as the person mainly responsible for the immense success of the Annual Meeting of the Student Movement in February, 1912.

This was a period of much discussion about the aims and basis of the Movement. In 1910 there was a long interchange of letters between Martyn Trafford, a Baptist, L. Johnston, an Anglican and a Fellow of Magdalen, J. H. Oldham, a Presbyterian, and Kirk about the principles and aims of the Movement. The correspondence was copied and circulated to leaders of the Movement, but unhappily no copy seems to have survived. Kirk was also chairman of a Commission on the Basis of the Student Christian Movement appointed in September, 1910, which produced a report discussed at Christmas of that year, and summarized by Dr. Tissington Tatlow in his *Story of the Student Christian Movement*.[1] Unfortunately it has proved impossible to discover any records of the discussions, and none of those who survive from that period of the S.C.M.'s history have any clear recollection of the part that Kirk played in the changes and his views at the time.

There was a good deal of travelling still to be done for the S.C.M. during vacations. Kirk was at a Conference at Montpellier early in 1910, and at the Baslow Students' Camp in July. The next summer he was at the Swanwick Camp, and in January, 1912, with his sister, at a Christian Students' Union Conference at Liverpool. He was also a Lieutenant in the London University Officers' Training Corps, and in camp with them for a fortnight each summer. Here, too, there was S.C.M. work to be done. In 1910 the L.I.C.C.U. had provided a tent as a reading and writing room, and where prayers were said daily, for

[1] Tatlow, *op. cit.* pp. 397 and 472.

the London O.T.C. Camp on Salisbury Plain. Later Kirk raised the question of the relation of these camps to the Movement as a whole and this resulted in a further extension of S.C.M. work. Kirk also found time to act in Dryden's *Siege of Granada*, and either to act in or produce *The Knight of the Burning Pestle*. With all this activity in addition to his work as Warden of Ealing Hall and Assistant to the Professor of Philosophy, it is not surprising that on February 16th, 1912 he collapsed and had to have four months rest.

There was another cause for Kirk's breakdown besides that of over-work. He was, among other things, a very capable administrator, and it was not easy for him to fit into the situation which had developed at Ealing in which Seton controlled the financial and general administra-tion of the Hall, and the Warden, though nominally the head, confined his activities to the personal care of the students. Mr. Wood, whom Kirk succeeded, felt at the time of Kirk's appointment that he and Seton were too much alike to work happily together. Friction in the Hall was made worse by the association of the two men in the affairs of the L.I.C.C.U. This part of the story is best told in the words of Dr. Tissington Tatlow. Writing of the development of the L.I.C.C.U. he says:

As the London committee developed its work rapidly and came in time to employ not only a London secretary but an assistant, and a special secretary for work among foreign students, adding to this a hostel for them, the question of continuity became important. The work was too extensive for one student committee to pass on to another student committee, also the committee found that it needed an office and a financial policy which it could only have if there was continuity, which constantly changing London secretaries could not provide. This led, in practice, to Walter Seton, who had become a member of the staff at University College, taking charge of the policy of the London Committee. He was its chairman and worked with great ability and devotion, built up its finances and made himself indispensable to the work in London. He was not, however, a man who found it easy to share his ideas with younger people and to accept theirs.

There is a subtle distinction between being a dictator and a leader. The leader of any group so democratic in its sentiments as that composed of British students must be clear that it is necessary to carry them with him whole-heartedly. To do this he must often sink his own ideas and must always be quite sure that he has a sympathetic understanding of the ideas of the younger group with which he is working. This Seton, with all his gifts, was not able to do and he tended to be a dictator rather than a leader. Kenneth Kirk, who became London secretary in 1910, saw this difficulty and strove to help Seton to adjust himself to the realities of the situation, but without avail. This ultimately led to Kirk's resignation before he had completed what was intended to be a long term of office with the Movement in London.

After Kirk left the tension between Seton and some of the younger men grew, with the result that he ultimately retired from the leadership of the London Intercollegiate Christian Union.[1]

When his breakdown occurred Kirk went to be nursed by a friend who lived on the South Coast near Hastings. After six weeks there he was, though still very feeble, well enough to be brought home, and then in the middle of April a friend from University College took him to stay at Cartledge Grange, Holmesfield. A fortnight in Scotland with his parents completed the cure, and he was able to return to Ealing at the beginning of June. He had, however, decided that he must resign, and his connexion with Ealing Hall ended on June 25th, and with it his work for the L.I.C.C.U. and S.C.M.

3

The unexpected termination of his work in London must have made a change in Kirk's plans for ordination. He had been at Cuddesdon Theological College for the Long Vacation Term of 1911, and no doubt was then intending to be ordained in London either on the title of his University post, or to a nominal curacy. Now his attention was turned to his own native diocese of York. He accepted a curacy at Denaby Main, a large colliery village close to Mexborough and about seventeen miles from Sheffield. On August 12th, he went to York for the Ordination Examination, and a fortnight later again to Cuddesdon where he had two more terms before being ordained deacon by Archbishop Lang on St. Thomas's Day, December 21st, 1912.

The Denaby curacy lasted in all nineteen months. Most of the time was spent under the incumbency of the Rev. S. F. Hawkes, the last few months under the Rev. H. B. Greeves. Mr. Hawkes was a priest of great ability and force of character. He had been decorated for gallant conduct during a pit explosion and was the kind of vicar, all too rare, who attracts a large crowd of men. Photographs kept by Kirk from those days show a choir of eighteen men and seventeen boys, two adult football teams, and a very extensive men's summer camp. This was different from anything that Kirk had tackled hitherto. He was supported by his usual earnestness and enthusiasm, but he confessed once to a friend: "I find after I have visited ten houses that I have had just about enough of it". Mrs. Greeves writes of the wonderful help that he gave to her husband on his arrival as Vicar in 1914, and of the

1 Tatlow, *op. cit.* p. 294.

very lasting impression that Kirk left on the Parish. She says: "He was simply wonderful with 'The Mothers' and I have one very happy recollection of him at a 'Mothers' Meeting outing' on a boiling hot afternoon, standing, holding the babies, in turn (in his shirt sleeves!) while their Mothers had tea."

Throughout his life it seems to have been a peculiar characteristic of Kirk's that he could express himself in the simplest and most memorable way to ordinary folk, making a deep impression on them. In a pamphlet on education called *The Way of Understanding*, which he wrote for the S.P.C.K. in 1920, he laid great emphasis on the importance of considering one's audience and being sure that the language and illustrations used would be such as to make points in a way which the hearers would understand and remember. His own preaching was always an object lesson in this difficult art.

He was not quite so successful with his fellow clergy to whom he gave lectures on philosophy, and particularly the philosophy of Bergson —no doubt material from his London courses. One of his hearers writes: "I can see the scene now after all these years. There was Kenneth so humble and earnest and there were the clergy with that strained look indicating that it was all to no purpose with the exception of the very small minority who could follow him afar off as it were."

Although Kirk had come straight from Cuddesdon the churchmanship of Denaby Main was by no means 'high' in externals. He delighted in later years to tell how on one occasion Mr. Hawkes had gone to take duty in a parish where vestments were in use. He arrived in the vestry to find the vestments laid out, and a server with a rather supercilious manner waiting to see what the visitor would do. Hawkes, though doctrinally a sound Tractarian, had never worn vestments before, and had not the slightest idea how to put them on, but with some presence of mind he turned to the server and said: "Well what are you waiting for? Vest me", which the boy proceeded to do, and, so the story went, ever afterwards it was the tradition in that parish that the server should vest the priest.

Hawkes remained a close friend of Kirk's to the end of his life. He is mentioned in the Preface to *Some Principles of Moral Theology* as having taken part with Kirk, Canon Streeter, Dr. Rawlinson and Dr. Hadfield in a conference on the relation of psycho-therapy to spiritual direction, and he was clearly a person whose judgement on pastoral matters Kirk valued enormously. Mrs. Sharp believes that Hawkes was one of the strongest influences on Kirk's clerical life, and that some of his greatness as a pastoral Bishop may be traced to this influence.

There is no doubt that Kirk in going to Denaby Main was directed to the right man at the right time.

It was obvious that Kirk would not remain long away from University life, and indeed it does not seem to have been his intention to do so, for in the summer of 1913 he entered for and won the Denyer and Johnson Theological Scholarship of £120 for one year. In 1913 also the Rev. A. E. J. Rawlinson, who was moving from a Keble tutorship to Christ Church, suggested Kirk to the Warden of Keble, Dr. Lock, as the man to succeed him. Dr. Rawlinson recollects that about that time he paid a short visit to Bishopsthorpe, and on arrival said to Archbishop Lang, "I am hoping that Kenneth Kirk may come from your Grace's diocese to Keble", to which the Archbishop replied "I will venture to pit my hope against yours". Nevertheless the offer was made and accepted, and it was arranged that Kirk should take up his duties at Keble with the Michaelmas Term, 1914. He would in any case have left the York diocese, for early in 1914 the new diocese of Sheffield was created and Denaby Main was in it. The first Bishop of Sheffield, Dr. Burrows, invited Kirk to be one of his examining chaplains, a post which he held for many years and which gave him great pleasure.

A friend of undergraduate days writes of him at this time:

It seemed to me, when I saw him a little later on, that the combined effects of his acquaintanceship with miners at Denaby Main and his encounter with realistic Latin theologians in Paris had given him an added maturity which, although new, was a development of his old characteristics: a firm grasp of the essentials of right-thinking, combined with a liberal outlook; an abhorrence of superficiality and rhetoric; a great capacity for sustained mental effort along with a practical business-sense which would have made him a successful banker or accountant; in churchmanship a firm adherence to the Catholic creed and practice proper to the Church of England; a determination not to suffer it that any partial or partisan diminution of our Christianity should usurp the place of sound and comprehensive doctrine; and all this rooted and grounded in a simple faith in Christ not less fervent than the faith which glowed in the young hearts of the undergraduate evangelicals of 1904 or 1908.

III

THE GREAT WAR

Kirk narrowly missed spending the whole of the Great War in a German internment camp. On July 27th, 1914, he had gone with his brother and another friend to Germany for a holiday course of study, being apparently unaware of the serious nature of the international situation. The rest of the story can be told in his own words:

When we first realised what was going forward we were at a place called Kaiserslautern, which is the military headquarters of the German Palatinate, 20 miles north-east of Strassburg. On Saturday, August 1st, things looked so sinister that, as we had no passports, we resolved to clear out. We got back to the Rhine to find that no steamers were sailing, and so we made our way to Cologne. The station there, which is a huge affair, presented an extraordinary scene. It was simply crammed with soldiers. Everybody was low-spirited. I am convinced that not a soul there wanted to fight.

We spent the night in the station, and on Monday morning we got a train for the Dutch frontier. At Oberhausen the train was searched for spies, and we had a decidedly unpleasant experience. An official backed by 50 soldiers, ordered us Englishmen out of the train, and searched us. On me they found a map of the Rhine country, the sort of thing you can buy anywhere for a shilling, and they thought that looked frightfully suspicious. Then I had a pair of military field-glasses, and that nearly finished me. The cry of "Spies" was raised, and the populace hooted us, but we were not seriously menaced. We were taken at once to the police-station, where we were fairly courteously treated, and after a delay of three hours were able to convince the authority of our harmlessness, and to establish our identity. We were sent back to the railway station, and once more boarded a train for the frontier.

After further adventures on the Dutch border the party eventually reached the coast and succeeded in finding a boat to Harwich. Kirk's final comment was:

From what we could see, the German people were as completely taken by surprise at the outbreak as we were, and we were very much astonished to learn the true situation from the English papers when we got home. There is an absolute conviction in Germany that the Kaiser is conducting a righteous war, into which he has been forced by Russia.

Both Kirk brothers had had connexions with the Army, and towards the end of September Leslie went into camp at Colsterdale with the Leeds Rifles, the 7th and 8th Battalions of the West Yorkshire Regiment in which, a month later, he was gazetted as First Lieutenant, and in December Captain. He was not, however, sent abroad until January, 1916. Kenneth's plans were for a short time uncertain. He went to Scotland on September 17th to do a fortnight's duty as private chaplain to Lord Rolle. By the end of the month it was clear that he would not be required or able to take up his Oxford appointment in October and so he applied for a commission in the Army Chaplains' Department.

Sometime in the middle of October he was sent to Hull as chaplain to the three Hull battalions, but a fortnight later was moved to Princes Risborough where he was billeted with a family called Stratton. The Misses Stratton remember his unremitting care for the physical as well as the spiritual well being of the troops, and his love of a good argument. They also noted his liability to frequent severe colds and had the impression that all the time he was driving himself harder than his physical strength could bear. From June to August, 1915, he was at the camp at Tring where the whole 21st Division was concentrated after spending the winter in billets. On August 13th they moved to Witley Camp near Aldershot, in preparation for their crossing to France on September 10th.

It was later recognized that the employment of the 21st Division in the Battle of Loos, consisting as it did of new and inexperienced troops, was most unwise. The Division suffered heavily losing something like fifty per cent. of its numbers. The preliminary bombardment for the battle began on September 21st, and the Infantry attack on the 25th. The 62nd Brigade, to which Kirk was attached, was sent at an early stage as a reinforcement to General McCracken in command of the 15th Division.

They were expected at 10 a.m. on the 25th, but did not arrive until 7.30 p.m. and then were "not in a condition fit to enter such a fight".[1] On the following days the Brigade suffered severely, losing 73 officers and 1,423 other ranks. At this stage of the war, it appears, most of the chaplains with the troops were sent to the field ambulances, as it was considered that with these units they could best be of service. One of the Staff Officers of the 21st Division writing from the front said: "Kirk and Keen (two of our chaplains) were splendid: working all night in Loos, collecting wounded under heavy shell fire, and no doubt saved a lot of lives."

[1] *Official History of the Great War, 1915.* ii. p. 207.

After Loos and during the winter and spring of 1915-16 the 21st Division were recuperating on 'quiet' fronts and being pulled together by a fresh G.O.C. They did not come in for any of the chief operations undertaken before the Somme.

Kirk appears to have been stationed at Armentières, at least it was from there that he came home for a week's leave after Christmas, 1915. He went back to France on January 3rd, 1916 but for most of that year there is little record of his movements. Mr. F. H. Kirk's health gave some anxiety and in the early summer he and his wife and daughter went to Newquay in search of convalescence. On the way home he had a serious lapse and had to be taken to a nursing home in Clifton where he died at the end of July. Kenneth was able to get leave and see him just before his death. In consequence the diary which Mr. Kirk kept comes to an end in 1916, his last entry being for January 19th, and, apart from a note about his father's death, Kenneth did not take it up until the following year. Even then he only records three incidents before his own demobilization in 1919. The War Office records for this period also have many gaps so that we are thrown back chiefly upon personal reminiscences and upon such references as can be gathered from Kirk's own later writings.

The 21st Division remained in the Armentières section until April, 1916, when it was moved to the Somme Front, and there can be little doubt that Kirk was with them all the time. He was involved in the Battle of the Somme which began in July. It is possible that later in the year he may have been given leave to come home and settle the family affairs consequent upon his father's death. At least he appears to have been at home at the beginning of 1917 when he was posted as Senior Chaplain to the 66th (East Lancashire) Division. This posting was made in February and Kirk was soon established at Divisional Headquarters at Béthune, where Fr. Wilkins S.S.J.E. remembers meeting him shortly before Easter. The Very Rev. H. W. Blackburne, who was Assistant Chaplain-General, writes that it was the impression made by Kirk's work when in the 62nd Brigade which caused him to be made Senior Chaplain of the 66th Division.

It does not appear that Kirk held this post for more than about nine months as by the end of 1917 he had returned to England and had been posted to Ripon where he remained with the R.A. Command Depot at South Camp, until he was demobilized in January, 1919. The reasons for his return to England are not known for certain and can only be a matter of conjecture. It is clear that they involved no aspersions on his work at the front. Everyone, from General Lawrence downwards had the highest opinion of him, and the General's A.D.C. writes: "I can remember him preaching some very effective sermons in the cinema at Béthune, and I always thought that he was particularly successful in organising services, including Communion, under rough conditions." The same officer writes: "For the first few months we were in the Béthune area, in the 1st Army. About June we moved up to the coast, east of Dunkirk, in preparation for an attack on the Yser which was never launched. In the autumn we moved south, to join in Passchandaele, and the Division went into the line there twice, with rest billets in the St. Omer area." He remembers that Kirk remained with them during Passchandaele. By this time it was becoming the practice to give men who had had a long turn of duty abroad a spell of home service, six months at least, and as Kirk had, save for short intervals of leave, been in France since September, 1915, it would have been natural for this arrangement to have been applied to him. There may also have been health reasons for his return. He had suffered badly from 'trench feet' and he had his usual throat complaints. The concert party which he later ran at Ripon is stated in a contemporary notice to have been composed entirely of men who had been invalided home, and this may have included the chaplain. There were also domestic reasons why he should come back to England. The loss of his father in 1916 had been followed in October, 1917, by that of his brother who was killed in action at Poelcappelle. There must have been much for him to do and to arrange when he could visit Sheffield.

Towards the end of 1917 a book was published called *The Church in the Furnace* edited by F. B. Macnutt and written by Seventeen Temporary Church of England Chaplains on Active Service in France and Flanders. The Preface is dated at St. Omer in September, 1917. The sixteenth essay in the volume was by Kirk, and is called 'When the Priests come home'. Kirk writes of a few of the dominant lessons priests had learnt in the Forces.

Foremost among them is the conviction that, hidden under the 'inarticulate religion' of the British soldier of which so much has been written lies a deep and intense reverence for the priesthood. Almost any chaplain can evoke it: the few who fail to do so fail because they do not reverence their own priesthood themselves. It is almost entirely independent of the chaplain's personality. To the soldier—officer or man—he is the emissary of a different world from that in which they fret and sweat and fight. He may be breezy or quiet, tactless or diplomatic, affable or retiring; he may preach well or badly; but still he represents another world—a better world—of spiritual things. Even though he be a drag on the mess and *de trop* in the billet, he is at all times looked upon as a repository from which can be drawn the peculiar benefits of religion. And this estimate is the lowest which even an unpopular chaplain need fear, unless he prove himself entirely and openly unworthy of his vocation ...

This then is the first of the things that every chaplain knows—that he is wanted, badly wanted, as a priest; even though he be unfortunate enough to be merely 'tolerated' as a man. He knows too—though it is hard to put the knowledge into words—exactly what it is he is wanted *for*. He knows he is indispensable, because he is the one representative of peace in an atmosphere of strife. To him men turn, as by instinct, for an antidote against strain, friction, weariness and depression. There are other antidotes, of course, some of them dishonourable, others blameless, but often hard to come by; yet even the dullest dog of a chaplain, so long as he can keep his own spirit equable, comes in the first rank among the influences that make life tolerable at the Front. He penetrates into every place, from the guard-room to the General's mess; and everywhere, by the slightest effort of courtesy, sympathy, and tact, he can smooth over the bruised or broken surface of the soldier's life. "I think the evenings you spent with us in the hut did me more physical good than gallons of doctor's medicine, and more moral good than if you had preached us a sermon every day of your life; and I know Jack and Jimmy say the same"— this is an extract (with amended spelling) from a very ordinary soldier's letter to a very ordinary chaplain; but I doubt if in a parish at home the same lads and the same chaplain would ever have got on to speaking terms at all.[1]

There is a striking similarity between these words of Kirk's and a passage in the *Official History of the Great War*:

An eminent French writer, Monsieur André Siegfried, has remarked as a fact which should never be overlooked in an estimate of the British Empire, that every Englishman is religious at heart, however little he may show or practise his belief openly. Certain divisions of the British Expeditionary Force fought with a religious fervour as strong as, or stronger than, their patriotism; but throughout the B.E.F. there was, besides the unseen inward reverence, an outward observance of religious duties more marked than in ordinary life in peace. The army chaplains were not only comrades sharing the common dangers, leaders in the outward observances, and comforters in sickness and death, called affectionately by the name of 'padres', but they seemed to be the connecting link with home, with that other life of peace, once known but perhaps never to be recovered. Nothing can be truer than that the troops liked having chaplains with them.[2]

Kirk went on to emphasize that the form of ministry looked for by soldiers was not one which could provide at best a momentary and elusive forgetfulness, but one that would give a permanent inspiration.

[1] *The Church in the Furnace*, ed. F. B. Macnutt. 1917. pp. 410, 413.
[2] *France and Belgium, 1916*. i. p. 135.

"The consolation expected of the chaplain—the peace for which his ministrations are invoked—is not a passive but an active thing." The distinction, he recognized, was not a new one, but it had been marked and underlined by what chaplains had seen at the front, and war-experience had taught many of them that it was perhaps the fundamental distinction between true and false religion. Kirk continued:

> Curiously enough war-experience has shown, also, that it may be the fundamental distinction between true and false art. A digression on this point, if it helps to make the argument clearer, is not superfluous. All down the British front, often under shellfire, are a row of 'gaffs' and picture-palaces, hastily improvised by soldier artists in huts or barns, or more worthily housed in genuine French theatres. The romance of these entertainments has yet to be written, and their high moral value to be appreciated. With few exceptions they present triumphs of scene-painting, lighting, music, and stage-craft under circumstances of the greatest difficulty. Their ideals are often in advance of those of more ambitious spectacles at home, and, if they can survive the crowning test of peace, might profoundly affect the artistic sense of the new England. That, however, is another question; what is important for us to notice is that they in their turn give an instance of this same distinction between the ministry that consoles alone and the ministry that inspires by its consolation. The cinemas, of course, are merely instruments of forgetfulness, and so are the greater number of the 'turns' (do not blame them for this; their function, though not the highest, is very high and laudable); but in almost every performance there are also passages of permanent creative value. Such passages may be either serious or comic. If the first, they raise the soldier out of himself to a higher plane of ideals; and no one responds more readily to the influence of good art than an audience on active service. If the second, they have an *intimité* of insight into the trials of trench-life which teaches the soldier not simply to laugh, but to laugh at his own troubles, and by laughing to rise above them. I have known performers of wide experience and eminent reputation fail with a trench audience, achieving a momentary success but forgotten in a day; whilst the lilt of a folk-song, simply sung by a soldier-troupe, has exercised an inspiring influence for weeks; and I knew one man at least who died more bravely because the words of such a song came into his mind —they had lingered there for months, and their memory was bright enough to strengthen him at his death.[1]

The troupe which Kirk undoubtedly had specially in mind in writing this passage was one known as the 'A.B.Cs.' which was founded by Major Shaw Page, A.S.C., and directed by Kirk, himself throughout 1916. Programmes survive for the 100th performance of the troupe on or about February 26th, 1916, the 150th on May 20th, and the 250th

[1] *The Church in the Furnace.* pp. 416-418.

on December 2nd. These establish that it is also to this troupe that the following passage from a book published in 1918 refers.

The place was one of those rough-and-ready theatres in which soldiers nightly perform to soldiers behind the front. The performance had gone the usual way of such things—ragtime, a parody or two, sentimental songs, duets, comedians, Jewish and Scotch—a performance clean, bright, and amusing. Just before the end there was a moment's pause, and then the orchestra played the unmistakable introduction to the *Keys of Heaven*—("Sounds like a bloody hymn," said a cynical gunner in the cheap seats behind). In less than five minutes the old folk-song had been sung through, not as a mere duet, but as a miniature drama. The 'girl' of the troupe—("Damned ugly, these French tarts," said the cynical gunner, and added that you needn't think he didn't know a girl when he saw one, and it was no good kidding him she was an adjectived bugler)—had shyly refused the advances of less worthy lovers, turning from them, as the curtain fell on the closing chords, to the one who offered her unreservedly the keys of his heart. It was perfectly simple and natural, without a touch of unreal sentiment; but words and air and acting together had an unforgettable effect upon the soldier audience, and their appreciation was shown not so much by tumultuous applause as by a certain sigh of pure content that ran from end to end of the long benches, in which even the caustic gunner joined.

This troupe, though far from being the most famous or most finished of the many that exist in France, stands high among them by virtue of *bijou* music-romances such as this. The "*Keys of Heaven*" is their greatest success, and men go night after night to see and hear it again; but they have other triumphs of the same order to their credit. They have an excellent "*Widdecombe Fair*," with a grey mare that dies in the most approved fashion, and reappears in a realistic storm as a truly satisfying ghost. They have lifted the "*Merryman and Maid*" song and dance bodily out of Savoy opera; and when the 'girl' (now resplendent as a gipsy dancer) sings the haunting minor phrases of the last verse, you might hear a pin drop. Round a medley of sea-ballads they have built a pretty romance of quay-side courtship; and they act the story of the "*Floral Dance*" with an old-fashioned grace and light-heartedness as rare as the melody itself.[1]

At Ripon also Kirk ran a very popular Garrison Concert Party, 'The Riponians'. Among his papers carefully preserved are programmes of their performances between January and June 1918, and photographs of the company and of some of the turns. On occasion both at Ripon and in France he appeared himself in 'The Optimist and the Pessimist'.

It will be apparent already that in Kirk's mind the running of these troupes was not a thing apart from his spiritual work as a chaplain.

[1] *A Study of Silent Minds.* pp. 43-45.

Some notes printed at the end of the book last quoted show an interesting by-product of the 'A.B.Cs.' He is writing of educational experiments with troops in the field and giving an account of work with groups.

The actual beginning of experience, he writes, grew out of a concert party. Its members (mostly amateur and of the class I have described) met two or three nights a week after performances to discuss future programmes, and so on. The leading spirits were in private life a collier, a builder's apprentice, and a joiner; occasional additions were a farm hand and one or two other colliers or ironworkers. They were mostly young, and almost entirely unread and thoughtless. After some months of concert work, however, the more enthusiastic decided that they required to know the principles of the art they had adopted; and this gave the impetus to an educational attempt. With such books as Stewart Macpherson's *Musical Appreciation*, and Plunket Greene's *Singing*, occasional copies of the *Music Student*, and so on, we developed a rough course, dealing not only with classical music, but also with the principles of light opera, comedy, and drama. A translation of the *Poetics* helped a good deal. The method was always the same, as far as it ever developed. The book was read by the unofficial leader, its main principles outlined by him and discussed; then various chapters were taken in detail. At all times the book was passed round among the men, and some of them read a good deal of it.

He continues:

The same process, with the same subject, was carried out later with a divisional band. Other groups with which similar experiments were attempted were the batmen of an officers' mess, a sanitary section, the signallers of one battalion, the stretcher-bearers of another. Among books treated in this way were *The Crown of Wild Olive*, *Lectures on Painting and Architecture*, *Ethics of the Dust*, *The Student in Arms*, *The Riches of Prayer*, Rowntree's *Poverty*, and so on. It is only fair to say that in some cases circumstances broke the 'course' off almost at its very beginning; but enough was done to shew that the system was capable of development.[1]

His experiences in France caused Kirk to think a good deal about the problem of 'working-class education', and his thoughts were embodied in a small book written most probably after his return to England and published in the last months (probably October or November) of 1918. It bears the title *A Study of Silent Minds*, and the sub-title *War Studies in Education*, and it is dedicated to the memory of his brother whose career as a school-master had been ended by his death in action in the previous year. Kirk argues that the English mind, in general, is characterized by a certain lack of initiative, originality, and creative

[1] *op. cit.* pp. 155-157.

self-expression. He supports this by illustrations drawn from life at the front, from observation of the way in which soldiers spent their time off duty.

Here and there is a man reading or writing; but for the most part they sit or stroll about quite purposelessly, and there is no sign that they are thinking or talking of anything much at all. Any slight novelty in their surroundings . . . will hold their attention for five, or ten, or twenty minutes. They will gaze steadily at the white burst of shrapnel four or five miles away, or at an aeroplane homing at sunset, or at a squad of grenadiers practising their deadly job. But as for purpose of thought or concentration—of these there is little evidence.[1]

In this, because the soldier off duty is no more than the Englishman at his simplest and most natural, Kirk finds a leading characteristic of the English mind at any time. But he emphasizes that it does not obscure all other characteristics and of these the one that seems to him most prominent is that the soldier's mind is made for friendship. In general, the soldier is kindly disposed towards all men and wants nothing better than to treat them, and to be treated by them, as friends. And yet there is something missing in these friendships. They seem unprogressive or unproductive. They rarely lead to any noticeable developments of character or of mind. Something must be wrong here, for friendship should be a powerful stimulus to human progress. The fact that in most of these cases it falls short of any such result points back to the fact that the minds upon which it has to work are for the most part empty, or it would be better to say passive, or receptive, or silent. They are childlike—taking in a great deal, but giving out very little—and, in spite of an infinity of foul talk and the presence of vice in varying degrees, essentially innocent. Another aspect of this childlike nature is a deep capacity for wonder.

All the details of his surroundings interest him; the language, religion, and habits of the French; the hints of Boche character to be gleaned from captured trenches; rumours of future movements magnified a hundredfold; stories from the Base, or from home, or from other theatres of the war. Above all, two things specifically connected with religion always come to him with the surprise of a miracle: the often repeated phenomenon of the crucifix standing untouched among ruins; and the strange vagaries of Providence, or fate, by which others have been struck down whilst he so far has been spared. Half his conversation, half his revolving thoughts, it might be said, are centred round the strange truth that one is taken and another left.

Such matters interest him; he notices and "studies over" them; exchanging second-hand truisms or—more rarely—hinting at original conceptions for

[1] *op. cit.* pp. 17f.

which he can find no coherent phrases; curious to know and understand them better; but unable, in most cases, through his racial passivity of mind, to find either the means or the energy to pursue any real train of thought or inquiry about them.[1]

This inactivity leaves the mind a prey, not only to temptation, but also to prejudice and blind impulse; and there is great waste because the possibilities for good, be they small or great, lie dormant and untouched. In the great increase in the number of chaplains, the official sanction extended to entertainments of various kinds, the semi-official position of the Y.M.C.A. and similar bodies, the regular distribution of free literature Kirk saw a recognition by the authorities of the presence of this danger and this possibility of waste. In these things he found an acceptance of the three means by which the silent mind can be safeguarded against the inroads of temptation—namely amusement, instruction and inspiration—a commonplace with educationalists. But, he maintains, only the third—inspiration—can be relied upon to avoid the dangers and the waste that the inactivity of the silent mind involves.

The difference between instruction and inspiration, he writes, seems to lie in this: that by instruction a man can learn how to handle the normal and expected; but only inspiration will enable him to deal with what is abnormal and unexpected, and especially with the most abnormal and unexpected of all things—his fellow men.[2]

Kirk then draws further upon his observation of soldiers off duty and at rest to indicate what they are capable of at their best. He describes the concert party, and the incident of *The Keys of Heaven* recounted above. He tells how a well-known elocutionist came to entertain troops in a hut near Arras, how he recited the chapter of *David Copperfield* in which old Peggotty learns of little Em'ly's flight, how he stopped with the last word of Peggotty's outburst, and how then there was, for what seemed a whole minute, an absolute and paralyzing silence, how at last the entertainer said nervously, "Perhaps you don't realise that that is the end of the selection?" and how the storm of applause then broke loose. Kirk comments:

What had happened was that he had underestimated the imaginative capacity of his audience. The story he told had captured their attention so utterly, that one and all had forgotten the war, and themselves, and the civilian who was entertaining them, and everything else in the world except old Peggotty with his horror, grief and shame. They were so lost in the drama

---

[1] *op. cit.* pp. 22f.   [2] *op. cit.* pp. 26f.

pictured for them, that the possibility of its ending suddenly—like the fragment from a book which in reality it was—never presented itself for a moment; they waited breathlessly for another outburst, or for some violent action to carry on the story.[1]

He then adds to these two pictures of the soldier's recreations two of his religion. One shows a chaplain arriving at Battalion Headquarters one day for a Communion Service, to find that one of his most regular communicants was a prisoner in the guard-room—his offence, that of lying to a sergeant. Scarcely had the service begun when the prisoner appeared under the escort of his best friend, a corporal of the same company. Questioned afterwards, the corporal said that he had seen no reason why Joe, though a prisoner, should not come to Communion. He had gone to the sergeant of the guard and put this view of the case to him, offering his own services as escort. The sergeant apparently agreed, and so did Joe; so prisoner and escort marched to the service together, received the Sacrament together, and together marched back to the guard-room.

The other picture is the following:

Imagine a French village schoolroom on a Sunday evening, the walls covered with maps and with those clever French placards which teach by picture and epigram the mysteries of citizenship, thrift, and family life. Fill it to the door with fifty or a hundred lads, fresh from battle, joining of their own free will by candlelight for a Sunday evening service. They are cramped in desks never built for their well-grown limbs; they cannot kneel to pray; many of them can hardly stand to sing without carrying their hymn-books into deep shadow; often they are wet and cold and dirty. The French are not slow to express their opinions of such things; and here is the judgment of the fat old *institutrice* who gave the chaplain permission to use the place, praising its *belle sonorité* the while. She stood at the door throughout, nominally to keep in check the crowd of whispering, inquisitive children; actually (for she certainly failed dismally in her ostensible purpose) to watch the scene herself. "Ah, Monsieur," she said, when thanked for her courtesy, "it is I who thank you. What seriousness! what devotion! If only we others could learn to pray so fervently and to sing with so good heart!"[2]

Finally he gives the text of a letter written by a young ordinary soldier who had been wounded at Loos and was in hospital in England. It is addressed to another soldier, a friend of several years, still at the front, and Kirk comments on it: "How many would have imagined that a commonplace, illiterate boy, could be moved by the power of friendship to such rapturous and rhythmical self-expression?"

[1] *op. cit.* p. 44.   [2] *op. cit.* pp. 46f.

If, he argues, the ordinary English mind is capable of such achieve-
ments as these it should be possible by wise educational methods to
lead it on to a point where movement on this high plane will be
normal and not exceptional. Minds such as these are by nature silent
and inactive, but they are certainly not inane, and therefore, given the
proper stimulus, their silence can be changed to self-expression, their
inertia to a living power of thought. English education, both secular
and religious, had so far largely failed to provide that stimulus, it had
failed to discover an appeal to which the pupil would respond.

To find such an appeal you must discover some primary disposition of the
mind which will inevitably grow and expand, provided it is given the right
food and led in the right direction; some thought-centre or vital interest which
will always react if the proper stimulus is applied.[1]

Looking at his five examples Kirk saw that in every one it was the
same interest that was aroused, and that an interest in people, and so he
came to the conclusion that "an absorbing interest in other people is
the one vital spark in the English soldier's mind." This conclusion he
then proceeds to reinforce by further observations drawn from Army
life, also bringing in evidence clearly derived from his work at Denaby
Main. He argues that English literature provides illustrations of the
same feature. Shakespeare's originality gave itself up so wholly to the
delineation of people that he could only spare passing attention for
the plot. Dickens, Thackeray, Meredith, Jane Austen, Trollope, are
remembered far more by their characters than by their narratives.
Macaulay, Froude and Gibbon are examples in the field of historical
writing of the statement that the Englishman's real interest is the study
of character. English training in for example the Universities and
Public Schools, and as distinct from English education, has, Kirk
argues, in countless ways been vindicated as a success, and this
because it is a discipline which appeals above all to the student of
character.

A boy is thrown, without previous preparation, into the society of a large
number of other boys, and expected from the first to study them and learn how
to deal with them fairly and yet firmly. At football or cricket, in house or
college life, he has to take his place and do his share, giving equal opportunities
to the rest; yielding place to those with greater ability than himself, taking
charge of those with less. He is expected to do this by instinct, and as far as
possible without any authority behind him except his own tact and insight . . .
How congenial this training is to the British temperament, and of what striking

[1] *op. cit.* p. 55.

results it is capable, the annals of the war, as of our whole Colonial history and Imperial Government, give ample proof.[1]

Kirk then proceeds to a criticism and analysis of the failure of liberal education in the past. That failure has been greatest on its intellectual side. For lack of a true philosophy of life the German character has been given over to the pursuit of untrue ideals, but for lack of any philosophy at all the English nature gropes blindly through life with no formed ideal to guide it.

The purpose of intellectual training must be, first of all, to implant in the mind true ideals, and to confirm them there by such weight of evidence and reflection as the individual is capable of making his own (for men cannot walk by blind faith alone); and therewith to draw out such powers of self-expression as will help him to pursue his ideals. By such means he will be fitted, as far as his intellect is concerned, to take his share in the business of life; and if his other powers (really inseparable from those of the mind), are developed at the same time and along the same lines, he will be enabled to take up that place in society to which his abilities, as well as his opportunities, beckon him.

Every theory of education, therefore, must be based upon a philosophy of life; and a man's ideals of education will be coloured by his opinions as to the purpose and aim of life.[2]

He considers whether the general agreement of human opinion has ruled out any objects or purposes as *not* being the true objects and purposes of life. He suggests that the considered opinion of mankind would absolutely rule out self-seeking as the end of life and that the popular ideal of life enshrines a belief that it must be of use to others. This leads to an examination of the place of self-sacrifice which, as a final goal, is definitely rejected. Here comes a passing reference to the Atonement, which we shall have to take up in another chapter. He reaches the conclusion that the normal ideal of life strikes a balance between self-seeking and self-sacrifice. It rejects a selfishness which disregards others entirely; but it also rejects a sacrifice which disregards self entirely. "Such a sacrifice may perhaps be demanded by abnormal circumstances; and if it is demanded, and freely given in answer, no human praise is adequate to reward its heroism. But the general conception of life is also that, given a universal acceptance of this ideal, such abnormal circumstances could not arise; and that no man has the right, by his own service, to deprive others of their share in the common service of all." He elucidates this by reminding us of two distortions of sacrifice, of the man who is for ever sacrificing himself in an

---

[1] *op. cit.* p. 73.   [2] *op. cit.* p. 77.

irritating and unnecessary manner in the pursuit of an exaggerated humility, and of the person whose sacrifice is ill-judged and mischievous, engendering in its recipients not a like devotion but a selfishness which is ready to take everything and give nothing. Self-sacrifice if pursued as a man's one aim, will almost certainly degenerate into one or other of these forms.

The highest ideal in life, Kirk maintains, is that we should aim at getting the best out of ourselves and out of others as well. Every man has a talent, however rudimentary, for influencing others to their mutual good; and his true business in life is to exercise that talent effectively within the most appropriate sphere. Where the talent is small the sphere will be no wider than the immediate family circle; where it is great, it may be as broad as the civilized world itself. For most of us the limits lie between these two extremes. We are each of us the centre of a certain circle of interests, and the function of education is to help a man to recognize the limits of his own circle, to inspire him to work within their compass as ardently as he can for the common good, and to equip him as fully as possible for the venture. We must look round for a type of liberal education which, both in its elementary and higher forms, will do what the traditional education aimed at but failed to achieve. Such an education must set certain objects clearly before its pupils.

(i) It must teach them the great need that exists for honest men to consider the problems of modern life without prejudice, and to work for their solution— for it is only by solving these problems that we shall get the best out of others and ourselves.

(ii) It must inspire them to take every opportunity of leading in this thought and work; either by embracing public life, in as wide a form as is compatible with their profession and abilities; or by influencing public opinion in the immediate circle of their fellow-workers, friends and family; or at the lowest by a discriminating and conscientious use of the franchise.

(iii) It must help them to understand that the smaller of two issues can only be decided by reference to the greater; that the civic problem will only be solved by those who appreciate the national; and the national only by those who are alive to the international.

(iv) It must develop their natural interest in human nature into a scientific study, so that they are secure against specious and self-seeking impostors.

(v) Finally, it must warn them against the insidious dangers of words and phrases; and teach them to discern the true bearing of an argument from its apparent meaning.[1]

1 *op. cit.* pp. 96f.

This programme Kirk regards as involving the study of institutions, of psychology, and of logic. By institutions he understands the state, the law, the nation, commerce, economics. Institutions and people together make history and so pupils are to be interested in institutions by teaching them history. Here he draws a lesson from the Old Testament whose writers succeeded in producing "a people passionately interested in its own institutions; unduly conservative, perhaps, but highly educated and deeply concerned in everything that genuinely affected the national welfare—a race of patriots in a very real sense." This, Kirk believes, is the true historical method.

Once you have given your pupil his background of events, select for his study the institutions and the problems with which his own life will bring him most into contact—problems of government and popular control, of industry and commerce, of the treatment of the idle, the criminal, the sick, the destitute. Trace the development of these problems and institutions through the centuries up to the present day, weaving your story round vivid pictures of the men and women by whose characters they were influenced, or by whose actions they were modified. Shew how time and experience rejected solutions that at first seemed successful, and revealed flaws that at first were undetected; and how new personalities arose to patch up the old systems or inaugurate the new. Such a method will breed an appreciation of the complex society in which we live, and a genuine desire to lend a hand in its development or administration.[1]

He considers the objection that we have tried to do this and that it has failed to interest our people. He denies that we have really tried, and he asks "Every civilized country has its national heroes . . . but who are the national heroes of England? At best we can only quote Saint George, King Arthur, and Robin Hood as having more than a passing hold upon the popular fancy—an alien saint, a mythical king, a legendary outlaw . . . It is because the method of the historical novel has never been scientifically applied to the teaching of history in schools, with a view to arousing in the scholar a true appreciation of our national problems, by giving him a living interest in our national heroes." The danger of parochialism must be guarded against, civic questions referred to national ones and national to international, so that a study of foreign history and of international relationships, conducted on the same method, must form part of this new scheme of education; and with it must be treated the influence of geography and climate upon national institutions.

By psychology Kirk meant "a practical classification of normal

---

[1] *op. cit.* pp. 100f.

habits of mind and types of character, and of the methods by which they can severally be brought under control." And he saw the main work in this field being done by introducing the student to the greatest creations of fiction. His criticism of current teaching of English literature was that it concentrated on too few 'characters' and failed to give a wide enough basis for real character study. Lack of training in logic, in the meaning of words and the validity of arguments, had been the most complete failure of modern education.

To a large extent the stagnation of our political and religious thought is due to this cause—that some of us will accept almost any argument, however futile; and the remainder—with a distrust as blind as their neighbour's trustfulness— dare accept no argument at all, however valid. And in each case the cause at the bottom is an ignorance of logic.[1]

Few successful experiments have been made in teaching logic, and Kirk suggests that a leaf be taken out of the classics and that we should try to teach logic and the meaning of words as Plato did, by dialogue. School debates should cease to be an optional amusement for out of school hours, and should become a regular and essential part of the curriculum. In this way, again, we should build upon the character-istic interest in people. "You will give the boy, at once, an audience whom he has to convince and an interlocutor whom he has to counter, and if you have a wise chairman who does not hesitate to point out fallacies or appeals to prejudice whenever they occur, your classroom may perhaps be noisy, but at least it will be interesting; and most of those present will learn something."

He is anxious, however, to guard against one great danger. A pupil should be confronted with the problems of life, interested in them, stimulated and equipped for their solution, but the teacher should avoid the temptation of presenting him with ready-made solutions. "However much you believe in a certain goal, never represent it as more than your own belief. Our business is to inspire thought, not to propagate formulae; to make pioneers of an undiscovered country, not tourists of a known one." The neglect of this principle, he believed to be one great cause of educational failure. A glib knowledge of fact more than a diligent habit of inquiry had been encouraged. Examina-tions had become the test of a retentive memory rather than of an alert mind.

A brief paragraph refers to the place that language study, mathe-matics and science will have in such a programme as he envisages. The

[1] *op. cit.* p. 106.

first is of inestimable value in all the three main subjects, and the more a boy can learn about foreign customs, foreign people, and foreign ideas, in their own language, the better he will understand his own. Mathematics and science are useful for his career, but of greater value is "the discipline of concentrated and connected thought and the intolerance of partial or *a priori* solutions for which they call". To these he adds, as an important subject, music. He had noted among the troops that wherever they were music was the one paramount thing next to their friendships and their food and tobacco that they seemed to need. In face of this he marvelled that music should have been left so entirely to chance in English education. Some children were taught to perform, "but the individual is not taught to appreciate, understand, or enjoy good music."

Kirk develops this theme by arguing that nothing resembles more closely the character of educated men than good music.

In good music there seems to be a fusion of four things: melody, rhythm, harmony and tone. The melody of a passage gives it purpose; the rhythm gives it balance; harmony enriches and extends it; tone gives it depth and colour and feeling. If each of these four is *good*, and if they are well combined, you have good music. Translate this into terms of human character. If a man has a high and well-defined purpose; if his outlook is balanced, so that his own enthusiasms do not carry him away; if he is neither narrow in method nor barren in thought, but has enrichment and grace in his character; if finally, all that he does and says is coloured by sympathy and feeling—surely he is the educated man of our dreams?[1]

He considers an objection that such an approach degrades the Beautiful to a merely utilitarian level whereas children should be taught to love Beauty, just as they should be taught to love Truth and Goodness, for its own sake and for that alone. He recognizes the force of this objection but points out that such a view needs to be carefully safeguarded lest it tend to make education a matter of pure selfishness, each individual trying to acquire 'culture' without reference to the needs of others. He adds that the desire for Truth, Beauty and Goodness can never be realized by anyone, individual or community, except through mutual encouragement and exchange of achievement, that these things are not personal but communal possessions. This leads to the assertion that those things alone are most true and beautiful and good which can be most widely shared, and that in teaching children to follow them we must show them only the paths which they can travel with the greatest company of friends, leading and being led in turn.

[1] *op. cit.* pp. 113f.

Therefore you will judge of a method of education—whether in music, art, literature, logic, or whatever else—according as it develops corporate progress —that is, gives the scholar both the desire and the power to share the results of his studies with others . . .

We may set this down without any fear of contradiction—that no spiritual activity, however great its triumphs may appear, is on the road to ultimate success, unless it is adding all the time to the corporate wealth and friendship of a City of Friends.[1]

In the final chapter of the book Kirk turns to the subject of religion which, being the sum total of all the bridges between men and God, must cover every channel by which men receive inspiration. He recognizes that there has been a failure in the presentation of Christianity in England and he suggests that it may be for the same reason as the failure in education "in that we did not appeal, first and foremost, to the English interest in people." He points out how successful the Church has been where it has contrived to impart the Lord's motive to seek the lost, appealing to the zeal aroused by taking the ordinary schoolboy to the school mission, the ordinary undergraduate to the college settlement. But these things are few and far between, and the Church as a whole has failed to communicate this sense of mission.

Kirk then considers teaching about the Church itself, and urges that we should put it before the child first and foremost as the Communion of Saints, a delightful society of saintly folk.

When he joined the Church at Confirmation, was he told, first and foremost, that he was joining a delightful society of saintly folk? Or that he must believe the Creeds, know the Catechism, keep the Commandments, and be regular at Early Services?

The latter, far more than the former, was the teaching most of us experienced when we were prepared for Confirmation. And—with the exception of the Early Service—what an appalling prospect! And even at the Early Service we were taught to ignore the other people, to "go to church silently, and come away silently, and not to look at the other communicants"; to think of it as an individual *commercium* between ourselves and God, in which the others, though undergoing the same precious experience, had no personal share. No wonder it all appalled our shy, sensitive, sentimental lads! No wonder they refused to be confirmed because they "wouldn't be able to live up to it!" No wonder earnest souls ask for a restatement of Christianity or for more dogmatic teaching! But what is wanted is neither dogma nor restatement, but a complete change of emphasis.[2]

[1] *op. cit.* pp. 119f.   [2] *op. cit.* pp. 133f.

He contrasts this with the greater willingness of the young man at the front to be confirmed:

He sees the chaplain—a man often gay himself, whose mission at all events seems to be to make the lives of others brighter—and around him a body of communicants, (one or two of them perhaps his own friends,) whose lives, in enough cases to make them at least a little conspicuous, are brighter and more buoyant than those of others around him; and though he knows nothing of dogma he feels that he would like to belong to such a society.[1]

He feels that he may be criticized as undervaluing the importance of dogmatic instruction. Dogma, he admits, is vitally important, and it would be a good thing if the ordinary churchman had a great deal more of it, but it is love and not dogma that will attract and hold a man to the Church. "Let him look for love first and find it; let the older members shew interest in him, and inspire his interest in return, and he will absorb almost by instinct such dogma as he needs."

Kirk supports this contention by describing the practice of many wise chaplains in France.

One in particular—by no means a shallow or careless thinker—though he went far towards understanding the thoughts of immature and silent boys, never ventured to give them more than a minimum of instruction. "I can't explain things to them," he said; "I don't understand them and they don't understand me—but they *do* understand each other,"—and therefore he handed each candidate over to one of his own communicants—preferably, if it could be done, the lad's own mate—and left them to hammer it out for themselves. Once he had assured himself of a lad's sincerity and given him the simplest possible instruction—"Go to Joe," he would say (if Joe was the chosen sponsor's name), "he'll tell you the rest better than I can." And you would see Joe and his catechumen sitting in a dug-out or on a fire step, fluttering a prayer-book between them; and what they talked about or how they settled the affair no one ever knew, but the result was clear. No lad confirmed under these conditions ever fell away; for Joe's love and interest, and the love and interest of the other communicants, kept him faithful; they taught him such things as he needed to know in their own strange language; they led his steps, in friendly fashion, along the path of Christian progress.

And the second result was this, that all the communicants of that unit grew eager to be sponsors; and one after another brought forward fresh candidates for Confirmation, or undertook the care of those who had no friends already in the circle. Their love and interest were aroused, and they grew quite naturally to be missionaries to those outside the Church, and pastors to newcomers within.

You could scarcely receive people into the Church at home in this fashion

[1] *op. cit.* p. 135.

unless it bore a greater resemblance than it generally does to that delightful society of saintly folk which is the Communion of Saints.[1]

He suggests that the reason why many churchgoers though saintly perhaps, are not delightful, and consequently do not interest the newcomer, is that they are not very interested in our Lord Himself. He realizes that such a statement needs justification and so he asks, What is the real test of interest? and answers not that you should always be talking about your subject; but that you should constantly be getting and shedding new light upon it, if only from the candle-rays of your own modest intelligence. And, he maintains, judged by this test the average Christian shows little interest in his Master. In this respect he finds a defect in the Church Services. With two marked exceptions—three suffrages in the Litany, and the customary Good Friday meditation on the Seven Last Words—none of them focus attention upon the character of Christ as revealed in His earthly life, or appear to draw their inspiration from that source. This may be one reason why they are so constantly criticized.

Certain it is that many modern innovations—legitimate and otherwise—in the Church of England aim either at a greater insistence upon the human character of our Lord—as in many popular manuals of devotion, and the Jesus-worship of some liberal theologians; or at a more limited and localized conception of His Divine Presence. Whether these innovations are wise or not, their tendency is clear—they are all of them attempts to interest the Christian a little more in his Lord.[2]

And so he concludes:

For religion to achieve its purpose you must make the Gospel and the Church and the person of Christ interesting to the learner. To interest him in the Gospel you must interest him in the people for whom it is meant; and that is easy, for they *are* interesting. To interest him in the Church, you must interest him in the saints; and that is harder, for the saints of to-day are often not very interesting. So, that they may become interesting, you must interest them, as well as their would-be companions, in our Lord Himself. And you cannot do that unless you yourself are interested in Him. That should be easy—for who could be more interesting? We only find it hard because we have never given to Him the thought we have given to other people.

It is strange that the Church should so have lost interest in her Founder, and this is not the place to attempt to account for it. But because it is true in the main, people have lost interest in the Church, and because they have lost interest in the Church they have lost—or never found—interest in the needs of others; and they have treated their fellows as curious spectacles, to be gossiped

---

[1] *op. cit.* pp. 138-140.   [2] *op. cit.* pp. 146f.

and wondered about, but not as living souls to be helped, strengthened, and developed. And this idle, purposeless interest—which is really no more than a languid curiosity—is what we called at the beginning the silent mind.

To call this silent mind to active self-expression—which was our problem—you must use its natural interest in other people (in some respects so vivid, in others so dull) to give it an appreciation of all the needs and problems of human life, and a desire to work for their solution. That was the object of the liberal education we sketched out. To strengthen that desire, to develop it to the heights of greatest passion, and to show the power by which it can be brought to realization, you must use this same natural interest to interest it in the Gospel and the Church; and to maintain an interest in the Church you must stimulate an interest in Christ Himself. When you have done that (and you will find that in this matter you must begin with yourself) you will have fulfilled the purpose both of religion and of education. You will have done all that human power can do; and you must leave it to the power of Christ to do the rest.[1]

Kirk preserved three reviews of his book. One, from the *Church Times*, concentrated rather on the religious content of it. The reviewer was in agreement with the general thesis, and also in particular referred to the last chapter as indicating one of the most satisfactory answers to the question "Why has the Church failed?". A reviewer in *The Times Educational Supplement* declared that Kirk had succeeded in stating a certain problem clearly and rightly for the first time. He recommended it to everyone who was interested either in education, or in the British soldier, or in human beings. The third review was in a church newspaper of the time called *The Challenge*, and it was signed with the initials W.T., which must stand for William Temple the founder and first editor of the paper. The review began: "Every now and then there is published a book which, small in bulk, is of really great importance. This is one of them." And it concluded "We have no doubt that Mr. Kirk's contention is just, and if just it is of unique importance. Certainly it is Christian; for the essence of Christianity is no acceptance of a body of propositions but devotion to a Person, through love to whom, called forth by His love to us, we strengthen our natural friendships and become friends of those whom we should otherwise ignore."

Such commendations show the extent to which Kirk's diagnosis was new, and the response that it evoked in contemporaries. It is strange, in view of that, that the book should have been so completely forgotten. Kirk himself seems to have lost sight of it in later years, and did not generally include it in lists of his published works. He may have felt dissatisfied with parts of it, and indeed, as some of the quotations

[1] *op. cit.* pp. 149-151.

that we have given will have shown, it breathes an atmosphere different from that of England after the Second World War. But it is unlikely that he ever repudiated the main thesis of this early book. A small work by him called *The Way of Understanding*, published in 1920 by the S.P.C.K. deals with the nature of education regarded from the point of view of one who would wish to educate himself. Many ideas from the earlier book are to be recognized there. As we shall see later, his concern as a bishop for the Church Schools of the Oxford diocese, and his work for the Woodard Corporation show him preoccupied to the end of his life with the problem of education. *A Study of Silent Minds* is valuable not only for precious glimpses that it gives of his war-time experiences in France, but also for its clear exposition of principles which guided his thoughts and work in later years.

IV

OXFORD AND THE STUDY OF
MORAL THEOLOGY

I

KIRK returned to Oxford to take up his Keble tutorship in January, 1919, and was quickly made a member of the Faculty of Theology. He was invited by the Regius Professor, A. C. Headlam, to give one of the courses of lectures then being arranged for the returning ex-service ordinands. In the Summer and Michaelmas Terms of 1919 he acted as Principal of St. Stephen's House, when it reopened as a Theological College. He had declined an offer of the Principalship, but agreed to run the House until the new Principal, the Rev. G. A. Michell, could take up his appointment. Thus began a close connexion with the House which lasted until Kirk's death, his last official engagement on June 3rd, 1954, being a visit to the House. In October, 1919, he was elected to a Fellowship after Examination in Theology at Magdalen College, but retained his Tutorship at Keble. Earlier in that year his family home had been moved from Sheffield to Oxford where his mother came to live at 39, Leckford Road.

In March, 1920, the Rev. G. B. Allen, then Dean of Pembroke, and Proctor for the year 1920-1, nominated Kirk as one of his two Pro-Proctors, and later in the year suggested him for appointment as Controller of Lodging Houses, an office which Kirk took up on January 1st, 1921 and held for the following twelve years. There were more men in the University than had been the case before the war and the problem of the provision and adequate control of lodgings for them presented considerable difficulties. In November, 1921, the Delegacy of Lodgings was set up, replacing the old Delegates for licensing Lodging Houses, and about the same time the work of the Controller was extended to deal with lodgings occupied by women undergraduates. Kirk was, therefore, in charge at a very important stage in the development of the Lodgings Delegacy. His memory for people was a great help. Landladies who visited the Delegacy office would be greeted at once by name and found that most of the facts about their houses were already clearly in the Controller's mind. He was assiduous in inspecting lodgings and strict in his requirement that they should conform to the official standards. Some years later he gave this advice about lodgings to a recently ordained curate. "When I was Controller of Lodgings and inspected Lodging Houses I would frequently stop with my hand on the front door knob as I was about to leave, and say: 'One last thing. May I look at the kitchen.' I knew at once by the response whether it was a good house or not. Let me advise you when you are looking for digs. Always ask to see the kitchen."

The additional income from this office enabled Kirk to marry. In May, 1920, he had become engaged to Miss Beatrice Caynton Yonge Radcliffe, second daughter of F. R. Y. Radcliffe, Judge of County Courts of the Oxfordshire Circuit and a former Fellow of All Souls. They were married in Oxford on March 30th, 1921 at the Church of St. Peter in the East, and after a fortnight's honeymoon settled at 10, Norham Road, Oxford, where they remained until 1931, when they moved to a larger house, No. 21 in the same road. Their first daughter, Hilary, was born in 1923, Joan in 1924, Patricia in 1926, their first son, Peter, in 1928 and their second son, Roger, in 1933.

In October, 1922, Kirk was elected Fellow and Chaplain of Trinity, succeeding E. A. Burroughs who later became Bishop of Ripon. It was not an easy job. His predecessor had not been very successful as a College chaplain and Kirk had to work hard to improve the chapel services and the attendance at them. Other people might have found an obstacle in the President, the Rev. H. E. D. Blakiston, who was a very remarkable character, but in a curious way the two formed a close friendship. After his retirement in 1938 Blakiston went to live on Boar's Hill and was a frequent celebrant of the Holy Communion in Kirk's private chapel at Sandridge. When he died as a result of a motor accident in 1942, Kirk, who was his executor, wrote in the Diocesan Magazine: "Of retiring disposition though he was, he was capable of very close friendships; and it so happened that he numbered among his friends every bishop of Oxford from Francis Paget onwards. (He must also have known Bishop Stubbs well, for the latter became an Honorary Fellow of Trinity in 1888; but the Bishop was the elder by 37 years, so there was little intimacy between them). When he resigned the presidency of Trinity, the undergraduates presented Dr. Blakiston with a fine silver tray, engraved with his arms and those of the College; this gift he has now bequeathed in perpetuity to the successive bishops of Oxford. It is to be further engraved with the coat of arms of the See, and is to record his happy memories of 'amicitia inter se et quinque episcopos Oxon: videlicet Doctores Paget, Gore, Burge, Strong et Kirk.' "

As a tutor Kirk taught theology for some other Colleges as well as for Trinity, and among his pupils were the present Chaplain of Trinity, Dr. A. M. Farrer, and the Lady Margaret Professor of Divinity, Dr. F. L. Cross. He also taught philosophy for P.P.E. in Trinity. One of his pupils in this subject recollects that he learned three things particularly from Kirk. First, that one should always, as far as possible, go to the original sources; second, that if one neglects to do this one should not expect to get away with it and fool intelligent people; and, third, that Christianity is a matter of life, not merely of argument. The truth of Christianity can only be found by living it.

As Kirk became known outside Oxford other appointments and engagements followed rapidly. In 1922 also Archbishop Davidson appointed him Six Preacher in Canterbury Cathedral. In 1924-5 he was again Pro-Proctor, this time to A. L. Poole of St. John's. In 1925 he was lecturing at Nottingham and Bristol. In 1931 there was more lecturing at Lennoxville in Canada, in 1932 at Bangor and Aberystwyth, besides numerous preaching engagements. All this was in addition to his work as a College chaplain and tutor, and to his activities as Controller of Lodgings, and yet it does not include that which was his main interest—the study of moral theology.

2

At the end of his contribution to *The Church in the Furnace* Kirk wrote these paragraphs:

If all men need our ministry, we must make ourselves accessible to all men. We must not burden ourselves unduly with organisation—the impossibility of losing himself in organisation has been one of the chaplain's greatest safeguards at the Front. We must be content to waste time wisely in the marketplace—gossiping like Socrates with all comers. But that this time may be *wisely* wasted in giving to all that spirit of serene activity which we have learnt to recognize as superlatively Christian, we must know, more than ever, the art of treating men as individuals. This art is given to some; but all can develop it with the development of their own souls; and those who are so developing it can forward its growth by study. Moral Theology has been much abused, yet it is exactly what is needed—the science of applying the broad principles of Christianity to particular cases. It seems to involve three branches—the discovery of general principles; the choice of the one most applicable to each particular case; and the skilful presentation of it in such a form that it meets with acceptance. In each of these branches much work has still to be done to bring them up to date. For the first we must study the special forms which sin,

temptation, and suffering take to-day, and know in general—not from book
learning but from genuine religious experience—in what way the Gospel is a
specific for each. For the second, the clergy must apply themselves to the study
of character and its diversities with far more industry than in the past; and
by fearlessly dissecting themselves must learn critically but sympathetically to
analyse others. It is pathetic that too often the vicar or the curate is the last
person in the parish to detect a hypocrite or rebuke an impostor; pathetic, also,
that he is the last to recognise excellence in an outward pagan or lapsed member
of the Church. For the third, we must learn to command acceptance of what
we teach not by virtue of our position ("It must be right because they do it at
St. George's"; "I know it's true, because the Archdeacon said so"), nor even by
the strength of logic, for logic never convinced an unwilling listener, and the
lesser educated of two men always suspects a trap in the argument of his
superior—but by the manifest truth that we have applied our principles to
ourselves, and that they have made us more peaceful, more charitable, and more
compassionate than before.

Equipped in some such way, the parish priest of to-morrow should be able
to undertake his work as a physician of souls with greater skill and a firmer
touch. Insight and training will have taught him to recognise the hidden causes
of spiritual disorders; he will be able to distinguish between the "feelings" or
"difficulties" of those who come to him for guidance, and the real needs of
which they are only symptoms; he will have learnt neither to mistake deep
humility for apparent callousness nor morbid self-denunciation for genuine
contrition. Experience will have shown him how to add discriminating treatment to wise diagnosis; when to be stern, when to be tender; what spiritual
exercises to recommend and what to deprecate in each particular case. And
lastly, sympathy and study will have fitted him to administer his remedies
in terms appropriate to the education and development of his hearers,
and in a manner that shall induce compliance without violating freedom
of choice.

When Kirk returned to Oxford he found that there were others
beside himself who had become interested in these problems, particularly the Rev. A. E. J. Rawlinson whom he had succeeded at Keble,
and Canon B. H. Streeter of Queen's. These two, together with Kirk's
former vicar, S. F. Hawkes, and Dr. J. A. Hadfield joined with Kirk
in a private conference on the relation of psycho-therapy to spiritual
direction. A little later, in 1922, at the suggestion of Archbishop
Davidson, Kirk and the Principal of Cuddesdon, Dr. Seaton, gathered
together a small conference on problems of Moral Theology. This
meeting was attended by the Rev. C. J. Shebbeare who later was to be
one of the examiners for Kirk's D.D. thesis.

Kirk himself lectured on Christian Morals in each Michaelmas
Term from 1919 to 1922, and in October, 1920, he published his first

big book *Some Principles of Moral Theology and their application*. This had grown out of a series of lectures delivered during 1918 to successive courses of temporary chaplains to the Forces at the Chaplains' Training Schools at Ripon and Catterick Camps, and it was dedicated to the Archdeacon of Richmond, H. Armstrong Hall, at that time Deputy-Assistant-Chaplain-General of the Northern Command. The Archdeacon had become a close friend of Kirk's and had encouraged him in his attempt "to present in systematic form the principles of the Church of England in the matter of conduct." Some seven years later Kirk described the book as follows:

In 'Some Principles of Moral Theology' I ventured to put forward a tentative scheme for the development and teaching of moral theology in the Church of England. The scheme was in the barest of outlines only; but it was an attempt to divide up the whole ground to be covered on a systematic plan, and thus to suggest a general background upon which clergy, and others whose vocation, interests or ideals led them to a study of Christian moral problems, might co-ordinate their thought and reading . . . [The book] borrowed its ground-plan (if that expression may be allowed) in the main from two sources—the 'Summa Theologica' of St. Thomas Aquinas and that adaptation of Thomist principles to the needs of the Church of England which underlies the writings of Bishops Sanderson and Jeremy Taylor.[1]

In the fifty years before Kirk wrote, only three books had apparently attempted to present the whole content of moral theology in such a form as should guide the theory and practice of the Church of England, and they were all out of print. Kirk followed them both in "recognising that the theology of St. Thomas Aquinas has a value for the Christian student of morals second only to that of the Bible and the Fathers" and also in never using later Roman Catholic writers except with the utmost caution. "The standing problem of all ethics", he wrote, "is the reconciliation of two apparently opposed principles, which may be called respectively the principles of law and liberty, or of authority and individualism." This was particularly the case with Christian ethics. A society with its roots in a divine revelation once given could not dispense with authority and law, and yet they must not interfere with the *true* freedom of the individual; he must be free to develop every part of his personality to its utmost in the service of God and his neighbour. "Christian theology then, above all other thought, is called to the task of solving this problem—the reconciliation of authority with freedom."

It was the great and abiding merit of St. Thomas Aquinas, Kirk

[1] *Conscience and its Problems.* p. xi.

held, that he attempted to effect such a reconciliation, but the Roman Church in later ages had not profited by his example. "If Protestant thought, as is usually held to be the case, has erred on the side of liberty and individualism, Roman Catholic theology has lapsed into an almost complete authoritarianism." For the student who was attempting to solve the problem of the relation between law and liberty there was little to be learnt from Rome.

The practice, therefore, of providing for the use of Anglican clergy handbooks of moral theology which are little more than translations of St. Alphonsus Liguori or his imitators, is one which can scarcely be deprecated too strongly. Should such a practice become at all common, it would give to Anglican moral theology a bias in the direction of legalism which might well be considered almost fatal.[1]

In the Church of England in the seventeenth century there had been a little group of divines—Hooker, Jeremy Taylor, Sanderson, Hall and their fellows, who had attempted to carry out St. Thomas's ideal of combining the principle of authority with that of freedom. "They had no doubts whatever as to the authority and divine commission of the Church, yet they rejected with finality the tendency of the Roman communion to push that authority to extremes." Kirk was not blind to their mistakes and limitations, but he believed that they had grasped and held fast the true ideal and deserved to be used freely in such a task as that upon which he was engaged.

Kirk was also insistent that there must be no sharp separation of moral from ascetic theology such as was not uncommon in Roman Catholic writers. "It is important in this matter to emphasise that theory and practice are very closely allied, and cannot be considered separately without great detriment to both." He quoted the emphatic words of James Skinner, the learned author of a *Synopsis of Moral and Ascetical Theology* published in London in 1882: "Whether a manual of moral theology for the use of priests in the English Church shall ever be compiled remains to be seen. But if ever it is undertaken, it must, in the largest sense, include spiritual and mystical theology. Otherwise we shall protract, among ourselves, the mischief of which the learned Benedictine, Martin Gerbert, complained in the middle of the last century: 'Huic enim divortio puto labem maximam theologiae debere: separationi quidem positivae a scholastica corruptiones theologiae theoreticae seu speculativae, separationi moralis a mystica corruptiones theologiae practicae tribuimus, *ubi mores Christiani sejuncti a virtutibus*

---

[1] *Some Principles of Moral Theology.* p. x.

Christianis fuerunt.' The whole end of our manual must be practical, not speculative."[1]

The survey undertaken in this first volume led Kirk to a special consideration of a problem which he formulated in the following terms:

The catholicism both of St. Thomas and the Caroline divines envisaged a Church clear in definition, authoritative in command, highly organised in administration and strict in discipline. The Church of England as we see it to-day, on the other hand, reveals a freedom of thought on the part of the individual, and a tolerance of that freedom on the part of authority, which would have startled both St. Thomas and his Anglican disciples. Is it fair, wise or profitable to attempt to adapt the principles of a closely-knit organism such as the Church which produced the moral theology of the past, to a loosely-knit association like the Church of England of the present?[2]

This problem he examined in *Ignorance, Faith and Conformity*, published in 1925, which is the least known of the three studies in moral theology and yet in some respects the most valuable. This book is mainly concerned with an examination of the concept of 'invincible ignorance' as it has developed in Christian theology. Kirk reached the following conclusions:

On the one hand, the Church of England has not abandoned any of the fundamental principles of the moral theology and canon law of the past, though some of them she has interpreted with a wise discretion; and others she holds, for the moment at all events, very much in reserve. And, on the other hand, the two factors of liberty of thought and of tolerance, which specially characterise contemporary Anglicanism, are not new phenomena in organised Christianity, though perhaps they have never before been seen in the same proportionate combination as to-day. Both factors were anticipated, recognised and provided for by the two principles of 'invincible ignorance' and of 'custom' which Christian experience has for centuries fully allowed and understood.[3]

He, therefore, held it right and justifiable to speak of Anglicanism as we know it, as within the limits of a legitimate development of the principles of Western Christendom as a whole, or as an experiment initiated within the legitimate bounds of true Catholicism; and he gave it as his opinion that this development or experiment, however strange and confused the circumstances which had conditioned it, was wholly

---

[1] *op. cit.* p. xii.   [2] *Conscience and its Problems.* p. xi.
[3] *ibid.* pp. xiif.

providential, and had brought to light new aspects of Christian truth of infinite value for the Church, which might otherwise have remained partly if not wholly unnoticed.

In 1927 Kirk published a third volume of moral theology called *Conscience and its Problems, An Introduction to Casuistry*. In the first part of this book, entitled 'Conscience and Casuistry' Kirk attempted to deal with some general problems of law and conscience. He recognized that it might have been more logical to have started a detailed approach to moral theology by a discussion of the purpose of life. "But", he wrote, "about the main principles of Christian conduct, as applicable to a civilisation like our own, there is little controversy. Difficulties only begin with the discussion of the subordinate precepts dependent upon these main principles; and such subordinate precepts can only be reached with any degree of assurance and unanimity if the rules of procedure adopted are both wise and commonly accepted. Here, therefore, at the point where controversy presses, a prior study of casuistry is all-essential." It might be held that these sentences belong essentially to the atmosphere of the twenties and show that Kirk's work in moral theology is irretrievably dated. Such a view would, however, be superficial. In all three of his moral theology books Kirk was grappling with problems that are real and continuing problems for Anglicans, as well as to some extent for Christians of other traditions also. He wrote with a good philosophical equipment, and against a background of knowledge of traditional moral theology as well as of current ethical theory which was equalled by few then and since. It may be safely predicted that any further work in Anglican moral theology will have to take serious account of these three books, and anyone who will take the pains to read them carefully, will find that his time has not been spent unrewardingly.

Although Kirk expressly disclaimed any attempt to discuss the purpose of life in *Conscience and its Problems* he did in fact treat of it in what is generally considered his greatest book, *The Vision of God*, which is an expanded form of the Bampton Lectures delivered in 1928. The thing that immediately strikes the reader of this massive volume is the quite extraordinary breadth of outlook and reading which lie behind it. In his earlier books Kirk had shown himself to have an unusual knowledge of scholastic writers and of the Anglican moralists of the seventeenth century. In *The Vision of God* he appears as a New Testament and Patristic scholar capable of taking his stand with any in the field. The Dean of Christ Church, Dr. John Lowe, in a letter to Kirk in 1939 wrote:

Perhaps I may be allowed to say, as a New Testament man, how filled with admiration I was at the knowledge of the modern literature in that field shown in the early part of "The Vision of God". It is rare enough in the professed teachers of N.T. in the English-speaking world to-day.

Perhaps the secret of it was that Kirk was, among other things, a 'professed teacher of N.T.'. Like other tutors he taught for the whole range covered by the Honour School of Theology, and from the Hilary Term, 1921, to the Trinity Term, 1937, with only one gap he lectured each year on the Theology of St. Paul. Moreover another course, which also became a regular one, on New Testament Ethics involved a detailed knowledge of current work in the field of New Testament studies. A comparison of the contents of *The Vision of God* with the Theology Lecture List down to the Michaelmas Term, 1937 shows, in fact, how closely that book was related to Kirk's teaching as a public lecturer and how he continued, after it had come out, to develop and expand its themes in his various courses. The present writer was fortunate enough to attend both the course on New Testament Ethics and that on the Theology of St. Paul in the last two terms in which Kirk lectured and his notes show how several of the themes of *The Vision of God* received then a developed treatment. Incidentally it may be noted that from October, 1924, to December, 1937, Kirk gave at least one, and sometimes two or three courses of lectures each term.

In *The Vision of God* Kirk disclaimed any attempt at writing a full history of the Christian doctrine of the *summum bonum*, but he came so near to doing it that any adequate summary of his book is impossible here. It is necessary, however, to outline the main theme which Kirk expressed in the following sentence:

It is suggested, therefore, in the chapters which follow, that the doctrine 'the end of life is the vision of God' has thoughout been interpreted by Christian thought at its best as implying in practice that the highest prerogative of the Christian, in this life as well as hereafter, is the activity of *worship*; and that nowhere except in this activity will he find the key to his ethical problems.[1]

Beside this may be set the following paragraph from the final lecture:

The doctrine that the 'end of man is the vision of God', as a practical maxim for life, implies that the Christian should set himself first of all to focus his thought upon God in the spirit of worship. It implies this of necessity, and of necessity it implies nothing more—nothing whatever as to the achieving of pleasures, rapture, exaltation in the act of worship. The only achievement man

[1] *The Vision of God.* p. ix.

has the right to hope for is that of greater Christian saintliness—greater zeal for service—coming from this direction of the heart and mind to God. It can hardly be denied that in so far as unselfishness is possible in this life at all (to anticipate for a moment another question), this is an unselfish ideal. To look towards God, and from that 'look' to acquire insight both into the follies of one's own heart and the needs of one's neighbours, with power to correct the one no less than to serve the other—this is something very remote from any quest for 'religious experience' for its own sake. Yet this, and nothing else, is what the vision of God has meant in the fully developed thought of historic Christianity.[1]

No one can study the course of Kirk's later life without seeing how this understanding of the primacy of worship was the centre of it all. That, however, is to anticipate. The Bampton Lectures are the crown of Kirk's work in moral theology. They illustrate the contention of his first book that moral and ascetic theology are inseparable. They remain a monument of organized scholarship and insight, one of the great and classic works of Anglican theology. It was, no doubt, this book above all that prompted Dr. Spencer Leeson in speaking to the present writer of the loss to the Church caused by Kirk's death to refer to him as 'the greatest master of the spiritual life of our time'.

The publication of Kirk's first two books and the work that he was doing in the University put moral theology forward as an academic subject in a way which had not been realized in earlier generations. In so far as it was touched on at all before Kirk's arrival it was the responsibility of the Regius Professor of Pastoral Theology whose duty it was to lecture *in Theologia quam vocant Pastorali quo nomine continentur Pastoralis muneris disciplina, conciones sive homilias scribendi et habendi ratio, Liturgicarum cum Rubricis historia, et alia ejusdem generis.* This Professorship had been founded early in the nineteenth century at a time when fresh attention was being paid to the problem of the training of the clergy and when by far the greater part of that training was still undertaken in the Universities of Oxford and Cambridge. Theological Colleges were barely heard of and regarded with suspicion. After the 1914-18 war things were very different. It became increasingly rare for men to be ordained without passing through a Theological College, and the subject matter of the courses on preaching, the Prayer Book and general pastoralia given by the Professor of Pastoral Theology was now all dealt with in those Colleges and seemed out of place in the curriculum of the University.

Moreover reform in the University was taking place in consequence

[1] *The Vision of God.* pp. 444f.

of a Royal Commission and the time seemed ripe for the Faculty of Theology to make some overhaul of its teaching arrangements. In May, 1925, at a meeting of the Theology Board, Professor C. H. Turner, the distinguished historian of the early Church and an authority on early canon law, moved the appointment of a committee to consider the Statute defining the subjects which fell under the Chair of Pastoral Theology. The committee consisted of the Regius Professor (H. L. Goudge), the Lady Margaret Professor (W. Lock), the Regius Professor of Pastoral Theology (R. H. Ottley), C. H. Turner, C. C. J. Webb, L. Hodgson and A. E. J. Rawlinson. In consequence of their recommendations, which were accepted by the Board and by the Hebdomadal Council, the title of the Professorship was changed to that of Regius Professor of Moral and Pastoral Theology, and the scope of the Chair was defined as follows:

The Regius Professor of Moral and Pastoral Theology shall lecture and give instruction in Moral and Pastoral Theology, in the duties of the Pastoral Office, and in such subjects as Christian Ethics, both Social and Individual, Ascetic and Mystical Theology, and the Study of the various types of Christian Experience.

A result of this change was to exclude the subject of Liturgies, on which the Professor had hitherto lectured, at least as regarded the Prayer Book, but the Theology Board in sending their recommendation to Council added the following note on that point:

In view of the fact that in this proposed modification of the Statute the subject of Liturgiology is omitted the Board wishes that Council should know that provision is at present made (and will, the Board hopes, continue to be made) by a University Lecturership for teaching in that subject.

The Regius Professor, Dr. Ottley, took the new title but was not expected to make any change in the type of instruction that he had given for so many years. Kirk was, however, in May, 1927, appointed University Reader in Moral Theology, the Board recommending him in these words:

The revived interest of modern times in the problems of Moral and Practical Theology has given rise to a demand (not at present being effectively met) for the provision of teaching in these subjects by the University. Dr. Kirk, whose first considerable work, *Some Principles of Moral Theology* (published in 1920), has been widely used as a text-book has shown by the publication in 1925 of a treatise of a more technical kind (*Ignorance, Faith, and Conformity*) that he possesses both the will and the capacity to find time for really learned and scientific research in his chosen field of investigation, and it is understood that a third volume (*Conscience and its Problems*) is in the press, and will shortly appear. As a pioneer in the study of Moral Theology upon lines which are not merely traditional, Dr. Kirk has already a growing reputation, and is widely consulted.

It was, therefore, natural and proper that when Dr. Ottley died Kirk should succeed him. He was nominated by the Crown at the end of March, 1933, and installed as Canon of Christ Church on April 22nd. There had been a good deal of talk about the possibility of his succeeding F. R. Barry as Vicar of the University Church, continuing to hold his Trinity Fellowship, but difficulties arose and the Professorship, which was obviously much more suitable, became vacant. Five years earlier he had refused the Principalship of Cuddesdon. A year later the newspapers made free with his name as a likely successor to Dr. Inge as Dean of St. Paul's. Whether he actually received the offer of the deanery or whether it was pure rumour does not appear.

The new Regius Professor of Moral and Pastoral Theology was just forty-seven years of age, and already marked out as one of the leading scholars of the Church, and a man who might be expected to occupy the highest office. In Oxford he was widely known as a man of great intellectual as well as practical ability but his very cleverness made him somewhat suspect. Then and later Kirk seemed to delight in finding a round-about and ingenious approach to problems which others would have tackled more directly. In consequence he was often thought to have ulterior motives, which was in fact not true, as those who knew him well testify. In ecclesiastical circles he made himself somewhat unpopular by supporting the abolition of 'Divvers' the examination in Scripture which all undergraduates had to take at that time. Many of those who were theologically of his way of thinking were often never quite sure where they stood with him. He was never a person of narrow interests or acquaintanceships, and some of those who were far removed from his doctrinal standpoint have testified to the friendship and real kindness which they had from him.

Those who came to know him well realized how intensely happy was his family life and how much enjoyment he derived from his children. When they were small he took endless trouble to amuse and instruct them, and they were all brought up with his interest in music and the theatre, and particularly in Gilbert and Sullivan. Every year there was a family holiday in some country or seaside resort where Kirk took a locum and, apart from his duties in the church, devoted himself entirely to the children. In addition in several years he and his wife had a further holiday alone together. Three of these were cycling holidays in France which he enjoyed immensely and often talked about. He had a real interest in literature, art, music and architecture, though his tastes were in the main rather conventional and conservative. His sermons frequently contained references which showed how he practised the recommendations that Bishop Edward King gave in his lectures on preaching: "Read the poets ethically . . . Read good novels. You will thus travel into circumstances, and conditions, and situations of life. This knowledge of man must exist in order to apply the other knowledge." Kirk's theology was never academic in the bad sense of that word. He was too much involved in the work of teaching and administration, and in the care and love of a family for him to be able to separate doctrine and life.

It was some time before Kirk was able to move into Christ Church. The house occupied by Dr. Ottley was not a convenient one for a family of young children and the chapter decided to divide the large house occupied by the Archdeacon of Oxford, making half of it into a convenient home for Kirk and his family. The new house was not ready for occupation until November, 1934, and in the meantime the great tragedy of Kirk's life had occurred.

His marriage had been very happy. His wife had proved the ideal partner for him, and certainly without the background of a happy and well-run home he could not have accomplished the remarkable amount of work already surveyed in this chapter. Both he and his wife were unwell during the winter of 1933-4, and early in May Mrs. Kirk became seriously ill with pneumonia. After a fortnight there was some improvement for three or four days but only to be followed by a second collapse and she died at 9.20 on the morning of Sunday, June 3rd. This was a blow from which Kirk never entirely recovered. The detailed account of his wife's death and funeral which he wrote with directions that his own funeral should resemble hers in all particulars as nearly as possible is some indication of his feelings. A letter written many years later and printed elsewhere in this volume[1] bears similar testimony. He was a lonely man for the rest of his life.

There were, however, immediate practical problems to be faced. He was fortunate in finding before the end of June an admirable housekeeper in Miss Harden who remained with the family until illness caused her retirement in 1941. Then there was the usual round of sermons and external lectures as well as the duties of the Canonry and Professorship. In 1935 he published a volume of sermons under the title of *The Fourth River*, words taken from the first sermon in the book

[1] p. 205.

which was on the text 'And the fourth river is Euphrates' (Gen. ii. 14).
These sermons in their combination of an ingenious and unexpected
treatment of the texts with acute psychological insight are typical
examples of his preaching at that time. Beautifully constructed as they
are they were mostly delivered without a note of any kind in front of
the preacher. During the years of Kirk's Professorship Christ Church
numbered among its canons a group of scholars of more than usual
distinction, several of whom were outstanding as preachers. The two
who were recognized as the most brilliant were Kirk himself and Dr.
N. P. Williams, the Lady Margaret Professor.

It has fallen to the present writer to give an account elsewhere of Dr.
Williams,[1] and little more needs to be said about him here. Williams
and Kirk were, in the thirties, the two outstanding representatives of
the movement of thought known as Liberal Catholicism, a movement
which may be said to have begun with Charles Gore and which centred
mainly in the Oxford Faculty of Theology, the somewhat analogous
Cambridge group of scholars being with certain notable exceptions
more akin in their outlook to Roman Catholic modernism. In the
Catholic movement in the Church of England there was at this period
no divorce between the scholars, such as Kirk, Williams, Darwell
Stone, B. J. Kidd, and the parish priests. A glance at the Reports of
the Anglo-Catholic Congresses of 1920, 1923, 1927 and 1933 will show
the importance attached by the movement as a whole to sound
theology, and the attention paid to the professional theologians. Kirk
did not either then or later have much connexion with the party
organization, but he was a regular speaker at the Congresses and other
such gatherings.

Some discussion of Kirk's contributions to the Congresses of 1923
and 1927 will be found elsewhere in this volume. The present chapter
may conclude with a reference to his address to the Oxford Movement
Centenary Congress in 1933. The title of the address was 'Truth' and
Kirk spoke of the achievement of the Tractarians as being the recovery
of certain great truths of Christianity which had been forgotten in the
Church of England. He listed among them the sacramental character
of the Church, the social mission of the Church, the personal holiness
of the genuine Christian and the pastoral authority of the Church.
The fifth and last of them was the truth of the Church's spiritual
independence. Of this Kirk said:

No Church can speak or act with spiritual authority which truckles to the
whims of party politics or accepts its mandates and its limitations from the

[1] E. W. Kemp, *N. P. Williams*. S.P.C.K. *1954*.

State. Spiritual dependence is as dangerous to a religious organism as temporal power. It is no accident that the Oxford Movement began with a sermon addressed wholly to this theme, nor that throughout its hundred years of history its opponents have consistently appealed to the secular arm. They recognized, as clearly as the Tractarians emphasized, its character as a challenge to Erastianism, which must culminate in the extinction of one or the other. The right of the Church to live her own life, to proclaim her own truths, to guide her own members, is a right which the great Leviathan has always denied; but a Church which does not assert it in season and out of season is a Church which carries the seeds of death within itself.[1]

He then went on to consider how far these truths had survived the test of time and to suggest certain weaknesses in the current witness to them. He concluded with the following paragraph on the question of the spiritual independence of the Church, a paragraph part of which is sometimes quoted but which needs to be borne in mind as a whole by churchmen of the present day at least as much as by those of a quarter of a century ago. Indeed, it might be said that if these words had been heeded at the time and acted upon, the Church would not be facing many of its present difficulties and humiliations.

We have time only to glance for a moment at the present and future of the fifth truth, that of the spiritual independence of the Church. Here, I believe, unless we take the matter seriously to heart, we are heading straight for disaster. Despite the prominence which this truth attained in the Tractarian struggle, it is one which to-day goes almost unheeded. We may speak of "disestablishment" or of "re-establishment", or what we will, but the fact remains that the matter is one of the merest academic interest to ninety-nine out of every hundred churchmen. When all due allowance has been made for the proper prerogatives of the Crown, or of Parliament, or of the nation as a whole, we have seen the temporality invade the sphere of the spirituality over and over again. And yet we are not alive to the danger, and those who speak of it speak to deaf ears. The crisis may come at any moment; for my own part I believe it will come almost certainly in the matter of marriage. The Christian principle of life-long monogamy will be flouted, if I read the signs aright, on some spectacular occasion in a manner which we cannot afford to ignore; and the whole question of the Church's right to make her own demands upon her members, and to exercise her own discipline if they refuse to comply, will flare up in a veritable pillar of fire. I do not know how many of us here know what we shall do when that challenge comes; but I am certain that the leaders of the Oxford Movement, had it seemed as close to them as it is to us, would have been alert to the problem. It is of *Truth* we are thinking this afternoon, and here is a truth which has been too long neglected. To think it out, to make

[1] *Report of the Oxford Movement Centenary Congress, July 1933.* p. 32.

it live, to bring it home to the consciences of churchmen, is a task fraught with the utmost difficulties. But the Tractarians saw that it was a truth upon which depended the whole existence of the Church of England, considered as a living witness to the teaching of her Master, and not as a State-controlled machine for the diffusion of conventional morality; and I believe that they were right. It is sometimes said that the sacrament of Unction is the lost pleiad of the Anglican firmament; is it not perhaps the case that, at the present day, the spiritual independence of the Church is the lost pleiad of the Tractarian truths? And if we recognize the fact and set ourselves to put it right, our review of those truths will not have been in vain.[1]

[1] *op. cit.* pp. 35f.

NOTE: For a fuller study of Kirk's moral theology see V. A. Demant: *Kenneth Kirk as Moral Theologian*, in *The Church Quarterly Review*, Oct.–Dec., 1957, and an unpublished thesis presented to the University of Lille by the Rev. F. Frost, in 1958, *La conscience morale dans l'œuvre de Bishop Kirk (1886–1954)*.

V

THE COHERENCE OF CHRISTIAN DOCTRINE

IT will be plain from what has been said in the preceding chapters that Kirk did not view moral theology in any narrow sense or regard himself as a specialist who must keep strictly to his chosen field of study. His mind was comprehensive and encyclopedic as well as penetrating and he was always alive to the importance of maintaining a close connexion between moral and dogmatic theology. In 1949 he delivered the Charles Gore Memorial Lecture taking as his text an oft quoted phrase of Gore's 'the wonderful coherence of Christian doctrine'. While recognizing that no human system of thought about the things of God can be wholly coherent because the mind of man is finite, and cannot grasp the plenitude of truth about the Infinite, Kirk nevertheless affirms that Christian doctrine is a unified whole and that if the Christian apprehension of any one doctrine weakens or becomes merely conventional, the disease will spread throughout the body. It was Kirk's own aim to try to keep all parts of his theology properly related. To some extent this was done in the lectures on the Theology of St. Paul, much of which appeared in print in 1937 in the Introduction to his volume on the Epistle to the Romans, published in the Clarendon Bible. That Introduction, however, does not give a full account of the course and in particular omits important passages on the Atonement and on Universalism. Kirk has been criticized for forcing St. Paul's thought into too systematic a form and no doubt his approach is not that of a present-day Pauline scholar, but as a comprehensive essay in Christian doctrine, based squarely upon the New Testament, the course was a masterly production.

In addition, Kirk lectured regularly from 1926 to 1933 on 'The Doctrine of the Trinity', and he contributed an important chapter on this subject to the volume *Essays on the Trinity and the Incarnation* edited by Dr. Rawlinson in 1928. Kirk's treatment of some of the patristic material has been criticized, notably by Dr. Prestige, but there is much else in the essay that remains of importance, as has been recognized, for example, by Dr. Hodgson in his own book on *The Doctrine of the Trinity*.[1] In 1935 in three lectures delivered in the new chapel of Lady Margaret Hall and later published under the title of

[1] See pp. 38 and 112ff.

The Crisis of Christian Rationalism Kirk surveyed critically some modern discussions (particularly in Archbishop Temple's Gifford Lectures) of the problems of Revelation and of the Malignity of Evil, before going on to the more strictly ethical subjects of Freedom, Happiness and Duty. This small book is less well-known than Kirk's larger works and deserves attention.

Towards the end of his life Kirk was, through force of circumstances, more particularly concerned with the doctrines of the Church and of the Ministry and in 1946 he edited the volume of essays called *The Apostolic Ministry* to which he himself contributed an important discussion bearing the general title of the book. This massive volume has been the centre of much controversy which it would be outside the scope of a biography to survey. Attention should, however, be drawn to the important new Foreword contributed by Dr. Farrer to the third impression of the book in 1957. A re-reading of Kirk's own chapter, in the light of subsequent controversy has somewhat surprised the present writer by how little of it he would wish to alter. Kirk wrote very carefully, probably rather more carefully than some of his collaborators, with the result that much of the historical criticism levelled at other parts of the book passes him by. His essay stands as a masterly and charitable exposition and it is devastating in its discussion of some of the more woolly official utterances on the subject of the Christian Ministry.

This short survey set beside the four big books of the twenties shows the breadth of Kirk's mind and theological interests. There is, however, one subject to which he is found constantly recurring, the doctrine of the Atonement. In the lecture 'The Coherence of Christian Doctrine' referred to above Kirk chose to illustrate his theme by a short survey of the relation of thought about the Atonement to thought about the Incarnation in the last hundred and fifty years and it is therefore of some interest that his first published discussion[1] of the Atonement should in fact be an address under the title 'God made Man' delivered to the Anglo-Catholic Congress in 1923 and printed in the Report of the Congress.

In this address starting from the Johannine text 'For their sakes I sanctify myself' which he interpreted in the Old Testament sense of 'sanctify' as 'For their sakes I become a priest', Kirk asked his hearers to think of the Incarnation in terms of a human ordination.

Priesthood attempts to bring God and man together, to mediate between them, to reconcile and atone. The priest brings sinful man to God with such

[1] Apart, that is, from a passing reference on pp. 82ff. of *A Study of Silent Minds*.

sacrifice as may be offered for his sin; and so our Lord presents men to the Father after paying for them the debt of sin which none but he could pay. Of that I say no more, for the subject is allotted to another speaker: and there is a second aspect of priesthood for us to notice now. Priesthood not only brings man near to God; it also brings God near again to sinful man. It restores to man that life of the Spirit, of communion with the Father, which we have broken and lost through sin. For be certain of this—sin is no passing cloud on a summer's day: it is a devastating tempest. It is no transient faintness; but a disease that brings spiritual death in its train. By sin each of us loses God. By sin we become *atheists* indeed, "without God in the world". But the priesthood of Christ Incarnate means that he has brought back and bestowed upon man once more the life of communion, of spiritual fulness, which should be ours by virtue of God's creative love.[1]

Four years later, at the 1927 Congress, Kirk was asked to speak explicitly about 'The Sacrifice of Calvary', and he tried briefly to answer two questions: 'Why did God need a sacrifice?' and 'How does Christ's death upon the cross satisfy that need?' With regard to the first he reminded his hearers that penitence alone does not wipe out the past.

God builds a beautiful temple when he creates a human soul; he writes a beautiful story when he plots a human life. But you and I by sin have desecrated the temple and spoilt the story in the telling; a new life—a converted life—may repair the damage (make reparation, as we say); it cannot efface it. "All for sin could not atone"; if God's need is to be satisfied, it will be satisfied only by other efforts than yours and mine.[2]

In going on to the second question, however, he rejected any suggestion that God's need was for more punishment to be meted out, more suffering endured, more wrath appeased; in other words he rejected all the crude forms of substitutionary theory.

These are not Christian conceptions. Revert once more to the figures we have chosen. The temple which God built, the story he planned, were marred and made impossible by sin; and in the temple and the story are signified the sinless human life lived, not by automatons, but by self-conscious free-willed men. Something of infinite value to God was defiled, beyond all cleansing by human effort; men whom he had made upright sought out, and degraded themselves with, the many inventions of sin. Only one thing could restore to God's sight the vision thus cloaked in darkness. That one thing was a Perfect and Sinless human life; and such a life was lived to its culmination in the obedience of the Cross by our Redeemer. He built a new Temple, more perfect than the first, which no hostile effort could destroy: he made a new

[1] *Report of the Anglo-Catholic Congress, 1923.* pp. 55f.   [2] *ibid. 1927.* p. 87.

story—a story which we still call the good news of Jesus Christ. If by no other figure, then perhaps by this we may perceive, as in a glass darkly, something of the way in which Christ's life and death satisfied God's need, and so became the perfect sacrifice for sin . . .

The Christian Church has seen the Son of God descend from heaven as Son of Man, to replace on earth that travesty of manhood which is all that sin has left of true humanity. All the conditions of a sacrifice for sin are here complete. It is needed; it is costly; it—and it alone—cancels the offence of sin. We look to a Redeemer, crucified in death, but crucified in life as well, by reason of his sinlessness in the midst of a sinful world; and we know that the offence of the past has been blotted out by God in his own sight; that his eyes see—as do ours also—nothing but the perfect Realization of the Man.[1]

In these passages Kirk is concerned with what is generally called the 'objective' aspect of the Atonement. A more extended treatment of this same aspect is to be found in section VII of his Essay on the Atonement in *Essays Catholic and Critical*, a volume edited by Dr. E. G. Selwyn in 1926. This section of the Essay is called 'Christ's Death the Price of Sin'. In it Kirk uses the parable of the two brothers (Matt. xxi. 28-31) to point the truth that where offence has been offered a mere cessation of the offence does not restore the original relationship which existed before the offence.

Even a complete reversal of behaviour can scarcely be thought to suffice, though it comes nearer to sufficiency. Something more is demanded—something in which the offender explicitly acknowledges his fault and asks for forgiveness and restoration, even though he knows that forgiveness and restoration are his without the asking. But when we come to say *what* it is which demands this reparation for the past, our limited knowledge of eternal truth makes it difficult to give an answer. Phrases have been multiplied to express the source of the demand . . . Perhaps we can do no more than borrow a theological term popular in many other connections; it is πρεπον, *conveniens*, "fit" that the past be explicitly acknowledged in this way, before we turn to the future with its hoped-for newness of life . . . [2]

When Christendom regains its appreciation of exact theology it will be possible to say plainly: "God, in no arbitrary or vindictive spirit, calls for acknowledgment of past sin as a piece of natural justice": and the conscience of man will recognise the essential truth of the statement without falling into the errors so common in modern thought.[3]

It is in the desire to make restitution or reparation that Kirk sees the essence of sacrifice. He goes on to make the further points, that it is not so much the actual as the symbolic value of the sacrifice that makes it

[1] *Report of the Anglo-Catholic Congress, 1927.* pp. 88f.
[2] *Essays Catholic and Critical, 1926.* pp. 263f.   [3] *ibid.* p. 265.

acceptable, and that if A has no appropriate sacrifice of his own that he can bring to the altar, he can avail himself of, associate himself with, B's offering. "Another's gift can still be offered validly, if the desire to offer sacrifice is there, and no other means avail."

To all who fail to find within themselves adequate means for that expression of real contrition of which we have spoken, the Church offers her doctrine that the death of Christ is the divinely appointed means of help in this respect . . . "On the cross," she says, "we see One wholly akin to ourselves offering a sinless life to the Father as representative for man. There is no confession of sin on His lips, for He did no sin; otherwise His sacrifice would have been, in its measure, imperfect as ours have always been. And if we attribute to the Father the intent to give His only-begotten Son for the world's salvation, we can scarcely be wrong in seeing in His death this purpose also, that man should be provided with an adequate sacrifice and symbol of penitence—a symbol sufficient to satisfy the demand of 'natural justice' or the 'fitness of things'."[1]

To this is added the further argument that sin is a corporate matter which cannot be adequately dealt with by the offering of a series of individual reparations. "Natural fitness, we may say, demands that human nature—if not universal nature too—shall in one symbolic corporate act express the conviction, shared by God and man alike, that sin is foreign to its ideal constitution."

Once we revert to the Pauline conception of the corporate character of sin, the absolute necessity for some such act as the death of Christ becomes transcendently clear. We are in a position to endorse the familiar statements that in Him humanity paid the price as a whole, and that He died as the Representative Man; for it is only a soul preoccupied with the thought of "my sin" to the exclusion of that of "sin" as a whole which can hesitate any more to confess that, without such an offering, the sacrifice demanded by natural fitness is still unoffered, and salvation, which must at least involve full and final reconciliation with the loving Father of all mankind, remains not merely difficult or doubtful of attainment, but completely and finally impossible.[2]

Kirk has, however, been criticized by Mr. G. W. C. Thomas in an interesting article in the *Church Quarterly Review* for 1957, on the ground that although he insisted on the need for Reparation he left the nature of the Reparation itself undefined. This is probably a fair criticism of the chapter in *Essays Catholic and Critical*, but we have seen that in his 1927 Anglo-Catholic Congress paper Kirk did go some way towards providing a definition. The lectures on the Theology of St. Paul throw more light on the problem. In discussing St. Paul's conception of Christ's saving work Kirk emphasizes, as he had done in an

[1] *ibid.* p. 267.   [2] *ibid.* p. 269.

earlier passage in *Essays Catholic and Critical*, the importance of the Resurrection. He then passes to the aspect of the doctrine which we have just been considering. The whole section of the lectures is given here as taken down by the present writer in the Trinity Term of 1937.

The great change which has come over the Christian is not attributed by Paul to one cause alone. It has its origin explicitly in the love of the Father. The fact that Christ died for us while we were yet sinners (Rom. v. 8), is a proof of God's love. The sacrifice of Christ was as costly to the Father as to Himself (Rom. viii. 3, Gal. iv. 4). This is the origin of our justification. The agent is the righteousness and obedience of Christ (Phil. ii. 8, Rom. v. 18, consult commentaries). 'Through one act of righteousness the free gift came to all men' (Gal. i. 4, ii. 20, Eph. v. 2). The specific method is the Cross and sufferings and death, the word of the Cross (1 Cor. i. 18, 1 Cor. i. 17, ii. 2, Gal. vi. 14, Phil. iii. 18). The sufferings find consummation in the Resurrection (Rom. vi. 9, 10, 1 Cor. xv. 17, cf. 2 Cor. v. 15, Phil. iii. 10). Therefore to separate the death from the Resurrection is entirely repugnant to Paul's mind.

The result of this series of activities on the part of God is the complete defeat of all the forces of evil, so that Paul can say that Christ had a triumph like that of a Roman Emperor (Col. ii. 15), in which each of the forces of evil is paraded stripped of power and reduced to contemptibility. Paul carries this idea out in Rom. viii. 3, 1 Cor. xv. 54, Rom. x. 4, Gal. iii. 25, Eph. iv. 8,—the Law has been annulled (Col. ii. 14, Gal. iii. 13, i. 4).

How are man's two great needs met by the death etc. of Christ? a) That God should be vindicated against the accusation of indifference to sin; b) that Man should be cleared from the sense of guilt. If these can be met Paul's gospel, *so far as it refers to the past*, is complete.

(*a*) Paul never deals with the first question in any extended discussion. It is clear that he believed that if God at the cost of His own Son's suffering and death engaged and triumphed over sin it is ridiculous to accuse Him of indifference to sin (Rom. v. 18, 19, viii. 3). He has produced the effect that the righteousness of the Law might be fulfilled in us. God has in the life, and death of Christ opened to man the possibility of a full life of righteousness. This refutes the view that He is indifferent to the struggles of the righteous.

The conquest of sin by Christ is not a mere demonstration but an act of power—it is the theory of Christ's Vicarious Victory. One like ourselves has died sinless in the face of malice and desertion—His victory is not His own sinlessness but His Resurrection; thereby death and sin have been deprived of their uniqueness—a gap has been made in the defences, and man through Christ can pass through unscathed. But the victory, though final is not yet complete— as in Col. i. 24. Nothing that remains can equal the battle Christ fought, and no local reverses can hinder the future universal conquest. Thus God is in no way indifferent to sin, but sent His Son to overcome it and offers His power to any who will embrace it.

(*b*) So the thought passes from the vindication of God to the justification of man; his relief from despair. Despair has no longer any valid place in human life; uncertainty, fear and suspicion have been replaced by newness of life (Rom. vi. 10, 11, viii. 6, 10, Col. iii. 1), joy (Rom. v. 11), peace (Rom. v. 1, Eph. ii. 14, Col. i. 20), exhortation 'boasting' (Rom. v. 2, Phil. iii. 3) and by continual consolations (2 Cor. i. 3, 4, παράκλησις). Paul so emphasises this aspect of the Christian life that he can leave on one side the word 'repentance'. That does not mean that the idea of repentance is foreign to him. He puts it in other forms (e.g. Gal. iv. 9, Rom. vi. 7, Eph. iv. 22, v. 14, Rom. i. 5, vi. 16, 17). He is so impressed by Christ's victory that he can speak as if in him humanity had already played its part in bringing the victory to completion: that is the meaning of his mystical identification of Christians with Christ, as in Rom. v. or vi, or 2 Cor. v. In this Paul is rhetorically anticipating the final triumph over all powers of evil which shall be manifest when all are identified with Christ or with Him have died to sin.

Because the victorious cross was infinitely costly it is natural that Paul should connect it with phrases connected with O.T. sacrifices (e.g. Rom. iii. 25), ἱλαστήριον, connected with the sprinkling of the blood of sacrifice over the mercy seat of the Day of Atonement, in 1 Cor. v. 7 our 'passover sacrificed for us', Rom. viii. 3 'concerning sin', 2 Cor. v. 21, God made Him 'sin on our behalf'—referring to the sin offerings of the O.T. because in the LXX ἁμαρτία is constantly so used. Christ is also a 'bloodless sacrifice' (Eph. v. 2). Christians are to present themselves in the same way (2 Cor. ii. 15, Phil. iv. 18). All this language would be quite natural and justified in connexion with the Atonement as a vicarious victory won by Christ on man's behalf, as it would emphasize the costliness of that encounter to Christ Himself, and so stimulate the gratitude and devotion of Christians. But in the history of Christian thought this sacrificial language, though not so strongly marked in Paul as in Hebrews or the Johannines, has led people to attribute to him a different doctrine of the Atonement from this.

The Justification of Man—his acquittal from guilt. Writers have taken the word 'justification' in this sense and have brought it into close relation with this sacrificial language, interpreting the latter in a crude and primitive sense. In the uncivilized mind two ideas are connected with sacrifice: a) it is placatory; b) it is substitutionary; i.e. it pacifies God by substituting an innocent victim for a guilty person. On these interpretations theologians have developed a doctrine of the Atonement which is transactionary, substitutionary, or forensic. Man is guilty of sin and cannot pay the price demanded by God—Christ has paid it, and God, indifferent to the question as to who pays it, remits the charge of guilt. If we add to this the doctrine that the Father Himself made as great a sacrifice as Christ did in the atoning work we are reduced to a more contemptuous conception of God—He is not only tyrannical, but so pedantic that, rather than that the fine should not be paid, pays it Himself, and in this case he pays it to Himself. The Atonement becomes a book-keeping transaction in which God keeps His accounts straight.

Has the substitutionary theory of Christ's death any place in St. Paul? Dr. Rashdall (p. 92) says it is impossible to eliminate it entirely. This is derived from 1. his use of sacrificial language; 2. (Gal. iii. 13) 'became a curse for us'; 3. the narrow sense of justification. Against this we must note 1. that the sacrificial language is incidental (except ἱλαστήριον); 2. that any reference to the wrath of God is avoided; 3. little is said about repentance, as if to avoid ideas of guilt and reparation; 4. 'reconciliation' is used as of man being reconciled to God—not vice versa; 5. while he does speak of Christ as suffering ὑπέρ ἡμῶν, he never speaks of Him suffering *in our stead*, as is required by the substitutionary doctrine. We are left with only two passages which could possibly support the substitutionary idea:—1. (Gal. iii. 13). The Galatians lived in an atmosphere of Greek culture where the idea of the family curse was a commonplace of tragedy and the only possibility was that some peculiarly perfect member of the family should take the burden of the curse on to his own shoulders to let it work itself out on him. Paul's use of the word is a happy illustration of his doctrine for Greek not Jewish readers. 2. ἱλαστήριον: a mysterious word belonging to a group of words used in the O.T. to solve the problem of sin: they can be used of man cleansing himself from defilement, or of God forgiving and being propitious. In Rom. iii. 25, it may be a reference to the Day of Atonement and may be connected with a substitutionary sacrifice, but this is not necessary. So one cannot say that Paul uses barbaric language about the death of Christ; only that by His death Christ won a victory on the part of man.[1]

Behind the substitutionary doctrine lies the idea that Christ did not merely open the door to man to a new status in the future but also corrected and adjusted something arising out of man's past sin. It is possible to make this addition to the doctrine without involving the immoral doctrine of substitution in the matter of punishment. There is a suggestion in Paul that man's sin had indeed been an act of injury to God which man could not correct, and that natural fitness demands that it should be corrected, and that Christ effected for man what man could not do, so that although there must still remain remorse for the past there is no longer a sense that something irreparable has been done. Rom. i. 23, summarising the whole of human sin says that man changed the glory of the invisible God—defaced or degraded it. By glory Paul means the visible manifestation of God in the temporal sphere. He is going back to the idea that man was made in the image of God and that his purpose should have been to retain that image and so continue to be the glory of God. But human sin has so warped human nature that it has ceased altogether to be the image of God, and therefore there is no longer in the universe a visible representative of the divine nature. Christ coming as the image of God (2 Cor. iv. 4, Col. i. 15), has restored things to their primitive state, has brought back the glory of God among men. That conception, which underlies also the prologue to John's Gospel 'we beheld His glory', is

[1] On this paragraph see also the Clarendon Bible Commentary on Romans pp. 65-68.

not obviously a doctrine of substitutionary punishment. It rectifies the past, not in the sense of paying a fine demanded by God, but in the sense of repairing a damage which man cannot repair and so satisfying the demands not of an exacting God but of natural justice or fitness. It may be given the name of Vicarious Reparation.

All the terms of Paul's thought about the Atonement can be summed up in the phrase Vicarious Victory and Vicarious Reparation. Here is a truly objective doctrine of the Atonement in so far as it insists that Christ did something for man, independent of man's efforts and merits, which man could never do for himself, and yet a doctrine which does not carry any of the immoral implications of substitutionary punishment or sacrifice which has so often been discovered in St. Paul and in the N.T. as a whole.[1]

These passages show how closely in his own mind Kirk linked the doctrines of the Incarnation and the Atonement. In his lecture 'The Coherence of Christian Doctrine' he pointed out how by the end of the nineteenth century attention was focussed upon the Incarnation, and the Atonement had slipped into relative oblivion, and how in the twentieth century this new interest in the doctrine of the Incarnation failed to retain the enthusiasm of English Christianity. The main reason, he believed, was that the two doctrines cohere, and therefore if one loses its light the other is bound to shine dimly, too. Given the occasion and the opportunity he would have gone on to show how the doctrines of the Church, Grace and the Sacraments cohere with these other two great doctrines, and indeed he hinted at this in the third paragraph of the lecture. There he quoted a critic of *The Apostolic Ministry* who had said that he could not recognize in the work of the authors of that book "any of the lineaments of the Christian God". Kirk imagined Gore, whose own doctrine of the ministry was akin to that of the book, replying to the critic: "That proves that your own doctrines of the ministry and of the Godhead, if they are in general agreement with each other, are in fact both of them sub-Christian. Go back to Scripture, and start your studies again."

[1] This account does not, of course, cover all the points of Kirk's thought about the Atonement, and the reader is referred to the whole of the essays quoted or summarized here, together with chapter two of *The Crisis of Christian Rationalism* and *Beauty and Bands* pp. 101-116.

VI

BISHOP OF OXFORD

I

IN the early summer of 1937 Dr. T. B. Strong announced his resignation of the See of Oxford. He had held it since 1925 after a short episcopate at Ripon. His whole adult life down to 1920 had been spent in Christ Church where he had been a beloved and successful tutor, and Dean. He was a person for whom the University, and Christ Church in particular, seemed to provide the natural and perfect setting, but he was not suited to the work of a diocesan bishop, and it was obvious how very boring much of that work was to him. A scholar himself, Strong followed the line of Stubbs, Paget, Gore and Burge, and there were those who, conscious of the deficiencies of his twelve years' episcopate, urged that the time had come for a break with tradition, that scholarship should take a back seat, and that the question of decisive importance should be to find a really pastoral bishop. Strong himself sent a memorandum to the Archbishop of Canterbury emphasizing this point. Like Stubbs and Paget before him he found that residence at Cuddesdon cut him off from the University, and that although in 1925 he returned to the diocese of whose cathedral he had been Dean, he could not resume his old close relationship with academic life. It is true that Christ Church was regarded, and regarded itself, as more of a diocesan centre than had been the case in the nineteenth century, but it was still far from becoming that focus for normal diocesan functions which other cathedrals are, and which it became to a much greater extent during Kirk's episcopate.

On June 11th, 1937, however, the Bishop of Chichester (Dr. Bell) wrote to the Archbishop as follows:

My dear Lord Archbishop,

Diocese of Oxford

Greatly daring I am venturing to urge the desirability of securing somehow that the appointment to the next Bishopric falling vacant should be the appointment of a first-class theologian. We are surely much weaker than we ought to be in theologians on the Bench just now. The recent appointments have been appointments of men of ability and distinction on the parochial or administrative side of the Church's life. There are very few Diocesan Bishops indeed who have produced real theological works, and some of the theologians on the Bench, like the Bishop of Gloucester and the Bishop of Carlisle, are growing old. I am afraid that some of our theologians of different schools of thought are feeling the lack of representation of theology.

Is not this vacancy in Oxford a very special opportunity? Your Grace knows that I am not lacking in 'cheek', so I would make the suggestion that Oxford really is the See for Dr. K. E. Kirk. He would be an immense enrichment of the Bench. He is a very good theologian, trusted and respected by everybody. He has the sympathy of the clergy, he is really pastoral, and he has had very considerable administrative experience. If Your Grace will do me the honour of looking at the footnotes on pp. 1,240-1,241 and p. 1,248 of my Life of Archbishop Davidson, you will see, from different points of view, the importance attached to scholarship on the Bench by Mr. Asquith, on the one hand, and French Roman Catholic scholars on the other hand.

We have now got a real gain in Convocation through the presence of Oxford and Cambridge University Proctors. It is all the more necessary to have University scholarship strongly represented in the Upper House.

The Archbishop replied the next day:

My dear George,

I am grateful to you for your letter of June 11th. I have received, and so I know has the Prime Minister, several earnest pleas from the Diocese of Oxford that the main consideration should be to appoint a really pastoral Bishop. The present Bishop has sent me a Memorandum strongly emphasising this point. He says that it is futile to consider that the Bishop of Oxford matters much to the University. Of all men he might have expected to have brought the Bishopric of Oxford into closer connexion with the University. But he tells me that this has been in vain, and certainly there is an almost unanimous feeling that what is wanted is someone who can not only supervise but give spiritual cheer and counsel to the multitudes of country parsons. At the same time I wholly agree with you that we do need on the Bench itself a strengthening on the Theological side, and in this respect certainly Kirk would be of great value. Also he is and ought to be pastorally-minded. On the other hand, he has steadily refused several offers which have been made to him. But I shall certainly include him among those about whom I talk to the Prime Minister when I see him next week.

Dr. Bell did not let matters rest there, but wrote again on June 14th:

My dear Lord Archbishop,

Very many thanks for your letter. I appreciate what you say about a pastoral Bishop. I think Kirk is really a pastoral man with a pastoral heart and experience. I wonder whether you would care to look at the little book he wrote as the result of his experience as an army Chaplain—"A Study of Silent Minds". But do not bother either to send back the book or answer this letter.

The Archbishop did, however, reply:

My dear George,

I thank you for sending me this book by K. E. Kirk. I hope I may be able to glance through it though I have no time for reading books. I shall bring his name before the Prime Minister when I see him, as I hope, on Friday.

Three weeks later, on July 5th, the Prime Minister, Mr. Neville Chamberlain, wrote to Kirk asking to be allowed to submit his name to the King, and at the same time Archbishop Lang also wrote to say that this approach had been made with his full knowledge and approval. The Archbishop asked Kirk to lunch with him on the 8th to discuss the matter. By the 21st Kirk had made up his mind and accepted the See. On hearing this Lang wrote:

I am very glad to hear that you have decided to accept the proposal made to you by the Prime Minister. I can fully realise all your difficulties and hesitations. But I feel sure that you are right in considering this as a summons to a special task which you could scarcely refuse.

I know that you will remember what I said to you that the Bishop should now be primarily a pastoral Bishop and regard the clergy and people of the large number of parishes in the Diocese—and not least country parishes—as having the first claim upon his time and thought.

Kirk's hesitations about accepting the See of Oxford are understandable. He had been a Professor for barely four years, and much of that time had been taken up by illness and by the domestic reorganization consequent upon his wife's death. He had five young children towards whom he now had a more than usual responsibility which the duties of a bishopric might make it difficult to fulfil. He must expect that the size of the Oxford diocese and its special needs would make it almost impossible for him to continue the task of constructing an Anglican Moral Theology to which he had set himself. On the other side there was the special call of Oxford which had been his home for nearly twenty years, the attraction of a return to a pastoral charge, and the opportunity of contributing his special knowledge to the highest councils of the Church.

The appointment was announced on the evening of July 26th and was in the newspapers the following morning. Kirk celebrated what was in effect his last day of freedom by taking two of his children to the Zoo. The appointment was greatly welcomed. On the previous Sunday evening he had broadcast from St. Matthew's Church, Westminster. One journalist who listened to him wrote:

I, along with many others probably, was curious to hear how a Doctor of Divinity and a Regius Professor would speak to the ordinary dwellers in St.

Matthew's parish, Westminster. And I was both delighted and edified. Dr. Kirk spoke in the simplest way of the children of the market-place, those who would pipe and dance and those who refused ...

No one listening-in realized that it was a future Bishop of Oxford who was talking, but we know it now. And those who know the diocese will realize from this address how Dr. Kirk will speak to the simple and unlearned in the hundreds of agricultural parishes scattered over that wide area. He is an exceptionally gifted man—learning, business capacity and deep devotion are not his least characteristics. And let me add this for the comfort of those struggling to maintain their schools, a fervent faith in the religious education of the young. He should go far.

The *Daily Express* was at the time running a series in which the Editor chose daily from hundreds of prints the face that had most impressed him. For the second of the series he chose one of Kirk in laughing conversation with some members of a clergy school at Hertford College, Oxford. He gave three reasons for the choice:

Because—
1: It has a smile that many bishops would be better for owning.
2: It has a broad nose suggesting humour.
3: The whole face reflects a kindly tolerance, inspires confidence.

Kirk continued in his Professorship during the greater part of the Michaelmas Term of 1937, lecturing on Christian Ethics and taking an Introductory Class in Moral Theology. The present writer attended the former of the two courses and remembers that Kirk concluded his last lecture (in the Chapter House at Christ Church) by remarking that that would be the last time that he would be able to speak in that place without asking the leave of the Dean and Chapter. His Election by the Chapter took place in October, and was confirmed on St. Andrew's Eve, November 29th. The Election of Dr. Francis Underhill to the Bishopric of Bath and Wells was confirmed at the same time, the ceremony being performed by the Vicar-General of the Province, Sir Philip Baker-Wilbraham, in Bow Church. The consecration took place on the next day in St. Paul's Cathedral. Dr. Underhill and Dr. Kirk were here joined by the Very Rev. A. A. Markham who was being consecrated to the Suffragan See of Grantham. The preacher was the Principal of Cuddesdon, the Rev. Eric Graham, and Dr. Kirk was presented by the Bishops of Lincoln (Hicks) and Chichester (Bell). In addition to the Archbishop of Canterbury thirty-one other bishops took part in the consecration. At noon on December 3rd Kirk attended at Buckingham Palace and did homage to King George VI. This ceremony was followed by the restoration to the new bishop of the temporalities of the See, and later in the month Kirk received from the Provincial Registrar a letter in the following terms:

My Lord Bishop,

I enclose the Letters Patent from the Crown to your Lordship granting the restitution of the temporalities of the See together with Writs to the Escheators of Berkshire, Buckingham, Oxford, Wiltshire and Dorset.

Your Lordship will simply retain the documents. No action of any kind is necessary!

Enclosed was a handsome red morocco pouch bearing the royal arms and containing a large sealed document addressed to "all and singular Knights Freeholders and all other Tenants of the Bishopric of Oxford" informing them that Kirk had been elected, that his election had received the royal assent, that he had done homage, and that the temporalities of the bishopric had been restored to him. It then commanded them "that to the said elect as your Bishop and Lord in everything as to the said Bishopric appertaining you be obedient and responsible aiding and assisting as it becomes you". The letters to the escheators commanded them to deliver restitution of the temporalities of the bishopric to the new bishop. There no longer existed, of course, any tenants of the see or escheators. The documents though issued in the name of King George VI bore the seal of King George V. The total cost of the restitution of temporalities was £40 : 12 : 0, £30 of which went on the Stamp Duty on the Letters Patent addressed to the non-existent tenants. The legal and other similar fees and expenses attending the appointment amounted in all to £259 : 9 : 8. The detailed account is set out in an appendix to this section of the chapter.

One of Kirk's first episcopal acts was the confirmation of a boy at Lancing on December 5th. The next day he received an official welcome—ruridecanal, civic and academic, at Reading. He was enthroned at Christ Church on the 8th, addressed the Diocesan Conference on the morning of the 9th and received a civic welcome in the Town Hall at Oxford in the afternoon. By a happy chance the Mayor of Oxford that year was Mr. H. S. Rogers the architect who had designed the new episcopal throne in the cathedral, which replaced the massive and cumbersome memorial to Bishop Wilberforce, and in which Kirk was the first Bishop of Oxford to be enthroned. On the 19th Kirk held his first ordination, and among those ordained priest on that occasion were Dom Augustine Morris, now Abbot of Nashdom, and the Rev. L. M. Styler later to be Fellow of Brasenose College and Secretary of the Bishop's Examining Chaplains.

In his first address to the Diocesan Conference Kirk spoke of his predecessor and his special gifts, then of his own sense of unreality at finding himself speaking as Bishop Strong's successor and his unpreparedness for the episcopal office. He found encouragement in the many friends and old acquaintances whom he saw before him, mentioning particularly Canon R. M. Hay (later Bishop of Buckingham) "the first person in Oxford who showed me kindness, for he invited me to breakfast the morning after my arrival here as a shy and callow freshman from the North." Another to be mentioned was Bishop Allen, whose Pro-Proctor Kirk had been. After these personal references Kirk passed to an account of the diocese itself with some reference to its history. He concluded with an outline of the immediate problems and challenges before them.[1]

Appendix I

1937

FEES AND EXPENSES ATTENDING THE APPOINTMENT OF THE RIGHT
REVEREND KENNETH ESCOTT KIRK, D.D., TO THE SEE OF OXFORD

	£	s.	d.	£	s.	d.
Home Office						
Stamp on Warrant	—	—	—	10	—	
Congé d'Elire	7	13	6			
Letter Recommendatory . . .	2	2	—			
Royal Assent	7	13	6			
Oath of Homage	1	1	—			
Restitution of Temporalities . . .	7	13	6	26	3	6
Crown Office						
Congé d'Elire						
Warrant	5	5	—			
Letters Patent	5	5	—			
Stamp Duty	30	—	—			
Docquet	—	2	—	40	12	—
Royal Assent						
Warrant	5	5	—			
Letters Patent	5	5	—			
Stamp Duty	30	—	—			
Docquet	—	2	—	40	12	—

[1] The address is printed in the Oxford Diocesan Magazine, January. 1938. pp. 5-16.

	£	s.	d.	£	s.	d.

Restitution of Temporalities

Warrant	5	5	—			
Letters Patent	5	5	—			
Stamp Duty	30	—	—			
Docquet	—	2	—	40	12	—

£148 9 6

	£	s.	d.	£	s.	d.
Brought forward				148	9	6

Election Confirmation Consecration and Installation

Archbishop of Canterbury's Legal Secretary's fee	21	—	—			
Vicar General's Office including disbursements at Bow Church . .	45	13	8			
Dean & Chapter of Canterbury for Licence of Alibi	—	10	6			
Registry of the Archdeaconry of Canterbury enthronement fees . . .	9	9	—	76	13	2
Messrs. Lee Bolton & Lee to passing papers and making payments including attendances at various Government offices, preparing documents of Appointment of Proxies, Certificates to the King, the Archbishop and Bishop elect for completion by the Dean & Chapter, lodging the Certificates at the Home Office, &c.						
Correspondence, &c.				27	—	—
Letters to Bishops of the Province advising as to Consecration, printing, postages and other incidental expenses . .				4	4	—
Paid Virgers at St. Paul's Cathedral .				3	3	—

£259 9 8

To this has to be added Dr. Kirk's share of the Cathedral fees for his consecration, amounting to £11 : 11 : 0, the cost of episcopal dress and robes, and the cost of moving house. It will be seen, therefore, that the acceptance of episcopal office in 1937 involved financial burdens of no mean order. It should be added that the Crown fees are now remitted, and the rest of the legal expenses paid by the Church Commissioners.

Appendix II

Unlike his predecessors in the see of Oxford Kirk was not made Chancellor of the Order of the Garter. This office, which had been secularized for some considerable time in the sixteenth century, had been restored to the Bishop of Salisbury (in whose diocese Windsor then was) "and his successors for ever" in 1669 at the petition of Bishop Seth Ward. When Berkshire was transferred from Salisbury to Oxford early in the nineteenth century the chancellorship went with it and was held by the Bishops of Oxford until the retirement of Dr. Strong, after which a layman was appointed. Kirk felt this as something of a slight to the see and for that reason used only a temporary seal throughout his episcopate, hoping that some day the episcopal seal of Oxford would again be enclosed in the Garter.

2

At the outset of his episcopate, indeed before his consecration and enthronement, Kirk was faced by the problem of where he should live. The episcopal residence of the see of Oxford had, since the seventeenth century, been in the little village of Cuddesdon, seven or eight miles from the centre of Oxford and very difficult of access by public transport. The pleasant manor house, which was the original Palace, had been extended in the nineteenth century by Samuel Wilberforce, but these very extensions were now a problem. Of Kirk's predecessors some, like Gore, had enjoyed the country life and proximity to the Theological College at Cuddesdon. Others, like Stubbs, had found the inaccessibility of the place and the establishment which life in the country imposed upon them almost more than they could bear. The views of Dr. Stubbs may be read at length in Hutton's edition of his letters,[1] here we will only quote one of the Bishop's characteristic verses:

[1] W. H. Hutton: *Letters of William Stubbs, Bishop of Oxford, 1904.* pp. 292-299.

F

I am Bishop of all I survey,
  Dean and Chapter don't matter a fig,
In the central demesne of the See
  I am master of Peacock and Pig.
O Cuddesdon, where can be the charms
  The Commissioners see in thy face?
Kettel Hall had been better by far
  Than this most inaccessible place.

For some time the Bishops of Oxford had kept a private room in
Oxford which they used for interviews, and Kirk quickly became
convinced that the whole administration of the diocese must be
transferred to Oxford. A memorandum dated October 11th, 1937,
outlines proposals for this. The diocesan office at 88, St. Aldate's was to
become the Bishop's administrative centre, for entertaining he could
use the Common Rooms of the Colleges of which he was a member,
and Cuddesdon Palace, considerably reduced in size, should be the
Bishop's private house, completely divorced from his official work.
On December 9th, ten days after his consecration, he explained his
immediate intentions to the Diocesan Conference:

I must pass on to give you a short official statement . . . as to the organization of my own activities. My plans in this respect have been shaped to a very
large extent by what I may call the problem of Cuddesdon. The first aspect
of that problem is the inaccessibility of the place itself. I am informed that on
three days of the week it is entirely without a bus service, and that only on
Saturdays and Sundays does any bus leave or return to the village after four
o'clock in the afternoon. This means that as a centre for interviews the Palace
is virtually useless. My predecessors have dealt with this situation by the only
possible method—that of having a room in the Diocesan Church House at
88, St Aldate's. I propose to carry the process a step further. Interviews cannot
be dissociated from correspondence and administration. I have therefore transferred the entire secretarial and administrative side of the bishop's work from
Cuddesdon to Oxford . . .

He went on to say:

There is, however, another aspect of the problem of Cuddesdon. No bishop,
especially in a diocese so large as this, can be expected to do his work efficiently
unless he is conveniently housed; otherwise a large part of his attention will be
distracted by domestic anxieties. Here I will speak quite frankly. Cuddesdon is
in many respects a fine building . . . But, judged by even the most modest of
modern standards, it is a quite unusually inconvenient house. That is not my
own view alone; it is based upon and confirmed by expert inspection and
examination . . . To bring Cuddesdon into even a reasonable state of

modernization, and make it a house which will not lay an overwhelming tax upon its occupier's efficiency and peace of mind, is a task which presents the most formidable difficulties, both technical and financial. I am at present considering, with the best expert advice I can secure, whether these difficulties can be overcome.

Meanwhile, of course, Kirk could not stay in Christ Church indefinitely, and it was necessary to find somewhere to live until the problem of Cuddesdon could be solved. Sandridge, a house on Boar's Hill owned by the University became available and in February, 1938, Kirk and his family moved into it. Announcing this in the Diocesan Magazine in April he wrote:

At present I am rarely at home, except occasionally for an hour or so at midday, between nine a.m. and eight p.m., and I see no reason to suppose that this state of things is likely to alter. Had I attempted to administer the diocese from my own house (whether at Cuddesdon or Boar's Hill or anywhere else) things would have been quite different. But so far as I personally am concerned (and I cannot speak either for my predecessors or my successors) such an attempt would have been disastrous.

I am convinced, in short, that the bishop's headquarters for administration must be the Diocesan Office in Oxford; and that he must be prepared to spend the whole of the morning there every day of the week, unless he is called elsewhere by more important matters. It must be remembered that modern ecclesiastical developments are throwing more and more responsibilities upon the shoulders of diocesan bishops, and that where (as in the Oxford diocese) there is no residence for them close to their diocesan offices, they must make some special arrangement to be in almost hourly touch with headquarters. The advantage of being able to conduct correspondence, have interviews, and attend committees with the least expenditure of time and effort, is overwhelming; and I do not think that the bishop's gain in being thus daily on the spot involves a waste of time, effort or efficiency to anyone else. When the moment comes for a final decision in the matter of Cuddesdon, all these factors will have to be taken into account.

These words were written after four months' experience of the administration of the see. Cuddesdon Palace was thoroughly surveyed and plans for alterations to it were drawn up and discussed but the conversion of a house with twenty-two bedrooms into a manageable modern residence proved a very difficult problem to solve, and no satisfactory conclusion had been reached by the middle of 1939. Then the international situation caused a number of organizations to make plans for moving out of London in the event of war and the authorities of Queen Anne's Bounty were glad to avail themselves of the offer of Cuddesdon, and to occupy the Palace until almost the end of the war. The black-out, petrol rationing, and the other restrictions of the period 1939-45 showed how fortunate it was that circumstances had caused Kirk to make his home on a reasonable bus route and within ten minutes drive of the cathedral and the Diocesan Office.

3

Soon after taking up the administration of the diocese Kirk noted that in four years' time would occur the fourth centenary of the appointment of the first Bishop of Oxford, Robert King, and he began to look forward to 1942 as a year when the whole diocese might be brought to an occasion of renewed self-dedication. This was expounded to the Diocesan Conference in November, 1938,[1] and the response encouraged the Bishop to begin preparations. "The intervening period", he wrote, "must be spent in a genuine evangelistic effort throughout the diocese." The Rev. C. W. Warner was appointed to act as Secretary for Evangelistic Work, and to be the centre of much of the preparations for 1942.

Two sad events, however, combined to frustrate much of Kirk's intentions. The first was his own serious illness. On February 16th, 1939, he returned home from the office feeling distinctly unwell, and a severe attack of catarrh and laryngitis quickly developed. All through March he was kept in bed, and early in April pneumonia set in. For some days his life was in the balance, but about the middle of April he surmounted the crisis and began to improve. No sooner had he begun to recover from the pneumonia, however, than an attack of phlebitis developed, and it was not until nearly the end of June that he was able to sit out of bed in a chair. It was August before he was able to go out of doors, and towards the end of September he was able to resume something like normal diocesan work. For the rest of his episcopate, however, his health was never good, and he was particularly liable to afflictions of the throat and of the chest which not only interfered with his public appearances but also made him subject to fits of depression.

The other sad event, if so inadequate a term may be used, was the outbreak of war in September, 1939. On Sunday, September 3rd Kirk issued the following message to the clergy and people of the diocese.

My dear Friends,

In this tragic moment of the world's history let us all keep clearly before our minds what is actually at stake. It is all summed up in the word 'freedom'—

[1] An important address printed in the Diocesan Magazine, December, 1938.

freedom of worship, freedom of thought and speech, freedom for happy intercourse in equal citizenship and service, freedom from constant fear of tension, crisis and war. Of each and all of these freedoms the unfortunate German people has been in large part robbed by its rulers; and year by year these rulers, intoxicated by their past triumphs at home and abroad, set out to destroy this same freedom among nations with whom they should live on terms of amity. If this robbery, this destruction of freedom goes on unchecked, all that we have known as Christian civilization is doomed to perish; honour, truthfulness, confidence and equity will be forgotten, and nothing survive except the reign of brute force.

As a Christian nation we are pledged to do our utmost to check this constant aggression upon the freedom of others, even though it involves us in all the agony of war. The wild lust for power at all costs by which the rulers of Germany are dominated has led them to reject all proposals for conciliation; the force to which they have appealed in one crisis after another during the last years, and in which they still put their trust, must be reduced to impotence if freedom is to survive. Once more we enter into a war without any desire for material or territorial gain; we stand only for the principles of justice, tolerance, and upright dealing among men, without which peaceful and civilized life is impossible.

We have no illusions as to the cost of our effort. It will demand of each one of us sacrifices greater perhaps than any which we have hitherto made in our journey through life. Many of us will have to pass through very deep waters before the end is attained. Stedfastness, courage, unselfishness, self-discipline— all these are required of us in the highest degree. If we are found wanting in any of them we shall not merely be traitors to our country and our cause; we shall make life all but unendurable both for ourselves and for all around us.

Since, then, so much is demanded of each one of us, it is right that all who believe in the power of prayer (and at a time like this not many are found to declare outright that prayer has no power) should earnestly ask God to give us the strength and endurance necessary for the heavy tasks which lie before us. In this hour, in which all human rights are threatened by the barbarism and arrogance of one man and the 'Party' which he has created as the instrument of his terrorism, it is right that we should dedicate ourselves to the cause of humanity. Let us pray for ourselves and for each other that we may always bear in mind that the true purpose of this war in which we have engaged is the defence of all that our religion has taught the world to hold most dear; and that, bearing this in mind, we may be of good heart whatever befall. Let us pray, too, that God will shorten this time of tribulation, and bring about— as only He can do—the speedy end of calamity, and the untrammelled supremacy of peace and justice once more. These prayers, dear friends, will not go unheard; and even in the uttering of them, we shall find ourselves moved to greater fortitude and resolution in the face of the calls that must be made upon us.

War is one of the most terrible of evils; but the enslavement of whole peoples is even more terrible. It is to put an end to this enslavement, and to do this alone, that we have chosen to declare war on Germany. I have no doubt that, tragic though it is, the decision is the right one; and I believe with all my heart that God will defend the right. Our part is to be of good courage, and to give our best in single-hearted endeavour, however hard our tasks, however difficult our circumstances, however great our sufferings. May God fortify each one of us to do our duty bravely in what may well prove to be the greatest test of our devotion to the service of mankind which we shall ever have to face.

Believe me, dear friends,

> Your faithful servant,
> Kenneth Oxon:

From this view of the war Kirk never wavered. He expounded it at greater length in a sermon preached before the University of Oxford on the Sunday before the Encaenia, 1940, and published by the University Press under the title of *The Menace to Faith*. True faith, he argued, is born from freedom, and faith and freedom of thought must always go hand in hand.

Faith gains its quiet unremitting confidence, its indomitable perseverance, from the appeal to reason. But no man can safely appeal to reason unless he knows that his mind is free; and that prejudice, convention, passion, fear, though their onslaughts may cause him to waver from time to time, have nevertheless been expelled from the fortress of his mind, and have no longer any permanent footing there. He then who robs us of our freedom has gone far to rob us of our faith as well. He has done all in his power to turn us into embittered sceptics, to whom no action seems worth while, no motive honourable, no friendship disinterested, no aspiration clean. Without freedom of thought, what we know as faith must either disintegrate into the mists of superstition and credulity, or be extinguished by the black clouds of unbelieving cynicism.

Throughout the darkest period of the war Kirk wrote constantly in the Diocesan Magazine, and spoke at the Diocesan Conference, on the spiritual problems and implications of the conflict in which the country was engaged. Two of the most valuable of these utterances have been reprinted in *Beauty and Bands*. One, *Prayer in Wartime*, was spread over the months February to August, 1940. The other, *The Atonement and the War*, was an address to the Diocesan Conference in May, 1941, published in two parts in the Diocesan Magazine during the following two months. In addition to these there was an Address to the Diocesan Conference in May, 1940, in which lessons drawn from the human experience of sickness were applied to the war,[1] and another address in December of the same year in which a warning was given

[1] Diocesan Magazine, June, 1940. pp. 79-87.

against any relaxation in spiritual vigilance with the passing of the immediate crisis of the autumn of 1940.[1] Among practical tasks in which the clergy and people of the diocese might engage the Bishop appealed for the raising of a fund so that a substantial gift might be made from the diocese to the dioceses of London and Southwark, to help them in the rebuilding of churches, and the reconstruction of Church life after the devastation wrought by German air-bombardment. In April of the following year this fund was closed at the figure of £3,845 : 7 : 8.

In 1944 serious moral problems were raised for many people by the mass bombing of German cities, and by the possibility of the bombing of Rome. Kirk wrote about these in three articles in March, April and May of that year. A correspondent had sent him a pamphlet with the title *What happened in Hamburg*, and containing an account of the horrors suffered by civilians during a bombing attack upon Hamburg. He asked, "I wonder if you still feel that war is the lesser of two evils for a Christian?" Kirk replied:

The pamphlet makes ghastly reading. But I must begin by saying at once and without qualification of any kind that its ghastliness is slight in comparison with what I have read not in one but in many documents, officially compiled by trained enquirers from the sworn testimony of eyewitnesses, descriptive of the cold-blooded tortures, inflicted by the Germans upon innumerable Russians, Poles, Czechs, and Jews of all ages and both sexes who have fallen into their power. *What Happened in Hamburg* makes one shudder; these other documents —far more authoritative in character, be it remembered—produce at first a cold nausea, which changes to an appalled realization of the satanic depths to which men can fall when they have once said, 'Evil, be thou my good'. Hence I have no hesitation in answering my correspondent, 'If war be (as I fear it is) the only alternative to allowing this German sadism to range the world unchecked, then war is beyond doubt the lesser of the two evils for the Christian.'

On the hypothetical problem of the bombing of Rome he wrote:

If it will shorten the war even by a day, and so be the cause of prolonging some thousands of human lives which otherwise would be cut short, let it be destroyed, tragic though we all recognize the necessity to be. The human race for which it perishes can rebuild the city in even more glorious shape than before. But if by sparing it we have taught men to think of human life as in no higher scale of values than material things, we have turned our back once for all not merely on reason but on the Christian religion itself; and that way nothing but chaos lies.

The dropping of the atomic bomb a year later caused many who had accepted as legitimate all other weapons of offence used by the allies

[1] Diocesan Magazine, December, 1940. pp. 178-185.

during the war to doubt whether the use of anything so destructive and terrifying could be justified. Kirk never discussed this problem at length, but he felt bound to refer to it in a sermon preached in the Cathedral at the Thanksgiving Service for the ending of the war with Japan. He fully recognized the seriousness of the moral issue, but for himself he felt that the use of the bomb was justified.

For months now the Japanese islands have been in a state of siege, the bulk of their armies cut off on the Asiatic mainland, their ships beaten back into the home ports, their air formations driven from the skies. For weeks the first blows of the assault have been falling on the besieged, but they have shown no disposition to abandon the conflict and thereby end the period of bloodshed. Two blows of unexampled magnitude have changed the whole picture. Our minds recoil before the carnage and devastation wrought by these blows; but to have withheld them, and condemned both sides to a siege drawn-out for months if not for years, would have resulted in casualty lists of far greater dimensions on both sides. Where all is horrible and poignant to the last degree it remains— so far as I can see—the more merciful course to have used the atomic bomb, than to have refrained from using it.

In publishing part of this sermon in the Diocesan Magazine of September, 1945, Kirk made it clear that he had spoken on the subject only with great hesitation, and that it was with equal hesitation and in response to requests that he published what he had said. He added:

I must ask anyone who reads what I have said about the new warfare to remember that it formed part only of an address whose main purposes were, first, to bring before the congregation the implications for peace of the Charter of the United Nations, so recently signed in San Francisco; and second, to urge them, in the name of Christian brotherhood, to support to the full every effort for the relief of suffering in the devastated countries. Anarchy rather than aggression is now the greatest menace to the peace of the world; and relief on the largest possible scale is the first bulwark that must be built against it.

At the end of August, 1945, Kirk was consulted by the Bishop of Chichester (Dr. Bell) about a suggested motion in the Upper House of Convocation asking for the appointment of a committee of moral theologians to consider the atomic bomb in relation to the laws of war. Kirk's reply is of interest for more than one reason:

My dear Bishop,

I have your letter of August 30th. The following points occur to me in connection with it:—

(1) I am quite clear that a reconsideration of the questions of weapons which may be regarded as legitimate in a defensive war would be both well-timed and instructive. It is, in fact, one of the subjects I hope to work on as soon as

I am able to relinquish my present post and get back to what I still regard as my proper sphere. However, that is a purely personal matter.

(2) I am equally clear that procedure by Commission would be fruitless. Unless the Commission were packed (not necessarily intentionally) to exclude the presentation of certain points of view, the result would at best be a Majority Report with one or more dissentient minority Reports, and we should be much where we are at present.

(3) For its Report to be really informative and weighty, the Commission would have to take into account the considered opinions of expert scientists and also strategists of eminence. To take the latter category only, this means that it ought to have among its members such devoted Churchmen as Keyes, Burrough, Montgomery, Paget, Smith, and so on; or at least would have to ask them for reasoned statements capable of being published in or with the Report. Anything less ambitious than this would merely add one more to the list of amateur and uninformed productions which pour from the press to-day. Obviously, however, to deal with the matter on this scale is going to involve a great expenditure of time and effort, and I think most of those whose opinions would be worth having are too heavily engaged with matters of extreme practical urgency to find time to take part in the research and discussions which would be necessary to give the Report any real value.

(4) The form of the proposed Resolution seems to me calculated to rouse the immediate and justifiable resentment of the pacifist. An unofficial theologian is, of course, free to discuss the question "Assuming defensive warfare to be justifiable, what weapons of defence are legitimate?" But if the Church officially propounds this question (as the Resolution does) it will be immediately accused of attempting to evade the far more important pacifist issue "Is war ever legitimate?" To the pacifist the Resolution would be as provocative as a Resolution to "consider the moral and spiritual implications of modern methods of arson" would be to you and me. All arson is wrong, and that being so it is misleading and pointless to discuss whether any one method of fire-raising is more wrong than another. I am certain that the pacifist would be vocal in accusing the Church of attempting to burke the fundamental question; and I am bound to say that although I am no pacifist, I should have a great deal of sympathy with him on this head.

So you see, I cannot support your Resolution. In this, as in so many other matters of faith and morals, I am certain that the main road of progress in the Church of England is by means of unofficial publications by groups of thinkers (or indeed by individuals), upon which, in the end, the mind of the Church passes its judgment in practice without official resolution. This is how *Lux Mundi* and *Foundations* were treated, and their influence is still felt; whereas the official Reports of Commissions have for the most part been forgotten within a few years of their publication.

The last paragraph of this letter is extremely important for an understanding of Kirk's mind and of his attitude to many aspects of

Church life and government. He was always somewhat sceptical about the value of Commissions, and on the whole gave little attendance at those on which he sat unless they were, as the South India Joint Committee, concerned with some immediate practical decision to be taken. In his later years he was doubtful of the value of the attempt at Canon Law Revision. He said to the present writer that most of the valuable parts of it would be defeated by the laity, and that in the liturgical field the problems had been greatly exaggerated and were much better dealt with by custom and natural development.

4

As has been said, the outbreak of the war, following upon Kirk's long and serious illness, caused any idea of a commemoration of the fourth centenary of the diocese, such as Kirk had originally envisaged, to pass out of view. Most normal diocesan activities either ceased or were greatly curtailed, and it was not until the very end of 1940 that a certain amount of them began to be revived. A year later the Bishop felt it possible to raise again the idea of some celebration of the fourth centenary. He was trying to bring about the revival of the suffragan see of Reading as the completion of his plan for the reorganization of diocesan administration, and this would fit well into a scheme for a general diocesan celebration. In January, 1942, he was able to issue an outline programme. The celebrations were to begin on Quinquagesima Sunday with the reading in every church of a Pastoral Letter from the Bishop, and Lent was to be marked by special prayer for the diocese and consultation as to appropriate action in the parishes. Early in May there was to be a meeting of the Diocesan Conference with a service of re-dedication in the cathedral at which the Bishop would give a Charge to the Diocese, and the period from Ascension Day to Whitsunday was to be observed as a time of invocation of the Holy Spirit to revive, strengthen and guide the Church. During the summer there were to be meetings and services in the various rural deaneries, and the Bishop hoped to visit a number of them to address clergy and laity of the neighbourhoods. Finally in the autumn there was to be a solemn celebration of the Holy Communion in the cathedral as a service of thanksgiving.

This programme was carried out more or less as outlined. In addition to the various services there were pageants illustrative of the history of the Church in the area covered by the diocese, and there was an important *Fourth Centenary Supplement* to the *Oxford Handbook of Religious Knowledge*. The celebrations ended on Wednesday, October

21st, when the Bishop celebrated the Holy Communion in the cathedral at 11.30 a.m. in the presence of the Archbishop of Canterbury (Dr. William Temple) who preached a Sermon at the close of the service.

5

The diocese of Oxford, consisting, as it does of the three counties of Oxfordshire, Buckinghamshire and Berkshire presents no mean problem of administration. When Kirk became bishop it contained something in the region of 850 parish, district and mission churches. He hoped to be able to visit every one of these at some time during his episcopate and indeed by January, 1949 he was able to report that he had visited 810 of them though this statement produced letters informing him of a further little crop of mission churches of which there was no official record in the Diocesan Registry. No doubt the war and illness were partly responsible for the fact that it took eleven years for the Bishop to come near the achievement of his object, but when due allowance has been made for those factors it will be evident how great a pastoral and administrative problem was constituted by the enormous size of the Oxford Diocese.

The division of the diocese into two or three smaller dioceses was an obvious consideration for anyone faced as Kirk was with such an administrative problem, and it is plain that during the earlier years of his episcopate he spent some time in going into the history of discussions of this subject during the first quarter of the century. In the Diocesan Magazine for March and April, 1942 he set out the results of his researches, but without any indication that he himself contemplated taking any action in the matter. He had, in fact, four years earlier given his reasons for thinking that the division of the diocese was not then a matter of practical politics nor indeed likely to become one for a good many years. He said, on that occasion:

I have during the past months been able to read some of the more important documents bearing upon that question—documents produced during the early years of this century for the various bodies which have discussed the matter. The impression they leave on my mind is that they are all out of date. The shifting of populations, the redistribution of wealth, the increase in facilities of communication, have changed the whole face of the problem: and when it is next discussed, it will have to be treated as in every respect a new one. That will mean a vast expenditure of time for those who embark upon it: and even so, if they reach an agreed conclusion (and no agreed conclusion has ever been reached before in the matter) it may well prove to be itself out of date by the time it is made public, so quickly do events move in the modern world. Further-more, no division of the diocese is possible at all without considerable increase in the available funds; and my own firm belief is that, if money for Church needs is forthcoming in anything like the required quantity, there are far more urgent purposes to which we shall all agree that it ought to be put. I do not in any way wish to closure discussion of the matter at any reasonably appro-priate moment. But I feel bound to say that, unless my mind changes, I have no personal intention of taking the initiative in this connection.[1]

The question of division having been thus set aside Kirk's thoughts turned in the direction of a reorganization of the diocesan staff.

When Kirk became Bishop his staff consisted of the Bishop of Buckingham (P. H. Elliott), who was also Archdeacon of Buckingham, the Archdeacon of Berkshire (R. Wickham-Legg), and the Archdeacon of Oxford (G. B. Allen) who was also in episcopal orders having been formerly Suffragan Bishop of Sherborne. From the first Kirk decided that he must work towards a system of three suffragan bishops. He wrote in the Diocesan Magazine for February, 1942:

It cannot be too emphatically stated that there are two very different con-ceptions of the functions of a suffragan bishop. The first may be called that of the 'assistant-suffragan', the second that of the 'administrative-suffragan'. By an 'assistant-suffragan' I mean a bishop who may fairly be described as the under-study of the diocesan bishop. He will take such ordinations, confirmations, institutions or consecrations, and preside over such meetings, in all parts of the diocese indiscriminately, as may be assigned to him from time to time by the bishop of the diocese. Apart from such *ad hoc* assignments he has in effect no duties. The case of the 'administrative-suffragan' is very different. To him is committed as a permanency a particular area of the diocese (indicated to some extent by his suffragan title), and so far as the law allows he is responsible both for the administrative and for the pastoral oversight of the area—subject of course to the right of the diocesan bishop to perform whatever functions within that area he may choose for himself. To secure some degree of legal recognition for the suffragan's position, the area committed to his charge is usually at least an archdeaconry, and he may very suitably hold the office of archdeacon as well as that of suffragan. This, however, is not essential.

At Oxford the plan decided upon was that there should be three suffragan bishops, one for each county, who should also be respectively the Archdeacons of Oxford, Buckingham and Berkshire.

The first step in carrying out this plan was taken in February, 1939, when the ancient see of Dorchester was revived to provide a suffragan title for Dr. Allen. This left Berkshire unprovided for. There had, however, been a suffragan see of Reading occupied by Bishop Randall

[1] Oxford Diocesan Magazine, December, 1938. pp. 324-325.

at the turn of the century, but no successor had been appointed on his retirement. In November, 1941, Kirk persuaded the Diocesan Conference to pass a resolution to the effect that it would welcome the immediate revival of the suffragan see of Reading, and also to make some financial provision for it. Two months later it was announced that the King had nominated to the revived see Canon A. G. Parham, Vicar of St. Mary's, Reading, and the new bishop was consecrated on February 2nd, 1942. At the end of March Mr. Wickham-Legg resigned his archdeaconry and Mr. Parham was appointed to it, so that within five years Kirk's plan of securing three episcopal archdeacons was complete.

So far as can be judged the system worked extremely well, but of course the burden on the diocesan remained very heavy. It was inevitable that the thoughts of a Bishop of Oxford should in this connexion turn to his predecessor, Samuel Wilberforce who is generally regarded as the originator of the modern type of English diocesan. Kirk observed that the centenary of Wilberforce's enthronement as Bishop of Oxford would fall on December 13th, 1945, and it seemed to him to provide, with the restoration of peace, a suitable occasion for stirring the diocese to new efforts, something that he had tried to do in connexion with the fourth centenary celebrations in 1942 but had been unable to carry out fully by reason of the war.

Writing in November, 1945, therefore, Kirk drew attention to the Wilberforce centenary. The Bishop's enthronement a hundred years ago was an event

Of the greatest significance both for the diocese and the whole Church. It inaugurated the diocese in its present form, bringing Buckinghamshire into ecclesiastical union with Oxfordshire and Berkshire under one bishop. It stabilized the critical situation brought about by the secession of Newman, a few months earlier, to the Roman Church. It inaugurated a model of effective organisation by archdeaconries, ruridecanal chapters, and central committees. It led to the foundation of Cuddesdon and Culham Colleges, and enabled some of the earliest modern Sisterhoods to be set up in Oxford itself and in Berkshire. Above all, by his personal example, Wilberforce transformed the popular conception of a bishop's activities and attitude towards his diocese. He abandoned the old slipshod methods of confirmation and ordination, and introduced reverence and a spirit of loving orderliness into their administration—in Burgon's words he became the 'remodeller of the episcopate'.

Diocesan celebrations were therefore planned for the Summer of 1946 and centred on two events—a commemorative service in the cathedral on May 14th, at which the Bishop of London, Dr. Wand, preached, and a visit by the Archbishop of Canterbury to the Diocesan Conference on July 3rd. The centenary provided Kirk with an occasion for some reflections on the suggestion made by one newspaper that the Church had run from the extreme of pre-Wilberforcian stagnation to the opposite extreme of over organization in which competence in administration had come to be regarded as the *sine qua non* in candidates for the episcopal bench. Kirk wrote:

There is no doubt that most bishops find their days fairly fully occupied; and for myself I am bound to confess that at the times of greatest pressure it is my systematic reading and study that suffer most. But I believe that most parish priests would say the same about themselves; and would add that the chief inroads upon their time were of a secular character—not least of all, the demands made upon them by the maintenance of house and garden when domestic help is either unprocurable or prohibitively expensive. Bishops, despite their larger paper incomes, are not altogether exempt from preoccupations of this character; and if, as is often suggested, they are less accessible than they ought to be, they, too, are entitled to plead the complexities and strains of modern domestic life as some slight extenuation of their misdemeanours.

Setting this aside, however, as to some extent irrelevant, we must observe two inescapable facts. The first is obvious. There are certain ecclesiastical functions—consecrations, institutions, confirmations, ordinations and so forth— which only a bishop can perform; there are others—dedications of buildings, of memorials, sermons for special occasions (as for example the centenary of the formation of a parish or the building of its Church)—for which he is in steady demand, and which he cannot decently refuse to discharge. These engagements make a continuous drain upon his time and energy, and no one can deny the propriety of his undertaking them; they are in no sense administrative, but quite definitely pastoral. Yet, exacting though they are, taken by themselves they would not by any means constitute an intolerable burden; and even when allowance is made in addition for those necessary secular preoccupations to which I have alluded, a bishop's life could be one of modest but adequate leisure.

I come then to my second inescapable fact. The heaviest, and, at the same time, the most spiritually important of the tasks which go to make up a bishop's day is imposed upon him by the incidence of his interviews and correspond- ence. Here he is called upon to exercise his highest duty, that of shewing himself a father to his diocese. Almost always the matter involved is a personal one— often it is anxious, poignant, distressing, or even tragic. I would not dare to guess how many hours the average diocesan has to spend in these duties every day. The weak have to be encouraged, the perplexed guided, the sorrowing comforted, the erring led into wiser or better paths. No doubt, if we were frankly realist in the matter, we should agree that many of these tasks could be assigned by the bishop to others more competent to perform them than himself.

But it is one of the most distinctive features of the episcopal system that everyone in a diocese claims the right of direct personal approach to the bishop himself; and a deep sense of injustice if not worse, would quickly spread if the bishop did not do all in his power to honour these claims, even when he himself is well aware that among his helpers there were experts far more fully qualified than himself to deal with the particular problem presented to him. He may, after being made aware of the issues involved, do little more than give his visitor or correspondent an introduction to a capable adviser; but he must first see the visitor or answer the letter sympathetically, and that is where time and energy are consumed.

All this means, quite simply, that many of the bishop's interviews will have to be thought over very carefully beforehand, and many of his answers to the personal letters he receives will have to be drafted over and over again, for a single word misplaced, a single sentence wrongly turned, may stultify everything that is attempted. I need scarcely point out that such responsibilities cannot be borne without constant and detailed prayer. Every parish priest is fully aware of that from his own experience, and indeed in this matter the conscientious priest bears exactly the same responsibility before God as his bishop. A parish may contain no more than a hundred souls; but the task of shepherding even those hundred through the gate of salvation is in itself so superhuman, that to say that a bishop carries heavier responsibilities still, seems to me to be introducing comparisons into a sphere in which they have no meaning. Any difference there is, is one of quantity not of quality. A bishop probably has to fit more interviews and letters into a period of time than many parish priests, but they are all of the same intimate personal type.

This being so, no bishop has very much time left for 'tramping from committee to committee'; and it would be crass folly, and worse, for those who choose our leaders to make administrative ability the first requirement when the time available for its exercise is bound to be small. Nevertheless, a diocesan is expected to attend a large number of committees during the course of the year, and it is a serious question whether this administrative burden could not be lightened in any way. At once it is clear that there are some discussions, at which his presence is entirely unnecessary. Technical problems—such as the kind of material of which a parsonage house or Church hall shall be built, or the particular security in which a legacy shall be invested—may often open up discussions not merely protracted but even embittered, to such debates most bishops could regard themselves as unqualified to contribute anything of value. Again, in regard to many diocesan Committees, it is enough for the bishop to exercise a generally benevolent supervision, or to lay down main lines of policy and leave details to be worked out by the experts. But all this depends upon the diocese being able to afford a sufficient number of experts (adequately equipped with office accommodation and staff); and this at the moment is an utterly impossible requirement. Even bishops can no longer afford, except in the rarest of cases, to keep domestic chaplains who were universal less than fifty years ago. Compared with the number of our parishes and the diversity of our undertakings, our own diocesan staff is ludicrously inadequate and (I am bound to confess) seriously overburdened with responsibilities; we trade upon their self-sacrifice and good-will to a degree of which we should be anything but proud. I know of no diocese of which the same could not be said with equal truth. Yet there are other claims upon the offerings of Church people which must have priority. Until much more has been done for the clergy of the past (and their dependents) by way of pension provision, for the clergy of the present by augmentation of stipend, and for the clergy of the future by training grants for ordination candidates, we must do without the administrative luxury of large, expert, and comfortably housed diocesan staffs. And so long as this state of things maintains, every diocesan bishop must be more or less of a jack-of-all-trades, helping his staff as best he can. No doubt, in his desire to help, he may sometimes prove a bit of a hindrance; but, human nature being what it is, he would think himself unworthy of the trust men put in him if he were not able to step into any breach at any moment without exhibiting glaring inefficiency.

But having said so much, I range myself wholeheartedly with those who insist that bishops must not be chosen primarily for administrative efficiency. That would be to give a secondary requirement quite fatal predominance in the life of the Church. If England is to be converted, it will not be the work of consecrated civil servants or captains of industry. In all ranks of the clergy we ask not for good organizers (though a little organizing ability may go quite a long way) but for inspired teachers, pastors and evangelists; this is as true for the episcopate as it is for the parochial clergy. And if, as is sometimes alleged, the protracted delays in filling up vacant sees is the result of putting efficiency first in the list of episcopal *desiderata*, then we cannot say too often or too emphatically that we shall be content with quite a modest degree of efficiency, provided we are given leaders of true spirituality and a real love for souls. *Finis autem praecepti est caritas de corde puro, et conscientia bona, et fide non ficta.* This is as true for bishops as for any other kind of Christian.[1]

Six years later Kirk returned to the subject in two articles on 'The Predicament of Church Government'. The predicament, an almost impossible one, in which the modern Church of England found itself was that of attempting to combine two systems of government—the patriarchal and the democratic. Kirk pointed out how Wilberforce, starting with the patriarchal tradition of episcopal government, whereby both pastoral and administrative responsibility lay wholly in his hands (administration of course including finance) began large developments towards democracy by holding frequent conferences of the clergy and by instituting Societies for Building Churches and Parsonages, for the Augmentation of Benefices, for the Provision of Additional Clergy and for the Education of the Poor.

[1] Oxford Diocesan Magazine, March, 1946.

Democracy began to take its place alongside patriarchal autonomy as a necessary feature in all really energetic Church life. I say 'began' intentionally; for though the diocesan Committees steadily assumed a more and more representative character, the bishop, in discharge of his patriarchal functions, remained the controlling influence in all of them. The inevitable result was the steady increase of episcopal burdens. On the one hand, if his pastoral ministrations were at all acceptable, the bishop found himself more and more in demand in the parishes of his diocese; on the other, with the growth of Committees, his administrative responsibilities took up more and more of his time.

As well as the example of Wilberforce, however, Kirk saw other factors at work, and one of them, the great increase in legislation on ecclesiastical business, attracted his special attention.

For some reason or reasons, which have never to my knowledge been fully explored, Parliament about 100 years ago began to take an unprecedented interest in Church affairs. The accession of Queen Victoria may be taken as a turning point. In the hundred years prior to that event not more than sixty Acts of Parliament were passed affecting the Church of England. In the next hundred and fourteen years (1837 to the present day) no less than three hundred and ten Acts and Measures have been passed, all dealing with the status, organisation, administration and discipline of the Church. The activity is not spread equally over the whole period. Between 1900 and 1920 there was relative quiet; only 37 Acts, all of them, except for the Welsh Church Act of 1914 and the Church Assembly Powers Act of 1919, of minor importance, came into effect. Since 1921, however, when the Church Assembly entered upon its legislative functions, ninety-nine Measures have been submitted to the scrutiny of Parliament and thereafter received the Royal Assent. This astonishing legislative energy, which began in the middle years of the nineteenth century and continues with ever-increasing fervour in the activities of the Church Assembly to-day, might almost be described, without prejudice, as an attempt to nationalise the national Church; and the student of contemporary affairs will notice with interest that the main result has been to stimulate private enterprise to an almost equal extent—sometimes in the form of opposition to and even evasion of the legislation enacted, more often, in recent times, by way of discovering how to implement its purposes and to use the powers conferred upon the Church, in certain directions at least, to the highest advantage.

One major result of this legislation had been to stereotype as official bodies with statutory rights and duties, many of the various committees and councils set up as voluntary organizations by the several bishops, and to bring into existence many other new official bodies. In some respects the bishop's administrative and financial autocracy had been clipped but in general his patriarchal position was as fully recognized as ever. He was *ex officio* the presiding authority of almost every diocesan committee and though he might depute his functions as chairman anyone aggrieved at the decision of any committee has the right of appeal to him. In the Diocesan Conference he forms in his own person one of the three 'authorities' who make up that body, and in many other matters also he has to give a separate concurrence to decisions already reached by a committee over which he presides. In theory it would be possible to confine the bishops to strictly pastoral functions, whilst transferring to elected committees the entire super-vision of finance and administration, but Kirk was sure that as far as the Church of England was concerned such a policy could not be carried through to any real effect.

Our ingrained episcopal tradition is so strong, that the bishop's words on administrative and financial matters—were he ever to speak on them at all—would probably outweigh in popular esteem anything that any Committee could decide. He would still be treated as a court of appeal by anyone who was aggrieved, and his pastoral influence would suffer a very grave blow if he declined to take up a worthy case on the ground that he had no status in the matter. Further, even a foolish and indolent bishop, provided he has the loyal assistance of his archdeacons and rural deans, must know far more about the personnel and needs of his diocese than any Committee can do; and he alone, as an *ex officio* member of all Committees, can co-ordinate their activities wherever (as so often) they overlap. His presence, therefore, at every Com-mittee whenever an important decision was to be taken would be under the new system as it is to-day. No doubt a highly qualified Diocesan Administra-tive Secretary, free from all detailed office cares which might prevent his touring the diocese continually, would do much to relieve the bishop's burdens. But even he could not take over the bishop's ultimate responsibility, for the simple reason that—not being himself the bishop of the diocese—he could not exercise that patriarchal influence which is inherent in the English episcopal tradition. And the cost of maintaining the staff which such an administrator would find necessary would for most English dioceses be altogether prohibitive.

Kirk reached the somewhat depressing conclusion that nothing more could be done than to accept the compromise between patriarchal and democratic government in its present form and to work it as well as we can.

It is clear from his words, and even more his actions, in other contexts that Kirk regarded the central legislative and administrative bodies of the Church of England as in large measure responsible for many of the difficulties of diocesan work. Elsewhere in this volume some of his dealings with the Central Advisory Council for Training for the Ministry, and with the Church Commissioners are set out. It was a view held very strongly in the Oxford Diocese that the Commissioners had a policy of de-centralizing the work and keeping a tight control over the purse-strings, thereby creating the most difficult of situations for the diocesan bodies. Kirk's business instincts and his great administrative ability made him very critical of any unnecessary expenditure of time and money such as he believed to be caused by some of the central bodies. It was a matter of pride to him that the Oxford Diocese had always made its annual budget of grants to the various parts of its work on the basis of money in hand, rather than on the basis of what it expected to receive through the Quota and other sources. He believed it to be almost unique among English dioceses in this, and his suspicion of the soundness of general Anglican finance was increased accordingly. Like many others he lamented some of the activities of the Church Assembly, as he wrote in a Christmas message in 1950:

The past twelve months have seen a greater pressure of diocesan administration upon those of us who are specially concerned with it than any in my memory. This is largely the result of what I cannot but regard as excessive legislation by the Church Assembly, together with almost remorseless pressure by the central bodies of the Church upon local administrative resources. We are reaching a point at which bishops, both diocesan and suffragan, are so much absorbed in office work of one kind or another, that they are hard put to it to discharge their proper pastoral responsibilities.

In one of his last major sermons, however, Kirk showed another side of his thought on these subjects. On the Feast of the Epiphany, 1954, he preached at the consecration of the Bishop of Swansea and Brecon, and took for his text Zech. xi. 7. "I took unto me two staves; the one I called Beauty and the other I called Bands; and I fed the flock." These two staves Kirk interpreted as the two main sides of the episcopal life. The pastoral ministry in all its many sidedness represents the happiest aspect of a bishop's work. "In such activities he is guiding the flock as a true shepherd should; can there be anything of greater beauty than this?" But beside the beauty of pastoral ministrations there are also the 'bands', the shackles and limitations laid upon the bishop by administrative cares and responsibilities. But Kirk asks whether beauty and bands are, as is so often suggested, inevitably opposed. He takes the example of the father of a family whose drudgery of office work, earning the money wherewith to provide for his family, is no less an expression of his love for his children than the rare hours when he becomes their companion and friend. Applying this to the episcopal office Kirk said:

As the leader of worship in his diocese, the bishop is charged with the duty of ensuring that the clergy who, under his guidance, call the faithful to serve, love and worship the Lord, are in things material as in things spiritual duly equipped for their task. It is for him to take care that their churches are properly furnished with all things necessary to the conduct of public worship; that they have adequate opportunity, accommodation and means for initiating the children of the parish in the doctrine and discipline of Christ; that they are not over-burdened by domestic cares or financial stringency, and so prevented from giving of their best to their ministry. As a bishop goes from Church to Church on his sacred errands—a sermon here, a confirmation there, elsewhere a quiet day, the inauguration of an evangelistic or teaching mission, or as occasion allows the celebration of the Holy Communion for the faithful people of some great urban centre or little country parish—the appointments of the Church, the response of clergy and people, will prove to him that the long hours spent in routine administration have not been altogether wasted. In them, as in his sacramental ministry he has expressed his love for his people; by this means, as by his public utterances he has fed the flock.[1]

6

As the last paragraph shows Kirk had a very strong sense of the liturgical functions of the episcopate, an aspect of the office which undoubtedly belongs to the primitive pattern of episcopacy but has been much neglected in the modern Church of England. A bishop's liturgical functions must, of course, centre on the church in which he has his *cathedra*, the cathedral, and the peculiar situation of Christ Church as both a cathedral and a college chapel had raised many difficulties for Kirk's predecessors. In addition to the college aspect of the problem was the fact that Christ Church is a royal foundation whose Visitor is the Queen, so that the diocese of Oxford possesses the only English cathedral of which the bishop is not the Visitor. Arch-bishop Benson in 1888 had written to Dr. Stubbs: "The Bishop of Oxford is not wanted in *that* Cathedral", and Dr. T. B. Strong wrote of Stubbs that "It is probable that among the details which vexed him in the position as Bishop of Oxford, one was the peculiarity of his relation to his old College". Strong had some verses which Stubbs had written to him as Senior Censor in 1895 when the Bishop, who was a regular guest at the Censors' dinner had been asked to return thanks for the toast of the Censors' Visitors:

> Though to dinner, dear Censor, you kindly invite us,
>   I cannot your Visitor be;
> For *incorporatus, annexus, unitus,*
>   You can't make a stranger of me.

[1] *Beauty and Bands, 1955.* pp. 13ff.

The Chapter and Dean must go to the Queen
  If they would their Visitor see;
The *Fidei Defensor* might visit the Censor
  If he should invite her to tea.

But I'm the old man of the See, dear Strong,
  You cannot eliminate me,
In the House I'm at home, as the Pope is at Rome,
  How can you exist without me?
However you treat me, you cannot unseat me,
  I am the old man of the See;
I'm W. Oxon, D.D., C.G.,
  You cannot disintegrate me;
Yes, I *am* the old man of the See.[1]

Kirk was fortunate in having been a member of the Chapter at the time of his appointment, and in that there had during the twenties and thirties been a considerable change in the attitude of the Chapter towards the diocese. Moreover during the four years immediately preceding his enthronement there had been great improvements in the furnishings of the cathedral and the ordering of its services, improvements for which his friend Dr. N. P. Williams was very largely responsible.[2] Williams was anxious that the great festivals of the Christian Year should be marked by a solemn pontifical celebration of the Holy Communion in the cathedral, and the Chapter and the Bishop accepted this plan. Kirk, therefore, took the 11 a.m. Sung Celebration on Easter Day, 1938, and thereafter officiated each year, when his health did not prevent it, at Christmas, Easter, Ascension and Whitsunday. In addition there were the ordinations in the summer (usually on the second Sunday after the University Term) at Michaelmas and in Advent. The ceremonial of the ordination was carefully worked out by Williams and E. C. Ratcliff, and later on was under the direction of A. H. Couratin, the Principal of St. Stephen's House. On the musical side there was helpful co-operation from the cathedral organist, Dr. T. H. W. Armstrong. In both music and ceremonial the Oxford ordinations became a model of impressive dignity. On the occasion of the fourth centenary of the diocese Kirk was given a full set of pontifical vestments which, with the consent of the Chapter, he used at these functions.

On Easter Eve, 1940, a further addition was made to the round of pontifical functions, and this was described by Kirk himself in the Diocesan Magazine some two years later:

[1] W. Hutton, *Letters of William Stubbs.* p. 302.
[2] See E. W. Kemp, *N. P. Williams, 1954.* p. 47.

I have been asked to give some account of the Easter Eve services at the Cathedral (including the solemn baptism of adults and infants), in order that parish priests may consider whether some adaptation of this most instructive ceremonial might not be introduced locally in future years. The ceremonies in question, which are now well-established, are based on two main principles. The first is the time-honoured custom of the Church to administer Holy Baptism solemnly on Easter Eve; the second is the principle that (unlike all the other Great Festivals) Easter still retains in one form or another its primitive 'vigil', and so has no 'first evensong'. The Lenten season continues until after the evening office of Holy Saturday. In so far as the joys of Easter Day are anticipated, the primitive method was to follow Vespers with a celebration of the Holy Communion, with the church decked out in its most festal array, and every light burning. At this service, *Gloria in Excelsis* was sung in place of the Introit.

In accordance with these principles, evensong of Easter Eve is said at the Cathedral with the utmost simplicity, the High Altar still being stripped and bare of ornaments. Immediately after Evensong, the procession to the font takes place, the choir singing unaccompanied the psalm 'Like as the hart desireth the waterbrooks' (Ps. 42). At the font stands the Paschal candle, which has been lighted before Evensong. The minister of baptism and his assistants are vested in purple copes. If the bishop himself administers the sacrament, he then confirms the newly baptised adults in the neighbouring Lady Chapel.

The procession is then re-formed, and returns to the choir singing the Litany, the newly baptised and confirmed now taking their place in it after the ministers, and so being symbolically ushered into the full fellowship of the Church. By this time the altar has been dressed for Easter with a full display of all its ornaments, and as the litany ends the ministers lay aside their purple copes in the Military Chapel, and put on the festal vestments appropriate to Easter. They then ascend to the Altar and the Collect, Epistle and Gospel of Easter are sung, *Allelulia* taking the place of the Introit. It would not, of course, be seemly for the first celebration of the Easter Day Holy Communion to take place before midnight; and so at this point the service comes to an end with the singing of the *Gloria*. The lights are lit throughout the Cathedral; the organ plays again for the first time since Palm Sunday; and (in happier days to come) the bells will peal once more. The *Gloria* ended, the officiant gives the blessing, congregation and choir join in an Easter hymn, and the Easter season has begun.

The large numbers who now attend this service each year seem to prove that, although it is admittedly only a local and modern attempt to solve the difficult liturgical problem of the observance of Easter Eve, it is not wholly unsuccessful.

Problems of public worship occupied Kirk's thoughts a good deal. He was determined that there should be no persecution in the diocese, but this did not prevent him from giving guidance and making requests. He was very careful to insist that he had no power to authorize any variations from the Prayer Book, but he was prepared to advise. In the months from October, 1940, to March, 1941, for example, he wrote a series of articles in the Diocesan Magazine[1] in which he tried to give an outline of the theology behind the problems connected with the Eucharistic liturgy, and proposed certain possible lines of advance. On this occasion he said:

I do not indeed think that a bishop ought to be asked formally to 'authorise' or 'sanction' any deviation from the Prayer Book of 1662. But I think he might quite well be invited to say whether he would regard any such proposed deviation with disfavour, as calculated to be harmful rather than beneficial on the whole.

In the course of 1941, however, certain action was taken in the Convocations with regard to the use of a revised Canon made up of the present Consecration Prayer, the so-called Prayer of Oblation, and the Lord's Prayer. This arrangement, as a temporary way of dealing with the problem, received support from the Upper House of the Canterbury Province. Kirk, therefore wrote in July:

In my original articles I enumerated four possible variants of the present Prayer of Consecration to which, in certain circumstances, I should not take exception. Now it is only in the case of *one* of these four (and that not, to my mind, the most satisfactory) that my proposed policy has received any endorsement. The other three have not been condemned (for they have not even been discussed); but no such measure of approval has been extended to them as to the one which simply adds the Prayer of Oblation and the Lord's Prayer to the Prayer of Consecration. It is only proper, therefore, that I should defer to this clearly marked preference on the part of the bishops, and say that it is only in the case of this particular variant that I can be expected not to take exception. For the sake of unity and order I hope that no one (whatever his personal predilections may be) will for the present raise the question of the other three.

In this connexion it should be recorded that four years later the Bishop recurred to the subject of the Prayer of Oblation on account of criticisms made by Dom Gregory Dix in *The Shape of the Liturgy*. Kirk strongly defended his earlier proposals in an impressive discussion of the doctrine of the Eucharistic Sacrifice in the Church of England, and the whole episode shows how far he was from being, as was sometimes suggested, wholly under the theological influence of Dom Gregory.[2]

In two articles in April and May, 1952, Kirk turned his attention to the problems of Village Worship, using as his starting point a letter signed 'Presbyter' in the January number of the Magazine. He was

[1] See *Beauty and Bands.* pp. 55-93.   [2] *ibid.* pp. 94-100.

concerned particularly with Mattins in a church where the congregation is very small and the choir non-existent. A paragraph in the first of the two articles shows his knowledge of the conditions of country life.

It would not be true to say that there is more work to be done in country cottages to-day than there used to be. In many ways work has been made much easier. Far less water has to be carried from the well or pump; far fewer oil lamps to be cleaned. The district nurse is a great standby in times of illness. Against this, however, must be set the vastly increased complications of modern life. The mere standing in queues not only in the market town, where shopping has to be done every week, but at the bus-stops from which the journeys between village and town are made, is a great source of fatigue. So quite a number of little jobs get left over for Sunday mornings; or where this does not happen there is a very natural desire to 'get out of the place' for a few hours. This accounts to a large extent for the great increase in motor-coach excursions on Sundays. It is easy of course to say that 'Church should come first'; but the truth is that there are far more difficulties and temptations in the way than there used to be when morning church was as established a piece of village-routine as anything could very well be.

The problem with which Kirk was concerned at this stage was how to help the faithful few who, in difficult circumstances, continued to come to church, so that they might derive the fullest possible inspiration and edification from the service. The service that he had in mind was Mattins, and he arranged his suggestions in five paragraphs. First he stressed the need to gather the congregation together, possibly in the chancel or a side chapel, so that it might be an assembly or family, rather than a number of detached individuals, under the same roof indeed, but scattered about the building. Secondly, with the congregation thus concentrated it would be better for the priest to abandon the pulpit and to give the address seated close to the people. "This would add to the homeliness of the occasion, and almost automatically the sermon would become much more like a Bible-reading or meditation (the congregation might even be encouraged to bring their Bibles and follow the exposition by reference to the text), or a simple homily on one of the great truths of our faith." Thirdly, Kirk asked "Does a congregation as small as that we are considering really want to sing very much?" He would like to see a considered experiment in saying the whole service, without any attempt to sing versicles, responses, psalms or canticles, and no intonation of collects by the minister, carried out over a period long enough to enable a serious estimate of its value to be made. But, fourthly, there was the question of hymns, and

probably there would have to be a compromise with tradition—
a couple of hymns, but no more. This absence, or severe limitation, of
music, however, left for consideration the problem of the organist,
and on this the final paragraph is worth quoting in full.

No one can be more loyal and devoted than many of our village organists.
But I doubt whether they find much enjoyment in grinding out familiar
chants and tunes week after week without a choir, and with a congregation so
small that (except for the undaunted few whom I have mentioned), the singing
is wholly drowned by the organ. If the organ and the organist, however, are
even moderately good, I think it might be possible to get the congregation to
accept an opening and concluding voluntary, suitably selected, as an integral
part of the Sunday worship, expressing in music what was to be said, or had
been said, in the course of the service. Once it was treated as integral to the
service, the congregation would tend to arrive in time for the opening voluntary, and stay, perhaps kneeling in quiet prayer, till the end of the closing one;
and once more it might find itself truly edified and helped by the experience. I
am even bold enough to suggest that a short and suitable composition might
follow the address or meditation, to enable those who were present to think
quietly about what they had heard. It is true that all this would be an innova-
tion into the tradition of 'family prayers' which we have taken as our pattern;
but no one could say that it was hostile to that tradition.

7

Kirk's knowledge of village church life was not only derived from his
observation of the parishes in the diocese. It had been his constant
practice from 1920 to the time of his consecration to take a locum in the
summer, for a family holiday, and generally the parish selected was a
country village. Of his very last short Easter holiday, six weeks before
he died, he wrote to a friend: "We had a pleasant week-end on Dart-
moor, though the wind was piercingly cold, and I was able to help the
local clergy—who are very hard pressed—by giving some sick-
communions, hearing confessions, and anointing one sick person."
Moreover, throughout his episcopate, he was a constant visitor to Sir
William and Lady Nora Fitzherbert at Tissington in Derbyshire, and
there, in the summer he often took duty at the village church. An
envelope labelled 'Tissington Sermons' contains notes of addresses
delivered there, some written for the occasion, others written for
parishes in the diocese and subsequently used at Tissington. Two
examples are given here, typical of Kirk's style of simple parish
preaching.

Matthew vii, 16. Ye shall know them by their fruits. (Trin. VIII)

A.1. Many names for Ch. (city-family-household-ship-army-temple). Here *orchard*. Trees of many kinds: 'hardy' apples, pears, plums, berries; 'tender' nectarines, peaches, apricots. 2. Each of us such a tree—to each God has given the things it needs—the right soil, rootstock (if grafted, protection against frost and winds, pruning as and when needed).
3. All the time is watching them—visiting—what kind of fruit? TEXT "He will know whether good or bad."

B.1. *Some trees good—year by year fine crop:* sometimes more, sometimes less; better, not so good (depends on weather—etc.). *Some bad*—crop grows *less and poorer year by year*. May be *diseased*—may be *dying*. 2. *Whatever cause*—external (blight)—internal (canker—grubs—rot—bacteria)—perhaps can be cured—perhaps not. 3. But till cured it is worthless—perhaps a danger—*not a real fruit tree—only a sham*.

C.1. *How true of religion*. How O.B.L. *hated shams*—*hypocrites:*—*Scribes and Pharisees—withered fig tree*. 2. *World points finger of scorn*—'churchpeople *no better than they ought to be*'—people of position who turn out to be *frauds and cheats*. 3. *"Fanny's first Play"* "if it's by a good writer . . ." *all wrong* . . . should say "if it's a good play . . ." That's Xtian. test—TEXT.

D.1. *Make sure religion isn't sham religion*. Baptized—confirmed—come to H. C. Splendid. 2. *Examine self*. Am I helping people to live happier, purer, worthier lives? 3. If not, ask God to cleanse and heal by his H. S. If so thank Him and ask that year by year fruit may be more pleasing in His sight.

1. Sam. vii, 16. He went from year to year in circuit to Bethel and Gilgal and Mizpeh; and he judged Israel in all those places.

A.1. *Old man going round in circles*—kitten—moth—goldfish—puppy—*idle useless life, fussy*.
2. *Not fair*—"while earth endureth . . ." (so man can get daily bread) Church's year—Sunday to Sunday—Xmas—Easter etc. So learn lessons—
3. *Good to know what to expect*—postman—baker's-cart . . . makes life easier, tidier, simple, more satisfactory.

B.1. *Much depends on kind of circle*—idle—finicky—vicious (men, women, young folk) . . . condemn . . . But if useful, friendly etc. difft.
2. Samuel *judged Israel*—(Hannah quarrels w. Judith; Job hits Eli; "Samuel's coming next week")
3. What is the circle of my daily life? . . . beautiful—valuable—worthwhile.

C.1. *Bethel* . . . *Gilgal* . . . M. 3 tiny villages . . . circle too narrow. cd. have widened . . . petty . . . unimportant—people got tired *"we want a King"*.
2. We *honour those who start in small way* and then take *more and more responsibility*—*small shop-keeper* becomes founder of Colleges and Hospitals—*errand boy* becomes U.S. President—Everest expedition.
3. *O.B.L.* . . . .

D.1. *Apply to circle of prayer* Always bound to be good.

2. *But is it wide enough?* (Korea) "God bless Mummy & Daddy . . ." (more if anxious or in difficulty) . . .

3. Year by year, month by month, day by day go on circuit in prayer . . . always taking in more and more people & needs (hear of them by books, papers, wireless).

In the early twenties Kirk spent several holidays at Polperro as one of a large family party. His preaching was so highly regarded that it became usual for the non-conformist chapels to close on Sunday evenings in order that their congregations might attend the parish church to hear Kirk preach. For one of his intellectual attainments and academic background he had a quite extraordinary ability to speak to ordinary people in terms that were immediately comprehensible and related to their circumstances of life. He was not a preacher in the grand manner, he did not indulge in the oratorical flights which made the sermons of his friend N. P. Williams so impressive, but he had a simple, moving and, in the best sense of the word, ingenious style of his own. His confirmation addresses were almost always based upon some quite short text which he offered to the newly confirmed as a sort of motto by which to remember their confirmation. The address usually extracted every ounce of meaning that could be got from the text. Very few preachers in recent times have been listened to with such careful attention by all classes of people as Kenneth Kirk.

The ability to speak to ordinary folk was not confined to the pulpit. Kirk had a remarkable memory for individuals and at parish functions really made those to whom he spoke feel that he knew and cared about them. The present writer has seen him after an induction in a working-class parish going round the parish hall at the 'bun-fight', making a point of speaking to everyone who was there, and leaving behind an ineffaceable impression of kindly interest and concern, and of a humorous delight in simple things.

8

It was this understanding and concern for people which, more than anything else, made him so greatly loved by the clergy of the diocese. As his coffin was carried out of the cathedral more than 300 of the clergy lined the south side of Tom Quad, from the cathedral doors to the gates. One of his suffragans remarked: "He would have known every one of them, and their wives, and all about their children". Kirk's remarkable memory of people was a great asset, but it was not a mere mechanical feat. Behind it was a real care for his clergy.

In one of his Visitation Charges Kirk went out of his way to emphasize the extent to which the whole work of the Church depends upon the parish priests. He traced the development of the organization of the Church into dioceses and of dioceses into parishes, and made clear the principle of difference between the parochial and congregational systems. In reply to the frequent saying that the parochial system has broken down, Kirk maintained that as long as the Church is so organized that the country is wholly divided up into areas each of them under a responsible priest, that saying is untrue. "What is true is that far more people live in one parish and work in another—possibly distant one—this creates all kinds of difficulties which used not to exist; but the system remains intact. Each parish is under a responsible priest; no other priest may minister in it without his permission."

The corollary of this, in his view, is that the whole of diocesan organization is intended to provide the parish priests and assistants with the help they need in their tasks. The various diocesan councils of Education, Moral Welfare, Church Extension and the like are merely ancillary to the parochial clergy whose responsibility is in no way limited or altered by these things. This, Kirk believed, is often misunderstood. If a particular branch is faced with lack of funds and the question of reducing the number of stipendiary workers is raised there is always the outcry "If the worker of this area is withdrawn, who will be responsible for such and such activities?", and the answer should be: "The men who have always been responsible—the parish priests of the area. They will be grievously hampered by lack of expert help no doubt; but the facts remain as they have always been. Under the bishop, the priest of each area is responsible for the spiritual well-being, in the widest possible sense, of all who dwell there."

From this it follows that the maintenance of the clergy in the highest possible state of efficiency—free from unreasonable strain on health, physical endurance, financial cares—is the first claim on all diocesan organization. Nothing else can come first. It is recognised in matters of Dilapidations and the Maintenance of the Ministry. In neither case are we doing one half of what we should be doing; but however badly our finances may decline in moments of real stress, these are the things which we must least allow to suffer. It is no use providing a priest with expert help in his schools if in the matter of diet for example he is below subsistence level; see that he has an adequate stipend, and though without full help his schools will of course suffer, still he will be physically and mentally strong enough to carry on with some measure of success.

Kirk deplored the attacks which are from time to time made on the zeal and efficiency of the clergy of today. He believed that the clergy of the Oxford Diocese were zealous, but many of them harrassed beyond endurance. The incidence of ill-health resulting from overstrain and in some cases undernourishment was a constant source of anxiety, and a situation which he desired to see ended at the earliest possible moment. He therefore welcomed the Challenge to the Laity issued by the Archbishop of Canterbury early in 1947, and in 1952 the Oxford Diocese was one of the first to raise its target from £500 to £600 as the minimum stipend for all incumbents.

He recognized, however, that the raising of new money was a long-term policy, and that, at least as a temporary measure, it must be accompanied by a reduction in the number of incumbents. But he was not enthusiastic about what he called "cumbrous methods of Pastoral Reorganisation", and much preferred the older method of pluralities. Comparing the situation in 1952 with that in 1937 he said that the number of incumbents had fallen by 60, that is ten per cent. "It is distressing beyond words that a parish that has had a resident priest for centuries should now have to do without, even though still receiving accredited regular priestly ministrations. It must be regarded as a temporary measure designed to meet the grave circumstances of the moment. The situation must be stabilized till the Laity Challenge Fund income has reached its zenith. Once that point is in sight we shall be able to build up numbers once more. Till then (a) a parish which can support an incumbent in reasonable financial security need not fear; (b) other parishes must be prepared, for the moment at least, to acquiesce with good grace in the temporary loss of a resident priest."

He realized that this reduction of the number of beneficed clergy would involve a considerable rearrangement of methods of ministry.

We have about 870 churches, parish, district and mission; at present about 540 incumbents, helped by about 110 curates, a fine corps of Readers, and very many retired priests of unfailing gallantry. Suppose that we have to reduce by another 100 beneficed clergy or even more, it will mean that the rural parts will to some extent become like areas in the Mission Field. Not every congregation will be able to expect the visit of a priest every week—evening weekday services may have on occasion to be substituted for Sunday ones. In many places it will be hard for the laity to accustom themselves to the idea that services must take place when the priest can come, rather than at times which have become traditional. Even the accustomed times of Holy Communion may have to be altered, and this will involve (as it has done for the R.C.s) a review of the ancient ecclesiastical rules about the fast before communion. (For an ecclesiastical rule, however laudable, must never be given priority over a divine precept; such as that most sacred ordinance of receiving the Sacrament). As I read in the records of missionary work to-day of the enthusiasm with which the priest on tour is received in the stations which he manages to visit—in most cases at considerable intervals—people driving 50 miles or more to receive the Holy Communion, I cannot help wondering whether a relative decline in the number of clergy for a temporary period, and the arrangement of their ministrations on a somewhat more itinerant basis (though nothing in comparison with the foreign missionary field, of course) might not produce a degree of enthusiasm, concord and coherence in the Church of England such as it cannot exhibit at present. That would be a very real and perhaps permanent asset to the Church, which would weigh solidly in the balance against a temporary reduction in the number of clergy available. It is for the clergy to do what they can to induce this sentiment and enthusiasm in the laity.

At the same time Kirk was anxious to encourage the laity to arrange services themselves, and to develop the system of Readers.

9

Kirk's sense of the great importance of the parochial clergy made him very ready always to defend them against criticism, and very loath to interfere with any incumbent's discharge of his duties. He had determined that throughout his episcopate the diocese should be free from anything that could be called persecution, and this determination was carried to such lengths that on occasion he failed to intervene and check abuses for fear that his action might be misrepresented.

The Rev. C. O. Rhodes in his book *The New Church in the New Age* has, however, quoted two letters of Kirk's as examples of how even a truly great and humane bishop could deal quite ruthlessly with a difficult clergyman.[1] The priest in question is an acquaintance of Mr. Rhodes and presumably supplied him with copies of the letters. The first of the two letters that Mr. Rhodes prints is as follows:

My dear Y.Z.

I have had some very disturbing accounts from various parishes of distress caused by passages in your sermons when you have been taking duty there.

I should be the last person, of course, to wish to condemn anyone unheard, but for the moment I have no alternative except to suspend the permission to officiate within this diocese which I issued to you some time ago.

I must therefore ask you not to undertake any work in this diocese until further notice.

Sincerely yours,
Kenneth Oxon.

Three weeks later Kirk wrote again. Of this second letter only the last part is printed by Mr. Rhodes and runs as follows:

[1] pp. 96-97.

I now make a definite suggestion. Are you prepared to promise:—

(a) To write out all your sermons, addresses etc. in full before delivering them?

(b) Not to deviate in the slightest from the written text?

(c) To submit to me the text of any sermon etc. to which exception has been taken?

If you are prepared to make this promise and to stand by it, it will enable me to cancel the suspension of your Permission to Officiate.

> Believe me,
> Sincerely yours,
> Kenneth Oxon.

On this Mr. Rhodes comments: "Some of us might think that sentencing to the pillory would be a lesser humiliation. Even when I was a new and inexperienced curate my vicar did not treat me like that. The incident is some little indication of what might happen to the clergy if ever they lost their parson's freehold."

It is, of course, possible to argue that Kirk should not have written the first letter without seeing Y.Z. personally, but in order to form any judgement on the matter it is important to be in possession of more facts than Mr. Rhodes has supplied. As regards Y.Z. himself, he had been an undergraduate contemporary and acquaintance of Kirk's. Subsequently, at the end of the First World War he had been ordained deacon by an English diocesan but after a short curacy in England ceased to hold any ecclesiastical office. Some years later he resumed the ministry abroad, and eventually, after a further period of years, was ordained priest by an Anglican bishop in the Far East. He returned to England at the end of the Second World War, and after two short curacies came to live in the diocese of Oxford in 1949, the year in which the correspondence referred to took place. In a letter to the author Y.Z. says that he stated definitely on paper to Kirk that he "was a member of the Communist Party . . . a worker for Peace on MOSCOW's Term . . ." The first part of Kirk's second letter is also relevant:

My dear Y.Z.,

I have given a great deal of thought to your letter and must say one or two things frankly:—

(1) You are wrong in supposing that the only parishes from which I have received complaints are B . . . and T . . . I have heard the same resentment against your services expressed elsewhere.

(2) Not one of these complaints has reached me from any of the clergy. In each case they emanate from devout laity of no party affiliations.

(3) I do not much mind your quarrelling with the clergy. They are usually

able to deal with offence given in this way. But I cannot have intelligent Christian lay folk disturbed, as you have been disturbing them.

(4) Whatever your experience of party spirit among the clergy outside this country may have been, you should be very slow to allow it to colour your views here. You have been out of England for a very long time, yet you come back with prejudices and obsessions which you proceed to apply irresponsibly to all and sundry here. Conduct of this kind seems to me as foolish as it is unjust.

I now make a definite suggestion, etc.

Three days later Kirk wrote again:

My dear Y.Z.,

Thank you for your letter and the promises you make in it. I have instructed my Registrar to cancel the suspension of your permission to officiate in this diocese.

Sincerely yours,
Kenneth Oxon.

A little more than a year later Kirk wrote again,

My dear Y.Z.,

To be frank with you, I have had certain complaints of the usual kind about your sermons during the last year, which would have to be considered if you were to apply for the renewal of your permission to officiate in this diocese. I did not think it worth while to take them up until then.

I will certainly answer any questions the Bishop of X. desires to put to me; bene discessits are not usually issued between dioceses in this country. I have, of course, no objection to your being accepted by another Bishop for work in his diocese.

Sincerely yours,
Kenneth Oxon.

After that Y.Z. went abroad again, but two years later he wrote announcing his impending return, and Kirk replied:

My dear Y.Z.,

I have your letter of September 3rd. I am prepared to give you informal permission to officiate in this diocese on your return. But I have got to remind you that last time I gave you permission to officiate, I received complaints about your sermons. I must therefore make it quite clear that the continuance of my permission depends upon my meeting with no further grounds for dissatisfaction or uneasiness.

Please forgive me for putting matters so frankly.

Sincerely yours,
Kenneth Oxon.

Three months later the Bishop wrote to Y.Z., now living at an address
in London:

My dear Y.Z.,

I am glad to hear from you and hope all goes well with you now you are
home again. I return your documents herewith which you so kindly sent me
to look at.

I am glad that you may be available for occasional duty in this diocese. If
you show this letter, it will be sufficient authorisation.

With all good wishes for the new year,

Sincerely yours,
Kenneth Oxon.

Copies of these letters were sent to the author by Y.Z. with a
covering letter, in the course of which he said: "Please do not mention
my name if you wish to use the enclosed letters of Kirk's". It had not
been intended to use them, but the publication of a part of the story
by Mr. Rhodes has seemed to make it desirable that such of the evidence
as is in the possession of Kirk's biographer should be presented.
Some might think that in this case Kirk, far from being arbitrary was
too ready to renew his permission to officiate.

10

Kirk could on occasion appear ruthless in his dealings with individuals. Some of this was undoubtedly physical in cause. He had a
constant battle against ill-health, and was subject to the kind of influenza and throat afflictions which induce moods of depression, and
could make committee work a strain. Part of it was also the result of
his own extraordinary ability. There is no doubt that in his grasp of
detail, his far-sightedness and his power of reasoning he was head and
shoulders above almost all of those with whom he worked, and this
made for difficulties in committee and occasionally in bodies like the
Diocesan Conference. Moreover it has to be remembered that for the
whole war period, when meetings and travelling were severely
restricted, circumstances placed the main burden of diocesan administration almost solely in his hands. His experience and knowledge of
the problems of the diocese were unique. From the start he was in the
closest touch with the day to day working of the Diocesan Board of
Finance. For two and half years after the retirement of Mr. C. A.
Chilton he acted as his own Registrar, with the invaluable help of the
Registry clerk Mr. E. A. Bacon. All this made it difficult to adjust
himself in the later years to the ordinary committee system. Members
of committees knew that the Bishop was far better informed about

most of the problems than they were, that he could see the consequences of any course of action much more clearly, and that he had
his own ideas of the right line to be taken. The result was that most of
them sat quietly and waited for the Bishop's proposals. Alternative
schemes were apt to be dissected and exposed rather like a college
tutor dealing with a faulty essay in logic. Throughout his life Kirk
loved an argument and, when he was not too tired or depressed, took a
real pleasure in his fights with the Commissioners and other such
bodies, but he was apt occasionally to use his intellectual superiority in
a bullying way, particularly in relations with his fellow bishops, the
central bureaucracy and some of the laity. Against this has to be set his
general dealings with the clergy. He liked to attend clerical meetings
as a theologian rather than a bishop, to put his ideas before them for
discussion, without the least attempt to impose them by the authority
of his office. He was always dignified, always respected, but few bishops
can have relied less upon their office and more upon their own inherent
qualities than he did. He was never pompous, he disliked being called
'My Lord', and his personal manner of life was simple and without
extravagance or ostentation.

It may be a fair criticism to say that he did not make the best use of
the more prominent laymen in the diocese. Most of his lay friends
were either in the University or in other parts of the country, and he
had not that close personal contact with the leading men in the towns
and countryside which would have enabled him to widen the basis of
diocesan administration. Moreover the extent to which the diocesan
machine was dominated by his own personality did not encourage the
more independent type of contribution. Some of this came to a head a
month before Kirk's death, when Colonel Leslie-Melville resigned his
chairmanship of the Diocesan Board of Finance. He felt that decentral-
ization and modernization were required, and that the laity should be
given more work and more information. "The Bishop", he writes,
"on the other hand, wanted to keep all the strings in his own hands.
(I have never been able to make up my mind whether that was inherent
in his nature, or the result of the war period when, for very good
reasons, he had run the Diocese almost single-handed.) He paid some
degree of lip service to my policy, but in practice always stalled, with a
good deal of success. In the spring of 1954, after some 5 or 6 years in
office, I told him that a point had been reached where, when pressed
by the Board for information about progress on this or that, I could
no longer tell them that 'the matter was in hand', and that either
we must march a little faster, or I must resign; and the decision rested

entirely with him. After a completely friendly discussion, he said quite frankly that he was an old man (though not old, he was certainly very tired), and was not prepared to change his ways. That being so, we reached a friendly agreement that I should resign."

Kirk was tired and ill for much of his last four years. His three suffragans were all older than he was and the successive break-downs of the Bishops of Dorchester and Reading threw extra burdens on him. When Bishop Allen resigned the see of Dorchester in 1952 Kirk took the opportunity to appoint a much younger man in the Principal of Cuddesdon, the Rev. Kenneth Riches, and when Bishop Parham resigned the see of Reading early in 1954, he chose as successor also a young man, the Rev. Eric Knell, who had been his pupil at Trinity. At that time Kirk spoke to Mr. Knell of his desire to surround himself with a new and younger team, and he clearly intended to remain in office for a further seven years.

II

No account of Kirk's episcopate would be complete without some reference to his confirmation addresses, for there can have been few bishops who were listened to with such attention by people of all ages. As a rule he chose some text that could easily be remembered and used as a kind of motto: 'I fall not away'; 'I am ready'; 'I will abide'; 'Thy King cometh'; 'The Lord is King'; 'Who shall ascend unto the hill of the Lord?'. Usually also the text was connected with some incident from the Bible or some secular poem or story—thus the last text in the above list was linked with the poem 'Excelsior', the motto of New York State. The addresses themselves were given at the end of the service and were short. Like all Kirk's sermons they were models of clarity. Almost all had four main sections, and in each section three points. The brief notes, which are all that remain, give a very in-adequate idea of Kirk's addresses, but those who heard him will be able to clothe such an outline as the following:

They came—they saw—they stayed. (John i, 39.)

A. 1. *Growing up* (cared for) (must care for other; told how to behave) (expected to know how to behave)—*So to-day into Church.* 2. *How did Church begin?* Andrew & friend—baptized & taught . . . came (hard) . . . saw (poor affair) . . . ABODE. 3. *Julius Caesar* . . .

B. 1. *So of us* . . . baptized . . . *came* (Sunday School) . . . *saw* (some Christians very poor affairs) . . . 2. *Can you stay?*—have promised . . . 3. Palm Sunday crowds . . . disciples . . .

C. 1. TEXT (I will abide)—'stand firm'—'witness'—temptations to envy—jealousy—bad temper. 2. unseemly talk etc . . . 3. Churchgoing . . .

D. 1. *New point*—they were fed in the little hut—promise of H.C. 2. Lapsed communicants. 3. Came—saw—stayed.

Choose ye this day. (Joshua xxiv, 15)

A. 1. Joshua *saw them falling away.*
   2. *3 ways of life*—riches: pleasure: God.
   3. *'I and my house . . . choose ye.'*
B. 1. TEXT. 'But have chosen & promised'.
   2. Yes. But *this* day. Every morning—
   3. All through day.
C. 1 *Examples* temptations.
   2. Language.
   3. Churchgoing.
D.   God's help.

In the whole diocesan year no occasion gave Kirk greater pleasure than the annual service on Whit Tuesday when children from every parish brought the 'Whitsun Farthings' they had collected and presented them for the work of the diocese. Here is the outline of the address that Kirk gave at this service in 1952.

A. 1. *Any birthdays here to-day? Sandy McPherson.*
   2. *Thursday—Queen's official birthday—Royal Standard Trooping Colour* (wireless? Television? Newsreels).
   3.
B. 1. *P.B. Birthdays—Kalendar—Saints—fill in w. names?*
   2. *Three great birthdays—Xmas . . . Easter* (Xtian religion) *Whitsunday* (Xtian Ch.)
   3. So in this Cathedral, *three great birthday-parties, Carols . . . Easter Eve . . . To-day* (Farthings).
C. 1. *Presents* at birthday party. *How in America: 'Happy birthday to you'.*
   2. *So to-day*—farthings your present—*what will happen to them?*
   3. *New Churches—old Churches—better schools—*help *poor—deaf—unhappy—* Thanks: 'Happy birthday to you'.

Kirk was conspicuously happy with small children. On the family holidays he devoted himself whole-heartedly to his own sons and daughters of whom at other times he saw all too little. He would sing Gilbert and Sullivan to them, make up stories, and at the same time teach them. The insight and simplicity which enabled him to do this with his own family availed equally with the children of the clergy of the diocese and with the heir to the throne whom he entranced by making rabbits out of his pocket handkerchief.

12

The great interest in education which Kirk showed in *A Study of Silent Minds* remained a constant preoccupation. As a College tutor he was, of course, directly concerned with education at the University level, but his activities in this field were early extended to the schools. In 1924 he began a long connexion with the Woodard Corporation, of which more will be said elsewhere, and his advent to the see of Oxford found that diocese already engaged in a strenuous attempt to raise £60,000 for the establishment of church senior schools. Kirk approached this whole subject with two firm convictions. First, that religious education is not, properly speaking, just a matter of religious instruction but should permeate the whole field of school life. Second, that religious instruction cannot properly be given apart from the context of a worshipping community. These two convictions made him a firm champion of church schools and a severe critic of un-denominationalism.

In an address to the Standing Committee of the National Society in 1943 he said:

Conviction is bred, fostered, and maintained by active and participating membership in a community. The man who stands alone is in far greater danger than he who walks in the company of the like-minded. This is as true in religion as in anything else. Thus the aim of religious education in school must be to 'lead on naturally to membership of the Christian Church, and as things are at present this means to one or other of the many Christian denominations.'[1] 'We can have no other ideal than this. But the history of the Cowper-Temple clause,[2] by which all Council school religious teaching is still regulated, shows that from the outset it was devised as a direct attack upon this ideal. Its main supporters in Parliament were the members of the so-called Birmingham League, whose declared object was to 'check the growth and weaken the influence of denominationalism, so that it might ultimately vanish from the land.' Nor was this all. Behind the League was the British Schools Society, whose only conception of religious education and practice was 'Bible reading without note or comments'. The League, it will be seen, had no interest in any existing Church, Established or Free; at best it set them all gently aside in favour of a non-existent, imaginary, Utopian Church, which no doubt it hoped in due course to bring into being. But the Society went further, and eschewed all Churches, real and imaginary alike; the Christian alone with his Bible was the only spiritual consummation at which to aim.[3]

[1] Sir Walter Moberly, *The Churches and the Teachers.* p. 15.
[2] The clause in the Forster Education Act of 1870 which provides that "No religious catechism or religious formulary which is distinctive of any particular denomination shall be taught in the school."
[3] Oxford Diocesan Magazine, July, 1943. p. 61.

Kirk believed that the operation of the Cowper-Temple clause had been responsible in large measure for the decline of religious and moral conviction.

Under such auspices, and with such avowed intentions, the Cowper-Temple clause was originally launched and operated. For three-quarters of a century the vast majority of our people (including, of course, practically all Council schoolteachers) have received no religious instruction in school except such as has been coloured by these ideas. We need not wonder very much, therefore, that religious conviction (which depends upon active and loyal membership in a worshipping community) has languished during this period, and that moral conviction is suffering from the same disease. For 'the education which does not attach a child to any denomination detaches him from all denominations'.[1] It may perhaps be said that Home and Church should make up what is lacking. But no one who realises the preponderating influence of School in a child's life, and the divinity which hedges the Teacher in his mind, can expect home and Church to effect much if the whole trend of the organised religious instruction which he receives on week-days is in the opposite direction.[2]

He acknowledged that in recent years the construction and use of Agreed Syllabuses had done something to improve the position, "to mitigate the stark undenominationalism of the Cowper-Temple clause", but he was not blind to their deficiencies, to the fact that in order to be 'agreed' they must gloss over or omit subjects which the Church considered to be of great importance.[3] Nothing less than a school directly connected with the worshipping life of the Church, therefore, would satisfy his ideal of education.

In his first Pastoral Letter circulated to be read in all churches in the diocese on Sexagesima Sunday (February 20th) 1938, the Bishop was, therefore, concerned to commend to church people the cause of Church Senior Schools. A new system of elementary education was being devised. The Public Elementary Schools were to be divided into two groups, one taking children up to the age of eleven, and the other, the Senior Schools, children from eleven to fifteen. The Senior Schools were to be central schools, and the State invited the Church to provide as many of these as it could, offering to help with up to three-quarters of the cost. Kirk stressed the novelty of this offer. He believed that it showed a recognition that Church Schools contribute something to the national life which no other schools can give. He did not wish to assert that in the Council Schools there was nothing but the most

[1] Canon H. J. Lewis, *The Church Gazette*, January, 1943. p. 4.
[2] Oxford Diocesan Magazine, July, 1943. p. 61ff.
[3] See *Beauty and Bands*. pp. 129-133.

elementary Bible teaching, no place for doctrine and worship, and he did not believe that the public education authorities wished for anything but the best of religious teaching in their own schools. He did, however, emphasize a difference between provided schools and Church Schools—"in the former religion may easily become no more than a subject to be taught, as history or French or arithmetic is; whilst a Church School must be a very bad one indeed if it does not make of religion a matter of personal life".

As was to be expected the amount needed for the new Senior Schools grew as the money was raised. There were diocesan collections on Sexagesima Sunday each year and the Bishop did not cease to commend the cause. In 1941 he felt it necessary to try to answer the objection "But surely in this time of war there are far more important charitable objects for our gifts than Church Schools; and what could you do with the money now if you had it? There is no school building permitted now". He asked critics to think ahead and to think deeply. The war, he maintained, was no mere matter of national, racial, or class supremacy, but a mortal battle between two opposite and irreconcilable principles of life—the Christian way on the one hand, the way of domination and force on the other. "We know that justice, liberty, truth—all the watchwords of our warfare—are bound up in the Christian religion. And we know that when soldiers and statesmen have closed this chapter of tragedy, what is to come afterwards must be wrought by the labour of men and women who have remembered, or learnt anew, that Faith by which even to-day we possess all that is worth having."

We look to Christ. Even now, in the midst of our preoccupations and anxieties, He must be doing His patient, healing work in the souls of men, if they are to have any hope at all. In Him is the only solvent of the world's disease, and it is as we know and believe in Him that civilization will be restored to health again.

How shall this great spiritual renewal be brought about? There are many agencies, and many means, which we can offer and God will use. But that which is readiest to hand, and most potent, is the training of the young. Observe what evil has been done in one generation in the dictator countries by those who have set themselves to corrupt the young. See what a monster of perversion and destruction has been created in that short time between the wars. Then why not good, instead of evil, by the same means? Is it surprising that attention is turning to the schools, and that people everywhere are asking why there should be amongst our young folk the lamentable ignorance of Christian principles of which we hear so often?[1]

[1] Oxford Diocesan Magazine, February, 1941. p. 26.

Dr. Iremonger has described in his life of William Temple how the kind of questioning to which Kirk refers here led to the making of the Education Act of 1944. In the course of 1942 a good deal of discussion took place in various quarters about a possible revision of the existing system of public education, and towards the end of the year the Standing Committee of the National Society published an 'Interim Report on the Dual System' which appeared to Kirk and to many other people to be extremely unsatisfactory. It ignored entirely, to use Kirk's words, "the growing demand that denominational teaching should be available in council or provided schools for all children (of whatever denomination) whose parents ask for it", and it asked for public money for the reconditioning of Church schools, offering in return certain concessions which were likely to result in the loss to the Church of a large number of schools. In the light of what Dr. Iremonger has written there can be little doubt that this paper represented the policy advocated by Archbishop Temple. The Archbishop, himself, in his Foreword said that the proposals were to be read "not as what seems to us the ideal method of arranging for religious instruction and education", but merely as "what we think the Church would be wise to accept if the government were found to offer it". In November after a long debate in which Kirk took a prominent part, a somewhat lukewarm resolution in support of the Report was carried by the votes of a minority of the members of the Church Assembly.

It was not clear how far this Report represented a thought-out policy and so the Oxford Diocesan Council of Education addressed a series of questions to the Standing Committee of the National Society which no doubt had some influence on the preparation of a further Report published in February, 1943. This, in Kirk's view, marked a welcome advance on the previous document. "It will be seen", he wrote, "that by these new suggestions, the Standing Committee has publicly embraced the principle that Church children should not be deprived of instruction in the tenets of their parents by the mere accident that they happen to live in an area where no Church school exists. I have always insisted that the recognition of this principle is a matter of elementary justice." The new Report was accepted unanimously by the Church Assembly, after a long debate in which Kirk again spoke, and he subsequently wrote in defence of it in the Diocesan Magazine in March.

We are *not* asking simply for Church teaching for Church children; we are asking for that, and also for Roman Catholic teaching for Roman Catholic children, and Congregationalist teaching for Congregationalist children, and Baptist teaching for Baptist children, and so on. And if the Congregationalists or the Baptists say 'Our children get all the teaching we want them to have in the Agreed Syllabus', our answer is obviously 'Perhaps so. *But ours do not;* and in common justice you ought to wish that we should be as well satisfied as you are' . . .

Take then the case of Church children. Ideally, their religious instruction should be given them, I suppose, in the parish church, where every doctrine can be brought before their eyes embodied in its 'ornaments', both in the technical and in the popular sense of the word. In practice, however, this is not possible. What then can we substitute? Our *Oxford Handbook of Religious Knowledge* and its *Fourth Centenary Supplement* give the answer. *First*, the child should be taught to handle its Prayer book and understand and appreciate the rites there set out, and the simple yet luminous explanation of them given in the Catechism. *Second* (as in the *Supplement*), it should be reminded of all the teaching to be found in the visible furnishings of its parish church; the significance of font, lectern, altar, bishop's chair, and so forth. Every one of these is linked up closely with the cardinal doctrines of the faith; and no instruction in those doctrines should be free from some reference to visible associations of this kind. For as the Bishop of Liverpool has wisely said, 'Truth must be introduced to the young in a form which out of their own experience they can naturally assimilate. They must receive it, if at all, in terms of life as they see life.'[1] And though the neglect of Church going is notorious throughout the country, there are still few children who have not found or cannot find their way to their parish church, where they can 'see' something at least of the 'life' of the supernatural Community to whose spiritual care their parents entrusted them at baptism.

Now the teaching of Church children by methods and with illustrations such as these has until recently been supposed to be forbidden by law in Council Schools. Latterly, the rigour of the law has been somewhat relaxed by Local Education Authorities; but more needs to be done (along the lines of the Church Assembly resolution) to make the situation tolerable—not merely, as I see it, for Anglicans, but also for all wise and far sighted Free Churchmen. For they, as much as any others, deplore the prevalent disuse of the practice of Church going, together with the laxity of much which seems to be associated with that disuse; and it is merely a matter of time before they realize that the cause of it all is the prevalent legally enforced undenominationalism of Council School religious instruction, which forbids a child (until he has safely reached the school leaving age) to be introduced to the loyalties and privileges of membership in the communion to which he belongs. Much could be said about this aspect of the matter; but I cannot dwell on it this month. I would only say, with all the emphasis at my command, that, if we want to discover the root cause of that modern English paganism which horrifies so many of us,

[1] *The Times,* February 15, 1941.

we need not look any further than to the rigid enforcement of the Cowper-Temple clause.[1]

In the summer of 1943 the White Paper on 'Educational Reconstruction' was laid before Parliament, and Kirk examined it in the Diocesan Magazine for August, September, and October. He noted immediately that on the main point of justice the authors of the White Paper were not prepared to move from the principles of the Cowper-Temple clause, although there were indications that its operation would be modified in practice. The provision that in County Secondary Schools where geographical factors made withdrawal for religious instruction in the faith of the parents virtually impossible the Local Authority would be required to provide facilities for such instruction on the school premises was one such welcome indication. Throughout the discussions Kirk was careful to keep this problem of Church children in Council Schools as much before the public notice as the problem of Church Schools themselves.

It must never be forgotten, he wrote, that four-fifths of the children of Church of England parents are in Council Schools. It is mere sentimentalism to suppose that 'What is to happen to Church Schools?' is a more important question than 'What is to happen to Church children in Council Schools?' and the focussing of the attention of all parties upon the first question, to the relative ignoring of the second, has been a grave misfortune.

By the time that Kirk wrote his second article the White Paper had been debated in both Houses of Parliament and in each received the general approval of an overwhelming majority of the members. He recognized that this was a factor in the situation which could not be ignored. "However much we may regret it", he wrote, "the nation as a whole feels itself committed to the anti-Anglican and anti-Roman policy of the Cowper-Temple clause, and does not recognise the essential ineffectiveness of religious instruction altogether divorced from membership in any worshipping community." Because of this attitude he saw no hope of bringing about, within the time available, such a change of mind as would cause the abandonment of the main principles of this part of the White Paper. "We must work to bring home the truth of the matter to the country in time for the next Education Bill in ten or fifteen years' time." The vote in Parliament had shown that attacks upon the main proposals of the White Paper would be futile and untimely, and might even result in the elimination of those tentative advances away from the Cowper-Temple principle

[1] Oxford Diocesan Magazine, April, 1943. p. 27.

which he had earlier welcomed. The efforts of church people should be devoted to trying to obtain somewhat better conditions for 'controlled' schools, and to raising the money needed to save for the Church as many as possible of the existing schools. In his October article Kirk returned to this subject.

I desire, finally, to say something on the question of the future of Church Schools. I pointed out in August that if we are to save these schools by modernizing them to meet present day standards, large sums of money will be required—not perhaps so much in this diocese as in others, where less devotion has been shown towards the needs of Church children in the past. I am shocked to discover how many Church people up and down the country are saying: 'The White Paper is the last straw but one. It prefigures the ultimate doom of Church Schools. In the next Education Bill they will be taken over lock, stock and barrel; to spend money upon them now is merely to throw it away.' Let me say once and for all that I regard this state of mind thus revealed as a piece of the most cowardly defeatism imaginable. We have great lessons to teach the country—the lessons that undenominationalism is the first step on the road to complete irreligion, and that true religion is only possible by virtue of active and loyal membership in a worshipping community. Our Church Schools are essential means towards making our witness effective; we must not let them go.

I believe that the barrenness of undenominationalism is already under suspicion in quarters where formerly it was regarded with enthusiasm as a truly pure form of Christianity; and that the country will steadily come to realize that there is a better way to a robust religion. But all this depends upon the Church remaining true to her divine vocation, and using her schools to bring up her children in the corporate faith which she professes and proclaims. Some schools, of course, we are bound to lose. But the loss of schools is not the loss of the battle, so long as enough remain to keep the way of Churchmanship before the eyes of the younger generation. If we are faithful now, it is in every way possible that by the time another Education Bill is required bureaucrats and administrators may have been so impressed by the excellence of the religious training given in Church Schools, that far more encouragement and help will be forthcoming than at present. Once more the question is one of tactical possibilities; but even a cautious appraisement of the situation makes it reasonable to say (as certainly Christian faith would have us say), 'Stand by the Church Schools now. Their day will come again, and then all our efforts and sacrifices will be seen to have been well expended.'

The Oxford Diocese responded to its Bishop's appeal in the next ten years as it had done in the past and very large numbers of schools were saved for the Church.

It does not appear possible at the present time to discover the full story of the negotiations and discussions which led up to the making of the 1944 Education Act. Kirk was a member of a small delegation led by Archbishop Temple which was received by the President and other members of the Board of Education in June, 1942. It was clear at that stage that there was a wide difference of opinion between him and Archbishop Temple, and there is little doubt that Kirk felt that after that date Temple tried to keep him out of any such negotiations. Whether this was so is not possible to say. The difference of view as to whether the Church could have got better terms in 1944 still persists, and it is held very strongly by many who were concerned with the matter at the time, that Temple could have used his great prestige to secure more sympathetic consideration of the Church's case by the members of the Free Churches. It was also considered that neither Dr. Temple nor the then Bishop of London, Dr. Fisher, fully appreciated the importance of Church Schools. Both had been headmasters of Public Schools and were, so men felt, inclined to think in terms of what is sometimes called 'Public School Religion', which they regarded as quite satisfactory. Religious instruction on the lines of an Agreed Syllabus together with a daily act of worship seemed to them much the same thing. Those who believed that more than this was needed felt that they were inadequately supported by the leaders of the Church against opposition from outside.

13

Kirk was appointed Examining Chaplain to the Bishop of Sheffield sixteen months after his ordination as deacon, and from that time onwards for the rest of his life he was directly concerned with the selection of candidates for Holy Orders. It was, therefore, with particular interest and long experience that he read the Final Report of the Archbishops' Commission on Training for the Ministry, published in the middle of 1944. In the July and September numbers of the Diocesan Magazine he examined the proposal that there should be a network of regional committees (each comprising the area of a number of dioceses) before one or other of which every candidate without exception must appear prior to his acceptance by a bishop or the principal of a Theological College. It seemed to him to show little realization of the nature of the work involved in the selection of candidates. The one thing that experience makes quite certain, he argued, is that the question whether a candidate has a true vocation for the ministry or not cannot be dealt with in the atmosphere of a committee room. "It demands intimate handling in searching private interviews; and the candidate must be assured from the outset that nothing said by him will be retailed, even to the committee, without his formal permission.

Thus a committee which desires to come to a decision as to the vocation of a particular candidate, will have to delegate the duty of interviewing him to one or two of its members; and will be bound to accept their verdict without question, because the evidence upon which it is based must remain to a greater or lesser extent unrevealed."

It followed from this that the Regional Committees would have to work through a number of small, informal sub-committees, whose decisions as to the fitness for ordination of the candidates they interviewed it must accept automatically. This being so the question followed as to the real necessity for the Regional Committees at all, and why the work could not be done as well by the existing diocesan machinery of Bishop, archdeacons, examining chaplains and so forth. He recognized that the main defect which it was proposed to remedy by means of the Regional Committees consisted of "the grave differences of standard between the dioceses". But there were bound to be as many, if not far more, differences of standard between the innumerable sub-committees which were to come into existence all over the country, and even in regard to the decision about intellectual and educational attainments Kirk held that the sub-committees would be needed.

Consider the humiliation which would be suffered by a boy who had first of all to face the nerve-racking experience of appearing before a committee of eight or ten people, so that they might have a cursory preview of his educational attainments; was then dismissed into an anteroom while his case was being discussed; and finally was brought back before the committee to hear the verdict, 'We doubt whether you are sufficiently educated to begin training for the ministry; you must take an examination'. We cannot recruit for the highest of all callings by methods such as these. Here again, then we come back to our innumerable tiny sub-committees, with their inevitable differences of standard, which the Regional Committees cannot by any conceivable machinery rectify or control.

He considered next the suggestion that these difficulties would be met by existence of a permanent full-time Secretary for each Regional Committee, who would keep the informal sub-committees up to the mark.

I have no such faith in the inevitable wisdom and competence of permanent full-time Secretaries as these words imply. Their own standards may be too high or too low; they may manage to impose their standards upon irresolute sub-committees, but fail to do so with strong-minded ones. If in the long run I must trust in permanent full-time officials, I am bound to say that the bishops —fallible though they no doubt are—are likely to be as good as any others.

They, with their bodies of experienced advisers, produce as good results as ever can be hoped for from this elaborate and expensive committee machinery; and even a very ordinary bishop recognises his paternal and pastoral responsibilities towards would-be ordinands in a way which is impossible to any artificially selected committee. The choice of candidates for the ministry is one of the most sacred obligations laid upon the Church; and nothing could be more dishonouring (nor, in my opinion, more dangerous) than to hand it over to the mercies of bureaucratic officialdom.

The scheme of Regional Committees was never carried into effect, but in the later years of the war and after the war Selection Committees run by the Central Advisory Council for Training for the Ministry, on behalf of the bishops, assumed more and more prominence. Kirk, like other bishops, found them useful, but he firmly refused to be bound by their decisions. Towards the end of 1952 he wrote to the Bishop of Rochester:

I am met more and more with the suggestion that Bishops are merely automatic ordaining machines, who must ordain anyone who has passed G.O.E. and is presented to them by a theological College recognised by C.A.C.T.M. The idea that the Bishop is responsible for decision as to the fitness of a candidate, and can reject, for example, on the ground of narrow-minded scrupulosity, is falling more and more into the background. My own feeling is that this is the result of the omni-competence with which we have virtually endowed C.A.C.T.M. But I may be wrong about this.

On more than one occasion he had sharp differences of opinion with C.A.C.T.M. about particular candidates, and an added seriousness was given to such clashes by the financial policy developed after the war, whereby dioceses were asked not only to finance their own candidates, but also to create a central pool. This new system began with the Appeal issued by the Archbishops for £600,000 for the training of Service Ordination candidates, the diocesan apportionment of which to Oxford was a total of £18,840 which the diocese was expected to provide over five years. This matter came before the Diocesan Ordination Candidates Fund Committee in May, 1946, and Kirk expressed his serious doubts as to the real necessity of the large sum involved. He considered that no account had been taken of the extensive Government grants that would be available for the education of ex-service men, and he was most reluctant to hand over large sums of money to be administered by a central body in whose financial policy he had little confidence. The diocese, therefore, under his guidance said that it was prepared to try to raise as much money as possible for the Appeal but that it proposed to keep the administration of the funds in its own hands. The Diocesan Ordination Candidates Fund Committee would spend the money in the first instance on candidates from the diocese, and after that were prepared to consider candidates from other dioceses recommended to them by C.A.C.T.M. This decision and offer were communicated to C.A.C.T.M. but no candidates were ever sent by them.

As an example of the kind of difficulty that might arise in a diocese such as Oxford was, with large rural areas, the following instance may be given. X. was a young man of between twenty and twenty-one who had left a Public School, after taking the School Certificate, and had completed articles with a firm of auctioneers and valuers in one of the more rural parts of the diocese. Against some discouragement at home he had become conscious of a vocation to Holy Orders and got into touch with Kirk and with C.A.C.T.M. It was clear that his intellectual abilities were not such as to make a University education suitable for him, and equally clear that his vocation would lie in a farming community. This was accepted by the C.A.C.T.M. Selection Board before whom he appeared, and they recommended him for training, but with two conditions attached, one that he should take further subjects in the School Certificate and complete qualifications for University entrance, the other that, as he had been rejected for National Service, on grounds of asthma and poor sight, he should do one year's lay work before starting his training for ordination. These conditions seemed to Kirk quite unreasonable in the circumstances. Particularly he could see no point in requiring a further year's lay work from a young man who had served his articles as an auctioneer. He therefore wrote to the Secretary of C.A.C.T.M. as follows:

I have now seen Mr X. and made the necessary enquiries about him. I am glad that the Selection Committee has recommended him for ordination and I propose to help him in whatever way I can.

I note from your letter that the Selectors make two conditional suggestions:—

(1) I understand that they recognise the point on which those who really know him all agree, that he is not capable of taking a University degree. I cannot therefore understand why they should suggest as a condition of his ordination that he should achieve University entrance. He has got his School Certificate, and with his particular vocation to ministry in a farming community this is quite adequate. I shall therefore waive this condition, should he ultimately desire ordination in this diocese.

(2) I do not understand what the Selectors mean by 'one year's lay work'. If they wish merely that he should give a further year to secular employment, I

should like to have a full explanation of their reasons; If, on the other hand, they wish him to be employed in Church work as a layman, I can no doubt arrange this. But, once more, I should wish to have a full explanation of their reasons for suggesting what, to my mind, would be a completely pointless delaying of his training for ordination.

Enclosing a copy of that letter Kirk wrote to the Secretary of the Diocesan Ordination Candidates Fund asking him to see the young man:

As you will see from the enclosed I propose to ignore the conditions put down by C.A.C.T.M. We shall probably have to find £50 a year for three years for him. But he is a very good candidate who will do admirably in country parishes.

C.A.C.T.M. will probably make a fuss about my waiving their conditions, but I shall take the line that their business is only to recommend or the reverse, and that whoever pays the piper will do the calling of the tune. If necessary we must send him to Lampeter or Edinburgh, so that no English theological college gets involved in the dispute. And I shall take full responsibility for ordaining him when the time comes.

Three weeks later another letter on the same subject ended:

I am having quite a brisk but intermittent correspondence with Y. (the Secretary of C.A.C.T.M.), who is very cross.

A financial problem arose because under a new and more comprehensive system for the financing of ordinands the diocese was now paying over considerable sums to the Central Grants Committee of C.A.C.T.M. and there appeared to be a real likelihood that the Bishop's waiving of the Selection Committee's conditions might result in the Central Grants Committee refusing to finance X. Eventually after an interview between the Secretary of C.A.C.T.M. and the Secretary of the Diocesan Fund the matter was sorted out, and it was admitted on the C.A.C.T.M. side that "If a Diocese decided to send all its apportionment to the Central Board of Finance then of course money must be paid out from the Central Board to any candidate who is finally accepted by the Diocesan Bishop concerned, and this, so far as I can see, would have to happen even if the man had been 'not recommended' at a Selection Board. He would to all intents and purposes become a Diocesan candidate, the Bishop in any case being the final authority in this matter." It will be understood that incidents such as this did not increase Kirk's liking for the central bodies of the Church of England.

Kirk had, however, other criticisms of the 1944 (Durham) Report besides that of its bureaucratic tendency, and these he expounded in a University Sermon on St. Mark's Day, 1944, taking as his text 2 Tim. iv. 11: "Take Mark, and bring him with thee, for he is profitable to me for the ministry." In this sermon he made a careful examination of the nature of the ministry as it is found in the New Testament. He emphasized the relation between worship and the life of Christian service to the community, to which he had drawn attention in his Bampton Lectures.

Ethical naturalism requires that a man shall be first and foremost a good citizen, active in the exercise of the social virtues. If he finds prayer and worship, whether public or private, ancillary to this endeavour, he may be allowed, without prejudice, to indulge in them in moderation. The Jewish Christian tradition is exactly the contrary. Man's primary privilege and obligation is the worship of God: as a preparation for the act of worship and as proof of its integrity, he must walk uprightly, and work righteousness, and speak the truth from his heart. (Ps. 15.1.) The be-all and the end-all of his creation is to dwell in the Lord's tabernacle and rest upon his holy hill: and the way thereto is clearly marked out by the Psalmist:—

Who shall ascend into the hill of the Lord, or who shall rise up in his holy place?

Even he that hath clean hands and a pure heart, and that hath not lift up his mind unto vanity, nor sworn to deceive his neighbour.

Against this background he argued that the work of the ministry is Godward, and that the more the thought of God is relegated to the background, the more the ministry becomes a purely humanitarian function, the needs ministered to are material needs and wants—the ministry is in danger of degenerating into a serving of tables.

When the Twelve, perceiving this danger, defined their own function in the Church as "continuing stedfastly in prayer and in the ministry of the word", they stated for all time the essential features of the Christian diakonia. At this point we reach a new stage in our enquiry. It is ninety years since Archbishop Trench pointed out that the word *proseuche*, here used for "prayer", is 'res sacra'. It is the only word in the rich New Testament vocabulary of prayer which is used exclusively of utterance addressed to God; the remaining synonyms are equally employable of requests addressed to men. We need not hesitate, therefore, to assert that the essential characteristic of the prayer to which the apostles were continually to devote themselves must be worship; for worship is the distinctive attitude which man must adopt in his approach to God as contrasted with his approach to even the greatest of his fellow-men . . . So the primary element in the ministerial life of the New as of the Old Covenant is the element of worship; a minister whose purpose is not set on worshipping and bringing his people to worship is a contradiction in terms.

The difference between the Old and the New Testament is that in the former the worshipper, as distinct from the minister, was bidden to stand remote and on his guard, fearful lest by a presumptuous approach to the Most Holy he should bring disaster upon himself; in the latter, he is invited to "draw near with faith", that minister and people may together unite in the supreme intimacy of a worship which they share with angels and archangels and all the company of heaven. Hence, in the Christian Church the "ministry of the word" takes an entirely different position from any which it previously had. In the Old Testament, it is the prophets—the free-lance agents of God—who stand outside the cultus and have no necessary place in the organised and official ministry— who deliver the word of God to the people; there is a sharp distinction between the prophet who preaches and the priest who leads in worship. In the New Testament, the ministry of worship goes hand in hand with the ministry of the word; they are integral to each other. The leader of worship must continually be delivering the words of God to his flock. He must expound to them the inner nature of that worship which comes first in the life of the Christian; he must overcome their reluctance and diffidence to engage in it; he must call them to repentance from the sins which obstruct true worship, and offer them the cleansing absolution of the divine Spirit; he must exhort them to that purity of heart and that vital fellow-citizenship with the saints both living and departed, that spirit of self-sacrificing devotion to the needs of others, without which worship is no more than a hypocritical mockery.

Kirk regretted that the compilers of the Report had not approached their subject more from this Biblical angle. "The cardinal truth that worship, the call to worship, and leadership in worship, form the Keystone of the whole building is never emphasized; the one fact which gives final meaning to the rest is all but wholly ignored." This deficiency affected everything that was said in the Report, and particularly the section on training. There were proposals for a more thorough training in teaching, for lengthier courses, and for enlarged opportunities for obtaining a first-hand knowledge of the needs of the laity. Experience of social work and an acquaintance with social theory and with national and local services were demanded, and recurrent changes of residence from one University to another, or from a detached college to a University town, were planned, but in the whole long section of the Report dealing with the training of the ordinand, worship and the inculcation of worship had very little place. "I doubt whether anyone reading it would carry away the impression that the curriculum was designed to turn eager but immature young Churchmen into clergy who recognise as their primary duty that they are called to persuade men to worship God". What was germane to the enquiry, and what seemed to have been quite overlooked was the double question: Is the training of the ordinand in the ways of worship what it should be? Is it such that besides becoming a true worshipper himself, he is able to persuade other men to worship God?

It was essential to the Report that the Commission should have devoted itself to this problem; but apart from one or two vague references it is never touched upon. I cannot doubt that it is the first preoccupation of every theological college principal, and that between them the twenty-six to thirty colleges in England could bring a wealth of experience, both of success and failure, into evidence. So, too, as I have hinted, could many parish priests or directors of souls—for the training of ordinands in the life of worship is not in principle different from the training of the laity, whether adult or children. Much could have been learnt as to methods which have proved helpful in stimulating and maintaining the devotional study of Holy Scripture, the ordered and intelligent practice of self-examination, thanksgiving and intercession, and the aspiring activity of worship centred round the eucharistic commemoration of our Lord's death in the Holy Communion.

The different schools of thought in the Church of England have far more in common in these matters than is often supposed; they exhibit similar excellencies, they fall into similar errors. A painstaking review of the books and leaflets of Scripture readings and the manuals of prayer and worship in common use, tested by comparison with the great classics of Christian devotional literature, would soon betray the lurking dangers of pietism, sentimentalism, unreality, and shallow self-hypnotism in which so many of them abound. The question that has to be solved is simply this: Are our theological colleges making the most of their opportunities in this matter: and if not where are they at fault? By this the Church will stand or fall; it is the acid test. It matters little whether a man is called High Church, or Broad, or Low: if he is a man of worship, none but the utterly prejudiced will fail to pierce through the superficial idiosyncracies of his up-bringing, and join him in the worship of God. But if he be not a man of worship, he has nothing whatever to offer the world. His scrip is empty, his words idle, his soul submerged in sleep.

The same defect Kirk found also in the section of the Report dealing with the selection of candidates, a section which, as we have seen, he had elsewhere criticized on other grounds also. Not once in the six closely printed pages devoted to the selection and testing of candidates did the words 'prayer' and 'worship' occur.

The Church must return to a conception of the ministry at once simpler and deeper than that which has cast its spell over the Commission. It must concentrate upon the primary requirement that its priests shall be men who have given and continue to give themselves to prayer, and are expert in commending prayer to others and leading them into its devious but salutary paths. They must detect in their own lives the point at which effective and recreative prayer is in danger of deteriorating into a barren and sensuous pietism; they must be continually on guard over their flock lest it fall into the like error. All this indeed is a matter for the most expert selection and training; anything else but this will at best produce only Christian publicists and propagandists, not men of God. The Christian ministry is primarily a ministry of Godward worship; to forget this cardinal truth is to abandon the Scriptural and Apostolic foundation upon which the Church is built.

14

After the war the problem of Cuddesdon arose again, and as Kirk has been much criticized in some quarters for his handling of this matter it seems desirable to set out in some detail the case as he saw it. The reasons which caused him to take a house on Boar's Hill in 1938 have already been explained. It is difficult to see what else, in the circumstances, could have been done by anybody but a very wealthy man. We have also seen how, at the outbreak of war, the Palace was occupied by the staff of Queen Anne's Bounty. In 1943 when the possibility of the Bounty staff moving back to London became apparent negotiations were opened with the Community of St. Mary the Virgin, Wantage, one of the principal Anglican communities for women, and in July, 1945, the Palace became a branch house of that Community, and the home of a new offshoot of it—the Community of the Salutation of St. Mary the Virgin, now established at Burford.

In the middle of 1948 the question of a permanent home for the new Community arose. Cuddesdon seemed in many ways ideal for an enclosed Order such as it had become, but the Bishop was bound to stipulate with them, as with his previous tenants, that the lease of the Palace would terminate immediately on his death or resignation of the see. The Community, therefore, opened tentative negotiations with a view to purchasing the Palace.

Here seemed the perfect solution to the problem of Cuddesdon. The extensive, costly and difficult plans for modernisation could be finally laid aside, the purchase money would make it possible to buy a house of reasonable size and more convenient situation, and there would be no fear of the Palace itself passing into alien or hostile hands. It appeared to Kirk that there were two alternative legal methods of disposing of an official episcopal residence. One was under the Ecclesiastical Houses of Residence Act of 1842, which provided that the Ecclesiastical Commissioners could, with the consent of the bishop concerned, sell the official house of any diocese. The other was under the Episcopal Endowments and Stipends Measure of 1943. This Measure provided for the vesting in the Commissioners of the whole endowments and property of a see, including the see house. If this was done the Commissioners then made a scheme under which a stipend, very considerably less than that formerly paid was allotted to the bishop, and he was also given an allowance to cover travelling and secretarial expenses. Under such a scheme the bishop had to pay rent to the Commissioners for his house. This Measure also provided that the Commissioners should have the power after consultation with the Diocesan Advisory Committee to sell the house of any see for which a scheme had been made, and to provide a new episcopal residence. The 1943 Measure was to apply in due course to all sees as they became vacant, but the existing bishops were allowed the option of applying for a scheme or not. Kirk, therefore, had to choose between asking the Commissioners to sell Cuddesdon Palace under the provisions of the 1842 Act, and asking for a scheme to be made under the 1943 Measure. The clauses of the 1943 Measure which concerned the sale of an episcopal house could not be put into operation apart from the rest of the Measure.

Kirk was one of a number of bishops who exercised their right to remain outside the operation of the 1943 Measure. He disliked the schemes that were made under it and believed that they did not operate to the financial advantage of the bishops concerned. He wrote, in 1952:

It must be emphasized that the Commissioners do not regard a scheme of this kind as intended to offer financial relief to the bishop, except in regard to the uncertainty of heavy and unexpected expenditure for dilapidations. Some bishops claim that though they are grateful to have been relieved of anxiety on this score, the reduction in their total income, the inadequacy of the allowance for expenses, the inability to claim income tax allowance in respect of excess official expenditure, and the rent charged for the new house of residence, means that they have to pay very heavily for this relief.

In approaching the Commissioners in June, 1948, about the Wantage offer he therefore expressed his desire to proceed under the provisions of the 1842 Act if it was eventually decided to sell Cuddesdon Palace. On July 1st the Secretary to the Commissioners replied that under the provisions of the 1842 Act they could, with the bishop's consent, promote a scheme for the sale of the episcopal residence, but that in the view of the Commissioners the Measure of 1943 had expressed the mind of the Church Assembly and that in these circumstances it would be inappropriate to use the 1842 Act unless there were special reasons.

After further correspondence in which Kirk made it clear that it had always been his intention to consult the Diocesan Board of Finance and possibly the Diocesan Conference before coming to a final decision, the Bishop wrote on November 25th pointing out that he could not proceed under the 1943 Measure without entering into the whole scheme, which he did not wish to do. He said:

I have neither the desire nor the intention of entering into the transactions to which, in the Measure of 1943, the disposal of a house of residence is made subsidiary. It follows that if the Commissioners maintain their refusal to allow procedure under the Act of 1842, they in effect shut the door to any sale of the property, however advantageous, during my tenure of the see; and their reason for doing this must appear to be a decision to use the possibility of a sale as a means of compelling a bishop to do something which he neither desires nor can be required by law to do. I cannot believe that the Commissioners desire inferences of this kind to be drawn.

He therefore asked for his request, together with these comments to be submitted again to the Commissioners. But on January 27th, 1949, the Secretary to the Commissioners replied:

I have re-submitted to the Church Commissioners the application which you made in your recent letters with regard to the future of Cuddesdon and the Board has directed me to explain that after giving careful consideration to the matter, it is not prepared to take action if all that is before the Commissioners is a proposal to sell Cuddesdon Palace.

A result of this opposition was that the Community concerned took advantage of the offer of Burford Priory and gave notice to terminate their tenancy of Cuddesdon. Kirk, notifying the Commissioners of this, wrote:

In a relatively short time, therefore, the palace will be unoccupied and the entire cost of repair and maintenance of the house and upkeep of the grounds must fall upon the bishop. It seems likely that this cost is in the neighbourhood of £500 a year. It is not, of course, possible to affirm that, if the Commissioners had adopted a less unhelpful attitude, the sale of the palace would undoubtedly have taken place. Nor is it certain that no new tenants will present themselves; though (as I said in a previous letter) those who know Cuddesdon recognise that the property is not of such a character as to make it widely sought after, especially in view of the limitation of tenure referred to above. Subject to these reservations, however, it does seem fair to say that the effect of the Commissioners' decision is to impose an additional burden of £500 per annum on the bishop until he finds himself compelled to ask for a scheme under the Measure of 1943. Nor is there as yet any evidence to suggest that the terms which the Commissioners might lay down for the implementing of the scheme would produce any improvement in the situation.

Subsequently in March, 1949, after Kirk had sent a copy of this correspondence to the Archbishop of Canterbury the Commissioners modified their attitude and expressed their willingness to consider a plan of sale which would ensure that the Palace should not pass into alien and unfriendly hands, and which would make provision for another and suitable see house. The chance of a sale, however, had been lost and did not recur. During the next two years Kirk was in correspondence with a number of societies and organizations with a view to finding a new tenant, but all fell through. Some found the difficulty of access a problem, with most there was the obstacle that the tenancy had to be terminable on the Bishop's death or resignation.

This question of the episcopal residence was one of the Bishop's principal worries during the last four years of his life, particularly as the house on Boar's Hill, which had been manageable under the labour conditions of 1938, became more and more difficult to run in the circumstances of post-war life. In the early summer of 1953 he bought a smaller house in Oxford itself, and found things much easier in consequence. But he recognized that that was no final solution to the problem, and indeed he touched on the matter in his last address to the Diocesan Conference. In 1952 he set up a Committee to go into the whole subject. Two of its members had an interview with a representative of the Commissioners and reported:

The Commissioners regard the making of a scheme for Oxford as intimately bound up with the future of Cuddesdon Palace. On this they hold strong views. They believe that Cuddesdon is the proper place for the Bishop of Oxford's residence; and they would require very strong arguments to convince them that such an arrangement was really impracticable.

The Commissioners' own note of the interview, however, attributes to one of the Oxford representatives the statement that there was strong *diocesan* feeling for the retention of Cuddesdon as the seat of the Bishop. On the Report of the interview Kirk commented:

A priori arguments cut both ways. No doubt there are strong general reasons for retaining ancient places of residence in episcopal occupation. In the particular case of this diocese, however, (if, let us say Cuddesdon were burnt down)[1] no one would advance the view that the bishop's residence ought to be situated eight miles from Oxford, accessible only by by-roads, with no railway station within three miles and only an exiguous bus service, remote from the Cathedral and all shopping, medical and other urban facilities, and above all from the diocesan office. This was said emphatically by a strong Commission which

[1] Since Kirk's death Cuddesdon Palace has twice suffered fire and is at the time of writing being demolished.

considered the whole matter somewhere about 1905; and the experience of the last fifteen years seems to me conclusive that, if future bishops of Oxford are required to reside at Cuddesdon, their efficiency for diocesan purposes is bound to suffer severely.

He himself always regarded the problem of Cuddesdon as connected with that of the diocesan office, and there can be little doubt that he would have liked a solution by which, as in some other dioceses, episcopal residence and diocesan office were in the same or in adjacent buildings. The experience of another diocesan who has tried both living away from and living beside his diocesan office confirms Kirk's view.

15

The decision not to live at Cuddesdon, and to make Oxford itself the centre of diocesan administration meant incidentally that Kirk was able to remain in much closer touch with the University than would otherwise have been possible. He, himself, often referred to the experiences of Stubbs, Paget, Gore and Strong all of whom had at one time held office in the University and all of whom had found on becoming bishops and living at Cuddesdon that they were largely cut off from their former contacts. He was more fortunate than all of them save Paget, in that he went straight from his professorship to the bishopric so that there was no break in contact, but by his continual presence in the city he was able still to take some part in the life of the University. He was a member of an unusual number of Colleges and in 1938 he was appointed a Delegate of the Clarendon Press, a post which he held until his death. He was in continual demand as a preacher in College chapels and on University occasions.

Another factor contributed to maintain his influence in the University. Mention has been made in an earlier chapter of the Oxford University Church Union as it was in Kirk's undergraduate days. This society, after undergoing some eclipse in the early twenties was refounded in 1928 by Dr. J. W. C. Wand, then Dean of Oriel. When Dr. Wand left Oxford to become Archbishop of Brisbane in 1934 Kirk was elected to succeed him as President of the O.U.C.U. and he exercised a very direct and important influence on its growth during the next three years. On becoming Bishop he asked that he might be allowed to retain the Presidency, but that a Chairman of the Committee be appointed to represent him in the ordinary day to day business of the society. This arrangement was readily agreed to and proved of the greatest benefit to the O.U.C.U. As a rule Kirk presided

at the meeting for freshmen held every year at the beginning of the
Michaelmas Term and he frequently spoke in the various courses of
talks arranged by the society. During the war years, when his own
movements were more restricted to Oxford itself, he was notably
helpful to those who had the immediate responsibility for the running
of the O.U.C.U. He was always ready, when his engagements
allowed, to come and talk at smaller or larger gatherings, and there was
no person of his standing who could so quickly put a room full of
undergraduates at their ease and discuss with them as one of themselves.

In addition to his public appearances in pulpits and his work with the
O.U.C.U. Kirk's other main channel of influence on undergraduate
Oxford was exercised through the confirmation services for members
of the University which he held each term in St. Aldate's Church.
These services were simple in the extreme. There was no music, the
Bishop wore a rochet and stole, the Prayer Book Service was read
straight through and at the end he sat in his chair and spoke to candidates for about ten minutes. These addresses will never be forgotten by
any who heard them. They were short, simple and direct, but the kind
of thing that no one else could do, as was only too painfully apparent
on the occasions when Kirk was ill and some other bishop had to
deputise for him. It can safely be said that Kirk made the Bishop of
Oxford count for something in the life of the University as none of his
predecessors had done for many years.

VII

MARRIAGE DISCIPLINE

As the leading Anglican authority on moral theology Kirk had for many years before he became a bishop been much involved in discussions and in writing about the problems of marriage, and of the most appropriate forms of marriage discipline for the Church of England. Sections of *Conscience and its Problems* touched on some of these questions, and in 1933 he published a small book called *Marriage and Divorce*. Within a short time, however, this book was made out of date by the publication of the Convocation Report on *The Church and Marriage*, and the subsequent enactment by both Convocations of certain of the Resolutions appended to that Report.

Not being a member of Convocation Kirk could not be a member of the Joint Committee which produced the Report, but he was invited to submit a memorandum, and in September, 1935 he wrote for the *Church Times* an article which examined the Report in some detail. He found much in it to welcome. "We have become so accustomed", he wrote, "to pronouncements in which motives are confused with actions, exhortation with legislation, secular with ecclesiastical jurisdiction, ethics with discipline, that the relief afforded by a document in which these obvious antitheses are kept clearly distinct is overwhelming. Common fairness demands that those who criticize the Report—and it cannot, of course, hope to escape criticism—should begin by recognizing that in this respect official Anglicanism has taken a very long step forward." In particular Kirk welcomed the recognition that while the legislative spheres of Church and State overlap, the Church cannot properly legislate for the State, nor the State for the Church. The Report stated that the Church "has a right to proclaim its own rules, and to deal with those who disobey those rules with its own discipline", and two Resolutions appended to the Minority Report insisted that these rights should be secured in all legislation with regard to divorce, "and that in particular the Church should be free: (1) To forbid the use of its buildings for any marriage when one of the parties has his or her former partner still living; and (2) to make its own regulations for the admission of such persons to the Sacraments and other privileges of the Church."

As Kirk pointed out, these words, if taken seriously, amounted to no less than a proposal for a drastic amendment of the conditions of the English establishment.

This means, in effect, that the King's Ministers must abandon their present customary prerogative of advising the throne to refuse the royal licence and assent to the legislation of Convocation unless or until Parliamentary legislation to the same effect is obtained, at all events when marriage discipline is in question; and that any canons which result from such legislation by Convocation must be respected as finally binding upon all members of the Church of England in any civil court which may find itself obliged to take cognizance of such matters. It means, further, that the Convocations must be prepared to set up canonical machinery to deal with marriage questions on a constitutional basis. These are very far-reaching corollaries to a Resolution whose form is simple enough. It is essential that the Convocations should be alive to them before adopting the Resolution; but it is also essential that, if the Resolution is adopted, Churchmen should hold the authorities to its full implications when the day arrives (as it certainly will arrive) to give them proper expression.

Kirk foresaw, rightly as events showed, that the main focus of controversy would be Resolution 5, which concerned the admission to Communion in certain circumstances of those who had remarried after divorce. Certain things said in the Report in connexion with this Resolution seemed to him sound and defensible. A clear line of distinction was to be drawn in discipline between those who remarried, and remained remarried, in 'invincible error' (i.e. with the conscientious conviction that they were acting according to God's will, whatever the Church might say), and those who could only be called 'deliberate and wilful wrongdoers'. Persons of the former kind were to be considered as eligible for admission or readmission to Communion. Kirk believed this to be sound in principle. He also thought it right in policy. The Majority Report stated that "the Church is entrusted with the duty of making allowances wherever possible for genuinely conscientious divergences . . . [and] there are many good Churchpeople who after earnest consideration are conscientiously convinced that the full rigour of the Christian code ought to be relaxed." As Kirk put it, to excommunicate all who had been guilty of such remarriage, however clear their own consciences might be, would, in fact produce so serious a cleavage on the moral issue as to make immediate chaos inevitable, and to bring schism into the realm of reasonable possibility; and the ideal of maintaining the unity of the Church was of such pre-eminent importance that, if it could only be realized at the price of a relaxation of discipline in this matter, the price was one that must be paid.

Unfortunately, however, these grounds, which Kirk believed to be soundly based, were obscured by another strain of thought which, by using the ambiguous phrase 'morally preferable' in the York version of Resolution 5, and omitting any reference to 'good faith' suggested that although it might be wrong to marry during a first partner's lifetime, it might nevertheless often be right to persevere in the second marriage, despite its initial wrongness. This seemed to Kirk equivalent to saying 'It is wrong to lie, but not wrong to remain in possession and enjoyment of whatever advantage your lie may have secured for you.' From this position it seemed only a step to the complete surrender of the primary doctrine that remarriage after divorce is prohibited by Christian principle.

Kirk was equally critical of the proposals of the Report concerning an extension of the grounds of Nullity. The most important of these proposed new grounds were later enacted by Parliament, and they are that one party at the time of the marriage knows and conceals from the other the fact that he or she is suffering from, or liable by reason of heredity to, certain classes of physical or mental disease; or that the woman knows and conceals from the man that she is pregnant by some other man. Kirk argued that the condition that one party must knowingly have withheld information from the other represented a confusion of thought. What vitiates A's consent is the fact that B was suffering from, or liable to, one of the diseases in question at the time of the marriage (for had A known this, he or she would not have contracted the marriage), and not that B was suffering from, or liable to the disease, and knowingly concealed the truth. "This concealment of truth might, of course, be made the basis of an action for damages, but it does not in principle affect the question of true consent at all. Thus any party who at any stage could adduce evidence to prove that the other, at the time of the marriage, was suffering from, or liable to, such a disease, whether he or she were aware of the fact or not, would have grounds for a nullity suit." This would put us straight back into the medieval confusion, and indeed into something worse, for the medieval canonists never allowed anything like so wide an application of the *error qualitatis* as this would be. "There were extremes to which the Christian conscience even in its laxest moments would not go in rendering the marriage bond insecure."

As a bishop Kirk was brought into immediate contact with the problems of marriage and divorce. He had a large and growing correspondence in the shape of requests for advice from other bishops in England and overseas, and the diocese of Oxford with its great size produced a vast number of matrimonial cases. In 1952 he wrote to a correspondent that he received requests to waive the rule against the remarriage of divorced persons in church, almost every day of the week, and he added "In a diocese half or a third the size of this things might be much easier". There was no relaxation of that rule, but in regard to the admission of remarried divorcees to Communion he was less rigid than was often supposed. In 1953 he wrote to a priest:

As you say, according to the principles which I try to administer in this diocese, I leave the question of approach to the altar to the consciences of the couple concerned, with the strongest possible emphasis on the fact that they ought to do nothing which might cause embarrassment or scandal, or compromise the Church's witness.

You will appreciate that in a diocese the size of this, with problems of this kind arising continually, in parish after parish, no other way of dealing with the matter is possible. To ask the bishop to investigate every case, would be an impossible burden upon him.

In another letter he wrote to a responsible and trusted parish priest:

So long as you are certain that no scandal is being given, and you yourself suffer no embarrassment, I should not take exception to the admission of the persons concerned to Holy Communion.

The question of the admission of such persons to confirmation was, however, viewed differently, as the following letter, written in 1949, shows:

In cases such as the one you lay before me my ruling is that the person concerned must not be presented for confirmation; but that if he is in good faith and no embarrassment or scandal will be caused, I do not forbid his admission to Holy Communion under the rubric as to persons who are "ready and desirous".

The grounds for this ruling are that confirmation is a formal act, completing the initiation of a candidate into the Church of Christ, and cannot, therefore, be granted to anyone whose circumstances are contrary to those required for membership, however clear his own conscience may be. Communion, on the other hand, is an occasional mitigation of ecclesiastical discipline for the benefit of the soul; admission can be refused at any time, should the person concerned prove not to be in good faith.

In other words, admission to communion is reversible—confirmation is not.

I only reached this determination of these particularly difficult questions after some years of very earnest consideration. Luckily they do not happen very often; and I can say that, so far as I know, the ruling I have given has been willingly accepted by those concerned, and still seems to satisfy the requirements of the problem better than any other.

In 1948 Kirk produced a second edition of his book *Marriage and Divorce* in which considerable sections, including the longest chapter, were entirely rewritten in the light of changes in the law and Church discipline which had taken place since 1933. In the previous year the Bishop had published a series of articles in the Diocesan Magazine, on the subject of *Marriage Discipline in the Church of England*. These were subsequently reissued as a pamphlet and frequently given by him to persons whose applications he had to consider, as they contain a short and reasoned statement of his position. The substance of the pamphlet appears in fuller guise in the second edition of *Marriage and Divorce*.

The following memorandum on a particular case submitted to him is a valuable amplification of Kirk's position about admission to Communion.

Draft

I promise to put on paper for you my views on the very painful question which you brought before me. I say 'painful' advisedly, for it is obvious that any decision whatsoever taken either by myself, or yourself, or the persons concerned, must give pain—real pain—somewhere; and that is why we must all think and speak of the matter with the utmost consideration for one another.

My view is, briefly, that where two persons, one of whom has a previous partner living, enter into a marriage contract, they should be urged most strongly to abstain from asking, or presenting themselves, for the Holy Communion.

Before I give my reason for this, however, there are two points that I want to make clear:—

First: In asking them to make this spiritual sacrifice (as on occasion at least it is bound to be) I do not imply that they have incurred the slightest moral or social stigma. I am only too willing to believe that they have followed the guidance of their conscience in a supremely difficult matter upon which, in the confused state of the modern world, divergent views are held by persons of the utmost integrity and thoughtfulness. And consequently, I should regard it as an unwarrantable breach of Christian charity if I myself, or any other member of the Church, altered by a hair's breadth the attitude we had towards either or both of them before they contracted their Alliance, or allowed that fact to create a breach in our friendly relations with them in all social and secular affairs.

Second: In urging them to abstain from presenting themselves for the Holy Communion, I do not wish them to dissociate themselves from the other services of the Church, or to refrain from co-operating with the Church and Churchpeople in all beneficent activities. It would not, indeed, in my judgment, be proper for them to hold official positions as Churchwardens, or members of the Parochial Church Council, for example, but as private members of the congregation I should wish their presence and their help to be welcomed; and I should regard any unfriendliness towards them in this connection as equivalent to the imputation of a stigma on their characters of the kind which I have disavowed in the previous paragraph.

Why, then, do I ask them voluntarily to abstain from the Holy Communion? For the reason that, to my mind, nothing is more important at the present day than that the Church should take the strongest possible stand against the levity with which the marriage bond is popularly regarded in so many quarters. To this end, those at least who form the innermost ranks of the Church's army— the Communicants—should be persons who neither by word nor deed have lent any colour to the suggestion that marriage is anything but a life-long contract.

Let me repeat; I do not accuse any particular couple either of whom has a previous partner living, of levity or callousness in this matter. In most cases, I believe, they hold to the main principle as strongly as I do. Further, I should be the last to accept the view that they were necessarily sinning against their own consciences. Where we differ I believe is in this: they consider that their own circumstances constitute an exceptional case in which this principle of a life-long contract does not obtain, so far as the previous marriage is concerned. And that is a plea which I find it supremely difficult to admit.

For my own belief, and it is shared by very large numbers of Church-people, is that the present moral situation is so critical that only in the rarest possible cases, if at all, should exceptions be allowed among Communicants, whom I have just ventured to describe as the "innermost ranks of the Church's army". That is why I ask persons such as the couple of whom you have told me, to refrain from embarrassing the Church, and weakening her testimony, by pressing the claims which they may believe they possess to continue to receive the Holy Communion. Let us grant for the sake of argument, that their case is really exceptional. Even so it is impossible for the nature of the exception to be explained to all and sundry. And so long as this is the case, their presence among the Communicants must inevitably lead to the inference, an inference fatal, in my mind, to the moral well-being of our nation, that the Church does not really care sufficiently for the principle of life-long mono-gamous marriage to take any real stand for it.

I would urge them, therefore, out of love and loyalty for the Church which has meant so much and can still mean so much to them, to abstain from pressing a request which could only be granted at the cost of weakening that Church's power to maintain the highest standard of Christian morality. I ask them to consider most earnestly whether gratitude for past blessings can properly be expressed in anything less than this.

But to help them in their consideration there is one thing that I must add, and I do it gladly and with confidence. I am convinced that, if they are prepared to make this personal sacrifice in order not to impair the integrity of the Church's witness, any grace which would have been vouchsafed to them in the Sacrament will be given them by God, in fullest measure, outside the Sacrament.

I am not asking them—I could not ask them—to cut themselves off from grace; I am only asking that they should not put themselves, and the Church, in a false position as concerns this vital matter. And I believe wholeheartedly that if they do this willingly, and for the sake of Christ and His Church, so far from losing spiritual blessings, they will reap them in a measure beyond all their highest hopes.

In October, 1953 the following motion was brought before the Canterbury Convocation by the Bishop of Rochester (Dr. Chavasse) and seconded by Kirk.

Where a man and a woman have contracted marriage before the Civil Registrar during the lifetime of the previous partner of either of them, this House recognises that the Church still has a pastoral responsibility towards them. It therefore deems it admissible for the parish priest to offer prayer to God with and for them in church, subject to the approval of the bishop as to the manner and occasion of his so doing; provided always that no publicity is attached to what is done, and that it shall be made clear to those concerned that it is in no sense a marriage in church.

Kirk's action in seconding this motion caused consternation in some circles and was misunderstood. Two retired bishops, among the many resident in the Oxford Diocese, wrote to ask what prayers he had in mind, and how, if they were said in church, it would be possible to avoid publicity. Kirk's reply was as follows, and it clears up his own position in the matter.

As you know, I am as anxious as you are that nothing should be done to weaken the Church's testimony in all marriage questions; and the resolution about which you write was carefully drafted to exclude from any approval by Convocation practices which unfortunately are on the increase, and which have exactly the undermining tendency which must be combated at all costs—e.g. public and advertised "services of blessing in Church" with all the embellishments of a festive social occasion; the issue by individual bishops of "forms of prayer" for such occasions; the re-admission of remarried divorcees to Holy Communion after a "period of probation" and so forth. The unanimity with which the bishops ranged themselves against such practices was very impressive, and cannot fail to have a salutary effect.

I think there are some misconceptions in your letter which I can clear away. First, none of us, of course can be "called upon" to pray in Church with persons in the conditions envisaged; the most the Resolution said was that in certain cases, under close regulation, such an action by a priest need not stand *ipso facto* condemned. But any priest is at complete liberty to tell those who approach him in the matter that he cannot reconcile it with his conscience to do what they ask; it is no "part of the pastoral duty attaching to clergy" that they should violate their own deepest convictions at the request of others. Second, as I said emphatically in full Convocation, the "kind of prayers" used in any case must depend entirely upon the exact circumstances of that case—especially the spiritual and moral needs of the individual; for what is suggested can only be regarded as legitimate if it will clearly operate *pro salute animae*. Any idea of there being certain "kinds of prayer" universally suitable in relation to this problem is, of course, purely chimerical. Third, like yourselves, I have no doubt (and I have said so repeatedly in print) that the home is in principle a better place for whatever is done than the Church; the difficulty is that it is often far harder to find privacy in the "home" (say, one bedsitting room) than in Church.—Your final point, about securing privacy in Church, does not seem to me a very real one. No parish priest of any experience or intelligence would find it difficult to make arrangements to satisfy this requirement.

It may help if I explain how things happen in this diocese. A priest will write to me giving details of a case, and saying that he is convinced that prayer with the persons concerned will be of spiritual benefit to them, without weakening the Church's witness to our Lord's teaching in his parish; and that he is willing (sometimes even desirous) to undertake the pastoral responsibility involved. (If he, as the minister most intimately acquainted with the parties and the parish, cannot assure me on these points, the matter of course lapses.) We then make an opportunity of discussing the whole matter; he tells me the "kind of prayers" which he believes will be appropriate and beneficial in this particular case, and we examine his proposals carefully, with a view to reaching conclusions which will satisfy us both in conscience. A vast amount, as you can see, depends upon his estimate of the parties—something also depends upon my own estimate of his powers of discernment in such matters. In any case this process eliminates, I believe, the dangers of easy emotionalism; and I can gladly testify to the fully objective character of the considerations which almost every priest who approaches me on this subject lays before me. Their sincerity and recognition of the dangers of the situation, and the care with which they have thought the problem out, invariably impress me more than I can say. It is difficult to believe that the Holy Spirit is not guiding them in a true approach to the determination of their pastoral duties in connection with these infinitely varied and always deeply poignant cases.

To sum up, let me say simply, first, that I should never require any priest to act against his conscience; second, that I should not approve any course of action along the lines of the Resolution in any case where the priest, with his intimate knowledge of the facts, could not give me the assurances I have mentioned.

Kirk was a member of the Commission appointed by the Archbishops in 1949 at the request of the Convocations to examine the laws of Nullity, and to give particular attention to the new grounds introduced in 1937, and to the proposal that the Church should establish some form of tribunal to investigate alleged cases of Nullity. As both his book and the Marriage Discipline pamphlet show,[1] Kirk was strongly opposed to the establishment of any such tribunals at that time, and in a speech in the Upper House of the Canterbury Convocation in 1950 he expressed himself very emphatically on the subject. In this field therefore, the eventual report of the Nullity Commission was in line with his views. In the same group of Sessions of Convocation, January, 1950, Kirk proposed that there should be a new clause added to Draft Canon XXXVIII, which would have had the effect of saying that the Church did not accept the ground of wilful refusal to consummate, introduced by the Herbert Act of 1937, as a true ground for Nullity. This proposal was referred to the Nullity Commission which again was in agreement with Kirk. It seems that he withdrew somewhat from the position of his *Church Times* article of 1935, and appears to have been ready to accept the other new grounds for Nullity introduced by the Herbert Act of 1937.

There can be no doubt that throughout all Kirk's thinking on the subject of marriage discipline what was uppermost in his mind was the urgent need to maintain and witness publicly to the Christian standard of marriage in face of the rapidly increasing laxity in sexual relationships which has been so apparent in the course of this century. In the Introduction to the second edition of his book on Marriage and Divorce he drew attention to the fact that in 1948 the annual number of divorce decrees issued was in the neighbourhood of 50,000, whereas at the time of the passing of the Herbert Act in 1937 it had been 5,000. He recognized that the war was partly responsible for this startling increase, and that a gradual reduction might be expected.

But, he wrote, not even the most optimistic observers believe that divorces in future will be less than twice as many as in the years before the passing of the Act; and most students of social conditions regard this estimate as far too low. Clearly, the Act must bear some responsibility for this. The vast extension of the grounds of divorce which it introduced, and the consequent ease with which a couple who have tired of one another can obtain a termination of their union,

[1] *Marriage and Divorce, 1948.* pp. 122ff.

have affected the national outlook very deeply. The result has been the almost complete extinction of the old sense that there was something discreditable about divorce: it has become too much of an everyday phenomenon to be condemned very seriously. To adopt what I have said below, "the moment any real strain arises in domestic relations the partners feel themselves free to look round for more amiable or attractive mates, secure in the conviction that, if they dissolve their union and seek a second (or often a third or even a fourth) marriage elsewhere, society will not hold them gravely to blame". A very potent inhibition against divorce and remarriage has thereby been removed. Persons who before the war might have made a serious attempt at reconciliation with one another now turn to the possibility of divorce as the simplest and most natural way out of their difficulties.[1]

He believed that it was the duty of the Church to do everything in its power to counter this laxity, and that the firm maintenance of the rule against the remarriage of divorced persons in church had, over fifteen years or more, done much to bring the Christian view home to people. He was not unmindful of the hard cases but he felt it right that people should be asked to make some sacrifice for the sake of upholding Christian standards, and he knew of many cases in which the sacrifice was willingly made.

It is therefore a fitting conclusion to this chapter to reprint an article from the Diocesan Magazine of April, 1946, an article which, though only partly concerned with Marriage, has nevertheless important things concerning the general subject of moral discipline in the Church.

When the Church says 'No.'

No one charged with the ungrateful task of attempting to administer such fragments of discipline, especially in respect of the laity, as survive in the Church of England can be unaware of the amount of dissatisfaction, criticism, and even resentment, which his decisions evoke. He is accused of narrow-mindedness, bigotry, legalism, hide-bound conservatism; he suffers from a tidal wave of abusive letters, many of them all the more unrestrained because anonymous. I am not speaking now of anything that could fairly be called irresponsible despotism; but merely of cases in which the person upon whom the burden of decision lies can quote chapter and verse for his verdict. Four instances occur to the mind at once:—

(a) The rubric at the end of the Order of Confirmation prescribes: 'And there shall none be admitted to the Holy Communion until such time as he be confirmed, or be ready and desirous to be confirmed.'

(b) Canon XXXVI of the *Constitutions and Canons Ecclesiastical* of 1604 enacts that 'No person shall hereafter . . . be suffered to preach . . . in any

---

[1] *op. cit.* p. vi.

Cathedral, or Collegiate Church, City or Market Town, Parish Church, Chapel etc.' . . . until he has subscribed the Declaration of Assent to the XXXIX Articles, and the Book of Common Prayer, and promised 'in public prayer and administration of the Sacraments' to 'use the form in the said book prescribed, and none other except so far as shall be ordered by lawful authority.'

(c) Three of the four Houses of Convocation (the fourth not having considered the question) agreed in 1935 that the Church should not allow the use of the Prayer Book Service for the solemnisation of matrimony 'in the case of anyone who has a previous partner still living'.

(d) The fourth instance is somewhat different. It is one form in which the scandal of what is called 'indiscriminate baptism' presents itself. The Prayer Book baptismal office contemplates throughout that the home environment of the child to be baptized is sufficiently spiritual to ensure that it will be trained in the practice and doctrine of the Church of England; the insistence upon the requirement of godparents provides an additional safeguard. But cases occur in which it is virtually certain that parents intend to send (or take) the children for their religious upbringing not to the parish church but to some sectarian conventicle (usually a completely freelance affair, without affiliation to any of the historic denominations) which is maintaining a continuous guerilla warfare against the Church. Surely, it is urged, the parish priest would only be acting in legitimate defence of the sacrament if he refused to administer baptism in such unsatisfactory circumstances? Those who take this view not unnaturally require the parents to give a clear undertaking that the child shall in due course receive such instruction in Church principles as is provided in the parish; in default of such a promise, and in view of the fact that the parents themselves, or the officials of the sect to which they adhere, are free to baptise, they refuse baptism in the church. For my own part, I believe they are doing Christianity a real service in their insistence upon the acceptance of these conditions by the parents, though I cannot say how the matter would be regarded by the Courts if it ever came into legal cognizance.

*   *   *

The examples I have given (and others could be added to the number) bring before us principles of discipline with varying degrees of authority behind them; and this affects the strength of the argument in the different cases. Nor is it possible to evade altogether a fire of criticism and contradiction aimed at showing that in particular cases the principle in question is inapplicable. Thus, even in the matter of the rubric which restricts the right to receive Holy Communion to those who are confirmed, or are 'ready and desirous to be confirmed', there are still some who maintain that it refers only to 'our own people' (presumably those of Anglican upbringing)—even though our own Bishop Shaw, in a most effective letter to the *Times* some years ago, pointed out that this would have the ludicrous result of excluding from communion an otherwise devoted Anglican who, through some eccentricity of theological outlook, refused to present himself for confirmation, though his Methodist wife, who was firmly determined never to be confirmed, would be free to communicate at the parish church altar as often as she wished. Again, those who do not recognise the high authority of the Canons of 1604, will point to the fact that certain recent resolutions of the Convocations purport to modify to some extent the strictness of the regulations I have quoted in the paragraph I have numbered (b). No doubt it is always possible to cavil at any particular instance that may be brought forward; but in general there is fairly wide agreement that on occasion it will be right for the Church to say 'No' to someone who desires to avail himself of the privileges of membership without in any way attempting to discharge the duties laid upon all loyal members of the Christian body by the teaching of our Lord and the authority of the Church.

What surprises me is the degree of shocked resentment, the sense of deep and embittered grievance, manifested by those who experience such a refusal. A very remarkable instance of this came to my notice a few months ago. It arises out of another disciplinary rubric of the Prayer Book. One who was beyond question 'an open and notorious evil liver, so that the congregation be thereby offended' had the temerity to present himself at a celebration of the Holy Communion in his parish church on one of the great festivals. There was no question as to the facts: the man openly paraded his evil manner of life in the village, and made a boast of his defiance of the laws of God. On the occasion in question, as he entered the church, a strong-minded churchwarden took him by the arm, and quietly but firmly led him outside again, debarring him from entrance throughout the duration of the service. The churchwarden's action met with universal approval; but the offender was not satisfied until he had lodged a complaint with the bishop of the diocese, and in a painful interview (in which the bishop expressed his full support of the churchwarden) insisted that as a confirmed Anglican he had an inalienable right to the Holy Communion, whatever manner of life he chose to lead. He maintained with passionate emphasis that as there were 'thousands as bad as himself' it was rank hypocrisy and unfair discrimination to exclude him from a privilege of which other parishioners could avail themselves freely and without scrutiny. That he had any genuinely religious desire for the sacrament may well be doubted. His dominant motive was no doubt a desire either to flout ecclesiastical authority, or else to secure by fair means or foul a kind of public exoneration for his sins. But of his intense indignation when the bishop ratified the churchwarden's action there could be no question.

* * *

This was an extreme case, no doubt, but a similar state of mind is continuously in evidence whenever the attempt is made to enforce principle (c) —the one which deals with the second marriage of divorced persons. Here again a secular or social element is often present—the desire to be 'married in white' can be so strong as to overthrow all recognition that what is proposed is stigmatized in our Lord's teaching as adultery. I do not propose, however, to argue in this article the rights and wrongs of the disciplinary enactments involved in any particular case. What I wish to suggest is that the root cause of all the trouble is a wholly warped conception of the nature of churchmanship.

Those who rebel whenever the Church says 'No' to them, regardless of the grounds there may be for such refusal of privileges in their case, are in effect treating the Church as though it were a department store. They think of themselves as entitled to ask over the counter for anything they may need or desire; and if it is in stock they hold that it is the duty of the salesman to let them have it without demur, and certainly without any enquiry as to their worthiness to enjoy the privilege demanded. This view of the relation of the individual to the Church is held by many Christians of real devotion and righteousness of life; they look to the Church primarily for the gifts and graces which God bestows through its medium to the earnest seeker. Here is an attitude of mind which is true to one of the most important elements in the Gospel. God is all loving and all merciful: He is wont to give more than we desire or deserve; He is always more ready to bear than we to pray. If we, being evil, give good gifts to our children, much more will He give the Holy Spirit to all who ask. 'Ask and ye shall receive, seek and ye shall find, knock and it shall be opened unto you'—here such Christians find the heart of the good news of Christ. And who shall say that they are wrong?

In fact, they are not wrong. But if they emphasise this truth to the exclusion of all others they are giving a very erroneous picture of the full Christian doctrine of the Church. The Church is not merely a channel of God's grace to the individual: it is also the body of Christ. Only those who adhere to the body, only the branches that remain in the vine, can expect the steady outpouring of supernatural gifts. To treat the Church as an emporium to which you may pay occasional visits as and when you need the goods purveyed there means simply that what is received, torn out of its true context, cannot be expected to help or satisfy. In the crudest and simplest allegory, the Church is a hostel in which only residents find what they need; it does not cater for the casual passer-by, in search of momentary refreshment only.

But more than this: the Church is the army of the living God—it demands willing service, loyalty, self-sacrifice—the virtues of the citizen soldier. Our first attraction to the Church may arise out of the desire to obtain something that it offers; but until that first impulse has been superseded by the overwhelming determination to contribute all we can and all we have to the Church's divinely appointed effort to save mankind, we have not really understood the principles of true churchmanship. We may be 'children', but we are not yet 'men' of God. Naturally, therefore, our first task must be to discover the principles of the Christian life of service, as administered in the discipline of the Church, and to live by them: not to ask for privileges whilst refusing responsibilities, or selecting for our own recognition only those duties which we think we can easily discharge.

The frailty of man has meant that throughout the history of our religion Christians have found it easier to think of the Church as an institution from which they can ask for what they need, rather than as one which makes vast demands upon them. I will not say that the emphasis must be reversed. But I insist that until the balance between these two conceptions has been radically redressed, the Church will never be the disciplined, harmonious and all triumphant body that is needed for the conversion of the world. The revolt from any form of regulation of which I have given instances is merely a side-issue of this maladjustment of teaching, but it is nevertheless a symptom of very grave significance. We need to combine to eradicate the underlying disease; for unless we are able to do this the accusation of impotence so often brought against the Church will never be capable of refutation.

VIII

SOUTH INDIA

THE long series of negotiations which led up to the inauguration of the Church of South India in 1947 are usually reckoned to have begun with a meeting at Tranquebar in 1919. They were watched with close attention by various groups of churchmen in England and a scheme of Union was carefully considered and given a qualified approval by the Lambeth Conference of 1930. From that date onwards, however, the anxieties of Catholic minded churchmen in England became more acute as further alterations were made and features of the scheme which had rendered it more tolerable to them were removed. Kirk was aware of these problems and in common with many of his friends at Oxford and elsewhere viewed the development of the South India Scheme after the 1930 Lambeth Conference with some concern. In a letter written in 1950 he says: "As long ago as 1933 I was present at a meeting at which Bishop Palmer was told quite definitely that the Scheme as it then stood must jeopardise the supply of funds from S.P.G. to South India: his enthusiasm, I suppose, led him to ignore the warning." He was also a member of a group of Oxford theologians who in 1932 protested against the practice of intercommunion among the negotiators in South India.

As a bishop and one who was looked to very much by the rank and file of the Catholic movement, Kirk could not avoid being drawn more and more into discussion of the problem. Dom Gregory Dix had some responsibility for this but there is no doubt that without that stimulus Kirk's own views and his perception of the issues at stake would have led him to decisive intervention. The probability is, indeed, that he exercised a moderating and restraining influence on Dom Gregory rather than that the latter stirred up an unwilling bishop. They were, however, at one in believing that the problems of reunion in India and in England were intimately connected, and in their anxiety that nothing should be countenanced in India which could later be used to undermine Catholic principles in the Church of England. It was certainly the belief of Dom Gregory and many others, if not of Kirk himself, that Archbishop Temple and one or two other bishops were trying to present English churchmen with a *fait accompli* in India which would be used to prepare the way for a similar scheme in England. Some countenance, as it seemed, was given to these fears by the way in which the Convocations were prevented from any full examination of the South India scheme.

Early in December, 1942, Kirk drew up the following memorandum in order to try to clarify some points about the implications of South India for England as people were already discussing the possibility of a High Church schism if the Scheme went through.

The South India Scheme

It has often been suggested that if certain dioceses of the Church of India enter into a so-called "union" with non-Episcopal bodies in South India, the constitution of the ensuing "United Church" might contain provisions which, because of the communion which has hitherto existed between the Church of England and the Indian bishops, clergy and laity who would be involved in this "union", would produce a serious crisis. The Church of England, it is suggested, would have to decide whether to treat these "ex-Anglicans" as any longer in communion with itself; and this would bring into open conflict strains of thought which are no doubt present in Anglicanism to-day, but have managed hitherto to so exist without producing a schism.

The situation, though confused and perplexing enough, is not however as serious as has been suggested above. We have to keep carefully before us the distinction between what is canonical and what is extra-canonical. Many things which are not strictly canonical happen extra-canonically, but so long as the authority of the canons is firmly recognised, much may be tolerated that is canonically irregular. From this point of view the following considerations seem relevant:—

i. *Interdependence between Churches:* The Church of India, Burma and Ceylon is, like the Church of England, autocephalous; and there is no canonical concordat whereby the two Churches have bound themselves to act together in all legislative and juridical matters of more than local importance. Whatever interdependence there may be between the two bodies is of custom and courtesy only. It is true that Indian bishops are at present summoned to the Lambeth Conference, and it might occur after the "union" that "bishops" of the United Church as to whose consecration or orthodoxy there were serious doubts should receive invitations. But the Lambeth Conference has no canonical status whatsoever; and at worst the attendance of such persons need be regarded only as a temporary abnormality.

ii. *Communicant status:* In the same way there is no canonical concordat between the Church of England and the Church of India, Burma and Ceylon whereby they have assigned communicant status to each other's members as such. An English diocesan has and will continue to have the responsibility of deciding, in accordance with Anglican constitutions, whether any peregrinus is competent to present himself for communion anywhere in his diocese. Only if the Church of England enacts canons depriving the diocesan of that right, or limiting his exercise of it, need he fear that his diocese may be forced into communion with a "Church" of doubtful Catholicity. Any such legislation is antecedently unlikely.

iii. *Ministerial status:* No one whatsoever can exercise a legitimate ministry in any diocese of the Church of England without the explicit licence of the bishop of the diocese. The "ministers" of the United Church will therefore have no ministerial status as such in the Church of England.

iv. *Benefices:* No English bishop can be penalized for refusing to admit to a benefice any person not ordained by, or on commission from, an English or Irish diocesan. Where however a minister has been ordained by a bishop of an English or Irish diocese,[1] a bishop who refuses to institute him to a benefice to which he has been presented by its patron is liable to certain secular penalties. Thus it might happen that an English bishop found himself obliged by secular law to institute to a benefice a clerk who, after valid and regular ordination in England, had spent some period in the ministry of a body of doubtful Catholicity. But it is to be observed that this adds little if anything to the problems of the Church of England; most bishops have from time to time to decide whether they will admit to a benefice a priest whose teaching or manner of life (present or past) they regard with grave disfavour, or will risk the secular consequences of refusal.

v. No doubt canonical irregularities will occur in respect of the communicant status, ministerial status, and admission to benefices, of members of the "United Church" who set up a domicile (temporary or permanent) in England. But by the nature of the case they cannot be many, and they will not differ in character from those which unfortunately take place in a number of dioceses already. It need not, therefore, be feared that any "union" entered into by the Southern dioceses of the Church of India, Burma and Ceylon, will aggravate the difficulties and problems of the Church of England. The real problem is that of the canonical irregularities which already occur in certain English dioceses. They are indicative of a non-Catholic state of mind which, if it were to spread widely, would imperil the Catholic status of the Church. A resolute criticism of and stand against these irregularities will both save Anglicanism from this fate, and will probably bring about in time a state of things in which the "united" Church of S. India will either have to conform to Catholic practice, or else abandon all pretensions to Catholic status.

vi. It will be noticed that this memorandum does not deal with three important questions:— (a) the degree to which members of the Church of England are entitled to attempt to influence the actions of an autocephalous Church; (b) the minimum amendments which would make it possible for the proposed scheme to be regarded with moderate equanimity by Catholics; (c) the advice to be given to Catholic societies carrying on missionary work in the dioceses concerned in view of the possibility of the scheme maturing. These are

---

[1] Col. Cl. Act, 1874, s.4 (N.B.—Sect. 5 apparently adds another category.)

questions of the first importance; but are entirely distinct from that which is here considered.

K. O.
December 5th, 1942.

In January of the following year a deputation led by Lord Quickswood and including Lord Sankey, Dr. N. P. Williams, Dr. Demant and Mr. T. S. Eliot went to Lambeth to express to the Archbishop of Canterbury (Dr. Temple) their disquiet at features of the South India Scheme. Later in the year the Superiors of Religious Communities for men in the Church of England prepared an Open Letter to the Archbishop, a letter which coincided with an enquiry formally addressed by the Metropolitan of the Church of India, Burma and Ceylon, to the other archbishops and metropolitans of the Anglican Communion. This enquiry asked two questions. First, whether in the event of the C.I.B.C. allowing four of its dioceses to go into the South India Scheme of Union their respective provinces would break off communion with the C.I.B.C. Second, whether they would refuse to be in communion with the new Church of South India. Dom Gregory was more particularly involved with the letter of the Superiors, Kirk with the replies to the Metropolitan's questions.

Towards the end of October Dom Gregory wrote a letter to the Bishop of which the following extracts give some idea of people's feelings at the time.

My dear Lord Bishop,

I very much hope that you are now better of the abominable cold you had on you last week, and that you did not suffer for attending to open the Parliament of Reverend Mothers. I stayed Thurs. night with Demant at Amen Court and discussed the situation with a small group of Convocation-men from both provinces, and others, all personally known to the Archbp. (save one.) It was unanimously decided to press the Archbp. to call a Round Table Conference of not more than 30 people—bps. & theologians—on S. India. This is to be done a) by a private approach next week. b) I was asked to include a request for this in the Open Letter of the Religious Superiors—which will be ready to go to him on Nov. 7th—c) I was to ask whether you would be prepared to invite certain bps. to meet you & discuss what measures can be taken . . . There was a great desire that a group of bps. should put out a memorial in favour of the R.T.C. to be signed by others. Apparently a number of "evangelical" archdeacons & canons have signed a somewhat similar memorial in the North.

I had three clear impressions from the meeting at Demant's. a) Consciences —and tempers—are becoming strained. There was some very plain speaking from some rather unexpected quarters as to the lack of any clear guidance from the episcopate. Your name and those of the bps. of Ely & Newcastle were mentioned with a good deal of criticism, and I found myself alone in the somewhat unaccustomed role of *laudator episcoporum*. b) If the Archbp.'s letter to the Metrop. goes as it stands & the Scheme goes through, a certain number of people are going to find the situation intolerable . . . c) It is *not* going to be the "extremists" but the people immediately to their "left" who will break away . . . And they are—rather curiously—making up their minds for "Rome & no half-measures", as one very "Prayer Book Catholic" said to me. I think this is probably because they have always had a stronger idea of discipline as Anglicans than the Romanisers. And now that they feel completely left in the lurch by everything they had trusted, Bishops, E.C.U., etc., they are going to stand by their principles and act accordingly. Any how, that is my impression. At the risk of becoming monotonous, I should still say that the greatest danger would come from doing nothing, followed by sporadic individual action & then disintegration. And I do not think that action by any group of priests will give any coherence. Why should it? And I don't really see what *action* the Lower Hse. of Canterbury can take to *block* the matter. For my own part, I do not grow less unhappy about the situation, I shall wait to see what my bishop does. But I am fairly sure that I shall never settle down with a good conscience in mediate communion with S. India (wh. is what the Draft Reply commits us to) though I think I should have an equally uneasy conscience signing up for *Apostolicae Curae*. So far as I can see I am not going to be very happy whichever I do. If it were not for my vows I might join the Balloon Barrage as a Roman Catholic private (with my insides so defective no other service wld. take me.) But that is equally against my conscience as things are. So the only thing is to await helplessly death by drowning in the last ditch.

The Open Letter of the Superiors was sent to the Archbishop in proof, in the hope that he might be able to make a reply which they would be glad to publish with it. The letter, however, contained a paragraph to which the Archbishop took strong exception, as it contained a clear reference to the possibility of schism. This paragraph was drawn up with a deep sense of responsibility and in the belief that Church leaders did not realize how serious the situation was.
On November 20th Dix wrote again to Kirk:

Dear My Lord Bishop,
Will you forgive me for troubling you once more about this everlasting S. Indian problem? I enclose a letter from the Archbp. to Fr. O'Brien which explains itself, I think. The passage to which His Grace takes such exception is on p. 61 of the accompanying proofs (marked X). It appears that I shall have to be one of those who have to decide whether to omit it or to dispense with a reply from him, when we go to see him, and I have already been consulted by two of the others as to what to say. Will you advise me a little?

I feel very reluctant to omit the passage. The discouragement & unsettlement of which the Archbp. speaks are already there—not in consequence of what we have said but in consequence of what *he* has *done*. I do not believe that our saying this will increase this feeling, though it may well bring it to a head. And I should regard that as desirable, because I do not believe that anything but a clear threat will stop the slide now. But a clear threat very well *might* stop it at this stage. And I do want to stop it, because the alternative is disintegration.

On the other hand it will be exceedingly difficult for us to resist the Archbp's. strongly expressed wish. He appears to be considerably shaken by the document, & from another letter to me about arrangements for publication exceedingly disconcerted at finding himself forced to do what he has hitherto avoided, namely discuss the Scheme itself in public—and rather cross. I have made it clear in a deferential way that if his letter altogether avoids the specific issues raised the Superiors will add a further "Rejoinder" underlining this fact, and people will draw their own conclusions. I can't quite make up my mind whether to omit the passage to secure his good will and try to bank on that, or whether to insist on it for the sake of the effect it will have in the church. And I don't know whether, even if the wise course is to keep it, I can carry the others with me against the Archbp's. pressure. Can you give me some private counsel? I will not use yr. name in the matter.

Unhappily Kirk's reply to this letter has not survived. The rest of his correspondence on South India suggests that he would have counselled caution and restraint. Certainly in a letter to Dix on the last day of 1942 he had pointed out some serious difficulties in the path of a plan for a non-juring Church which Dix had outlined.

The Archbishop asked the Superiors to go to Lambeth to discuss the Open Letter with him, and the visit took place on Friday, November 26th. Three days later Dix wrote to Kirk to describe the Lambeth meeting.

Dear My Lord Bishop,
    This is just to let you know what happened on Friday.
    The Archbp. received us at 2.30 p.m. & was, as always, very kind & fatherly. He questioned us exceedingly closely as to the amount of disquiet & distress we thought there was among the *laity*. This went on for some time. I think we were able to convince him that he had underestimated this. Then he proceeded to read us his proposed Reply. It was very long—more than twice as long as the document sent him—and almost pure hot air. He answered none of the criticisms of the Scheme we had put forward on dogmatic grounds but said that he recognised this as "*our* formulation of the Anglican tradition" (it was pure Prayer Book)—and was vague & more embarrassed than I have ever known him to be. Then he again begged us to remove the offending para., told us that he would oppose anything on the lines of a S.I.

Scheme for England, but more or less intimated that what was to be worked for here was "a gradual approach to intercommunion" (I will not swear those were his exact words, but I think so) not fusion or combination. You couldn't "fuse the Methodist Conference with the Church Assembly". Then he gave me the "copy" of his document for the printer, & gave us all his blessing, at 4 p.m.

Opinion before we went was v. uncertain as to whether to omit the para. & print his answer, & we made no final decision beforehand. Opinion when we returned was unanimous at once to *retain* the offending para. and not print his reply. It was with some slight difficulty that I persuaded the Superiors even to read His Grace's typescript again after tea. I was therefore left with the ungracious task of returning the Archbp.'s MS from the Dacre Press with regrets that we could not print it, as the Superiors had decided to keep their letter in its original form. (Surely an unique experience for a publisher!)

It struck me that he really was becoming a little anxious as to the size of the split he is provoking, though determined if it seemed likely not to be disastrously big to carry the thing through. Everything seems to depend now on convincing him that he is going to create a *big* disturbance. He is still relying on the *fait accompli*, though with less assurance. I think if you could have seen his proposed Reply you would have agreed that the Superiors were right to refuse to bowdlerise their letter for the sake of securing it. At all events, he thoroughly convinced even the most hesitant of those who were there that he has made up his mind to 'shed' the Catholics if it can't be avoided, rather than give way to any objections. He will do it with regret, & will hope to retain some of them by blandishments if he can manage it. But he seems to think it would be *wrong* now to put any obstacle in the way of S. India, & he will follow his conscience. There is no choice for us but to follow ours. I feel utterly miserable about the whole affair, but much more determined than before that I *won't* accept, come what may . . . I do hope your throat is better.

This correspondence should be compared with the account of the affair given by Dr. Iremonger on pp. 592-593 of his *William Temple*.

Meanwhile Kirk himself was in correspondence with the Archbishop over the reply to be made to the Metropolitan's questions. Dr. Temple had prepared a draft reply to these questions and it was circulated to the members of the Upper House of Convocation eight days before the beginning of the October group of sessions. Kirk unfortunately had one of his periodic attacks of throat troubles and was unable to go to London. On the day before Convocation met, therefore, he wrote to the Archbishop in the following terms.

My Lord Archbishop,

It appears unlikely that my doctor will allow me to travel to-morrow, or even on Thursday. I must therefore respectfully ask you to excuse me from attendance at Convocation this week.

I do this with all the more regret because there were certain aspects of the draft letter to the Metropolitan of India to which, if no one else did so, I desired to draw the attention of the Upper House. If, therefore, I am not present, I should be most grateful if you will indicate to the House the problems which I had in mind. No doubt many of them would have been elucidated had I been able to be present at the debate, but unfortunately, as I have said, the chances of that are poor.

(1) I take it that this is perhaps the most critical constitutional issue which has been before the Church of England since the days of the Non-Jurors. A hasty decision might very well lead to something approximating to schism, if not in the Provinces of Canterbury and York, perhaps in that more amorphous body which is called the Anglican Communion.

(2) In spite of the critical nature of the issue involved, this is I believe the first occasion on which the Scheme for union in South India has been brought before Convocation for discussion in any form. Perhaps I am wrong about this, as I know little of the activities of Convocation before 1937. But unless I am wrong, the facts seem to warrant our proceeding with the greatest circumspection.

(3) Many members of the Upper House were not in Episcopal Orders at the time of the last Lambeth Conference, and so have never heard or taken part in a full dress debate on the subject. It is true no doubt that they may be said to have had opportunities of familiarising themselves with the pros and cons of the matter since the Scheme came before the Lambeth Conference. But they have mostly been fully occupied with other matters during the last twelve years, and it is possible that they expected the matter to lie dormant until the next Lambeth Conference. They are thus (and I frankly confess this to have been the case with myself) ill equipped for the immediate and final decision at this moment for which it appears that they are asked.

(4) The present time is scarcely suitable for raising a new and vehement controversy in the Church of England. Some of us last year were induced on these grounds to lay aside a cause which we had greatly at heart—that of the enrichment of Eucharistic worship in the Church. This was a minor matter as compared with the present issue, and we are surely entitled to plead that the same principle should be observed in this case?

(It is to be noticed that by a wide and informal use of economic inter-Communion with the so-called Uniting Churches, the South India dioceses could, for the time being, secure the most urgent practical results envisaged by the Scheme without plunging the Church in England into the kind of controversy we should all deplore).

(5) Despite the considerations I have outlined, all of which should lead us to caution, the present draft letter to the Metropolitan of India is laid before the Upper House with only eight days notice—a time surely too short to allow busy men to do more than skim the surface of the problems involved.

(6) With these considerations in mind, I hoped, had I been present in

Convocation this week, to move a resolution in some such terms as these:—

"That a committee be appointed to review in detail the Scheme of Union in South India in the light of Holy Scripture, the teaching of the Fathers, and the Principles of Christ's Church as embodied in the formularies and liturgy of the Church of England, and to report."

It is in particular this intention of mine, now defeated by my indisposition which I hope your Grace will kindly communicate to the House.

(7) I should like to emphasise that this is no merely vexatious delaying resolution; it is a serious proposal designed to give those of us who have not been called upon directly to face the problem before, time and material for reaching a responsible judgment in the matter.

(8) I venture to press this suggestion all the more strongly because the oftener I read through the proposed Scheme of Union, the clearer it becomes to me that it ignores, if it does not actually contravene the teaching of Holy Scripture on many points of first importance. I had a preliminary list of six such points which I desired to lay before the Upper House with the necessary comments upon them; as things stand, I cannot do more than indicate that only one of the six was concerned with questions of Orders and Ministry.

(9) It may be said that even though my intention is not to delay proceedings, the proposal I have outlined above will have this effect. But if, as I understand, the Metropolitan of India is approaching every Anglican Metropolitan throughout the world with a similar enquiry, it is not likely that they will all have sent in their replies before we meet in our next group of sessions. Further, it appears to me that the responsibility for any delay will not lie with this house. The Church of India, Burma and Ceylon could have consulted your Grace at any time within the last twelve years had it wished to do so. If it chooses to wait till the eleventh hour before final decisions have to be taken in India, the blame cannot be imputed to England.

(10) I am puzzled and distressed at the possible implications of the Metropolitan's questions. They do not touch matters of principle, but only matters of expediency. If the Church of India, Burma and Ceylon is certain that it would be doing right in endorsing the Scheme for Union in South India, it ought to do so whatever the consequences might be. If it is not certain, it is obvious that Convocation could willingly advise if it were asked to do so. But the Metropolitan's questions deal with the possible consequences of certain actions, and not with the Scriptural and theological principles of the Scheme; and so suggest that the Church in India is more open to considerations of expediency than to those of duty. I should be the first to wish to have this suggestion repudiated; but I must frankly admit that I am always frightened of hypothetical questions taking the form "If I do so-and-so, what will you do". There is a very real danger that they may import into any matter under discussion considerations of worldly prudence and not of Christian idealism.

Forgive me for putting this lengthy letter before you, but I should not have felt I had done my duty by Convocation in the regrettable circumstances which make it impossible for me to attend, had I not taken this opportunity of opening my mind to your Grace and the members of the Upper House.

In Convocation the Archbishop's draft reply was given general approval by the Upper House sitting in committee, so that no record of the discussion there was made and it is not possible to know whether Temple communicated the contents of Kirk's letter to the other bishops. It was, however, decided that although the reply was not to be a formal Synodical Act the advice of the Lower House should be asked about it. The Bishop of Dorchester, Dr. G. B. Allen, moved in the Lower House that a Committee be appointed to consider the best advice which the House could give, and this was carried with only two dissentients.

On October 19th, Kirk wrote to Dom Gregory Dix the following letter:

Dear Gregory,

Like yourself I have been going through the Draft Answer more carefully than I have felt well enough to do for sometime past. It is all very puzzling, but I am inclined to say the following:—

A. *The Canonical Position.* This is not actually given away by the Draft Answer, provided that certain interpretations of the Answer are recognised as allowable:—

(i) It is the inalienable right of a bishop to refuse permission to officiate in his diocese any episcopally ordained minister without giving a reason. It is equally his right to refuse it by giving as his reason that the minister in question is accredited by a Church of doubtful orthodoxy. Nothing in the Answer abrogates these rights in the case of either present or future English Diocesans, though the quotations from the Lambeth Encyclical letter ("Its bishops will be received as bishops") is dangerous. However, the quotation is not endorsed in the Answer.

(ii) The last 8 lines of answer (a), first page are very sweeping. They depend however on the interpretation of the words "within its competence". These lines are not germane to the answer and should be deleted; but provided it is recognised that the ambiguity or want of definition of the phrase "within its competence" robs them of any real meaning, no grave harm is done by them.

(iii) The Lambeth Conference Report page 125, expresses the hope that "no Church of the Anglican communion will establish Churches or congregations in the area of the Union apart from the United Church." It is to be noticed that nothing in the Draft Answer endorses this hope.

In any future discussion in the Upper House on the Draft Answer, I should endeavour to make these points absolutely clear.

B. *The Dissenters.* In spite of your letter I doubt if they expected much more than the Draft Answer. What will really upset them is point (iii) above. That

L

is why it should be very fully stated here and now, so that no accusation of bad faith will be made later on.

C. *The Committee of the Lower House*. What are they to do? I imagine they must simply roam over the ground generally, drawing out the unscriptural and uncanonical features of the Scheme, and urging the greatest caution.

D. *Your Open Letter*. I am more puzzled than I can say as to the right shape for this to take. I wonder if it might not take the form of a meditation on the Scheme plus the Draft Answer, pointing out:

(i) The limitations of the Draft Answer so far as the Dissenters are concerned;

(ii) Then its general unsatisfactoriness of character;

(iii) Then ending by reserving the rights of the Communities, as Communities, to adopt whatever attitude they may think fit towards the ministers of the United Church, and also of the Church of India, Burma and Ceylon.

*   *   *

Here are one or two other points:— (1) I should greatly like to know what you think about this, especially *C* as I am being pestered for advice on questions of the Committee's line of action.

(2) I should dearly love to have information on the following. What Catholic Missions are there in South India which may be expected to refuse to enter the Scheme? I suppose there are some. In that case some Bishop or other must be prepared to take them under his wing. Presumably Colombo is the obvious person; but if he did not, then I suppose it might be done by an English Diocesan or by the Scottish or Welsh Provinces?

(3) Have you any light on the line which the Provinces of Scotland and Wales are going to take? If you could make contact with them it would be a great thing, as they could strengthen our hands considerably.

By the middle of December his mind had become clear as to the points in the Draft Reply which caused him most concern, and on December 16th he wrote to the Archbishop suggesting two amendments to the Draft Reply.

My Lord Archbishop,

While I have been in bed I have been thinking a good deal about the South India question and your reply to the Metropolitan. I should like at least to send you, as I do herewith, a memorandum of two amendments which, very diffidently, I would put forward with some brief explanatory notes.

It may be that the Bishops having given general approval to the draft reply, these suggested amendments must be regarded as out of order. On the other hand, I suppose they might be moved during a discussion of whatever resolution were based upon the report from the Lower House which is coming to the Upper House.

I should like to make it clear that I am acting entirely independently in this matter, and have not discussed these proposed amendments or shown them to anyone as yet.

SOUTH INDIA REUNION
THE DRAFT REPLY TO THE METROPOLITAN OF CALCUTTA

Proposed Amendments

I. For answer (a) substitute:—

"(a) As regards the first of the two questions to which we are asked to reply, our answer is simple; our answer, as at present advised is 'no'. Such a rupture of fraternal relations as the question envisages could only be brought about, on our side, by an Act of Convocation passed in the most formal manner possible by both of our Houses. There is not the remotest indication that any member of either House would, in the event of the consummation of the Scheme of Church Union in South India, put forward a proposal for such a rupture; or that were he to do so, he would have the slightest hope of obtaining any support for it.

"But it would be disingenuous to say this without drawing attention to the limiting clause 'as at present advised'. Not one of us in England but prays most earnestly that the new United Church of South India, if or when it comes into existence, may prove in every respect as loyal to the Scriptural and Apostolic truths of Christian faith and order as the Church of England has always striven to be. But if, through the folly or frailty of men or the wiles of the devil, it appeared that the granting of these prayers might be long delayed, it might well be that our Province would feel the need to redefine its attitude. We cannot believe that, in such a dire emergency, the Church of India, Burma and Ceylon would not find itself in agreement with whatever steps this Province felt bound to take; but we must recognise that there is at least the possibility of disagreement here; and unite in prayer to God that His Providence will safeguard us all from such a disaster."

2. *For Canon (b) of the three canons of administrative action in answer to question (b)*

"(b) A Minister of the United Church, the validity of whose Episcopal ordination (whether as regards matter, form, or intention) was above question, would be qualified . . ."

NOTES

On amendment 1

(a) The Reply as drafted assumes that it is "within the competence" of the Church of India etc: to approve the Scheme without further consultation with the other Provinces of the Anglican Communion than has actually taken place. This raises problems of constitutional principles, both in general and as regards this particular Scheme, which might lead to acute controversy. Hence the amendment avoids any question of principle, and merely considers the likelihood of a resolution for the rupture of Communion being moved in Convocation at this juncture.

(b) There is, I think, a fear that the Reply may be taken as committing the Province of Canterbury unconditionally to approval of the Scheme, and/or to tolerance of the Church of India's approval of the Scheme, however the Scheme may work out in practice. The amendment, by allowing for the possibility that circumstances may change, and that, if they did so, the Province must be free to reconsider its attitude, would help to allay this fear.

On amendment 2

So far as the ministry of the United Church is concerned, it seems clear that any controversy which arises about its validity will turn primarily on the question of intention, even where a valid matter and form have been observed in ordination,—of the Bull *Apostolica Curae* in reference to Anglican orders. We ought from the outset to show ourselves aware of this, so that if by any unhappy chance we have to draw attention to the point at a later stage, we may not be accused of raising a wholly new issue.

Temple's reply has unfortunately disappeared, but it evidently criticized some points in what Kirk had put forward, as appears from the following written on the last day of 1943.

My Lord Archbishop,

South India

Thank you very much for your kind letter of December 20th. I am very anxious that anything I propose should have, if possible, your Grace's goodwill: so I have thought over the suggestions of that letter very carefully, and now venture to write about them:—

(1) I gather with relief that you would not take strong exception to the first proposed amendment; so I should like that to stand as it is. I agree that the language is rather formal, but would accept verbal changes very readily.

(2) As regards the second amendment I am rather in a difficulty. It seems to me that the problem of validity (with special reference to the question of intention) may arise as soon as the Act of Inauguration has taken place: for at any time thereafter someone ordained in South India may apply to the Archbishop of Canterbury for written permission to officiate in England under the Colonial Clergy Act. I would very gladly indeed accept your suggestion on this point if you felt it possible to read "So soon as the Act of Inauguration has taken place it would be of course the duty . . ." *instead* of "When the Scheme was complete and in working order . . ." If you think this possible, I will try to phrase the amendment satisfactorily . . .

(3) There is a third and allied point which has impressed itself on me whilst

I have been thinking about the matter. It is mainly a legal question, and so is not primarily my concern; and I have no doubt that your Grace's advisers have considered it and would give me the answer. It is as follows.

The Colonial Clergy Act (referred to in your Grace's draft reply to the Metropolitan) explicitly deals with persons ordained "priest" or "deacon" overseas. But no one in the United Church is to be ordained "priest". The word does not appear in the Scheme; they will be ordained "presbyters". As an Act of Parliament is concerned, it would surely be dangerous for any Archbishop to give to a South Indian "presbyter" permission to officiate as a "priest" in the Church of England until some competent Court, or an amending Act, had declared South Indian presbyters to be priests for the purposes of the principal Act. For if, in default of such a declaration, the Archbishop were to take the step in question it would still remain doubtful in law whether such a person were a "priest" or not; and this would involve doubts as to whether he could legally be admitted to a benefice, or even whether he could validly solemnise a marriage. (If he had been ordained deacon in India, no doubt he could, with the Archbishop's permission solemnise a marriage in England as a deacon; but not all presbyters of the United Church are required by the Constitution to pass through the diaconate—chV. para 11).

No doubt there is a flaw somewhere in this; and I should be most grateful to be told where it is. At present, it seems to me that, unless *either* the United Church is prepared to use the word "priest" in its formula of ordination, *or* the Colonial Clergy Act is amended in some way or another, "presbyters" coming to England from South India will be in an intolerable position as will also the Archbishop of Canterbury for the time being, and all his suffragans.

I hope you will forgive me for raising the question, but I cannot think it wholly irrelevant.

This correspondence is important because it shows that at this very first stage of synodical discussion about South India, Kirk forcibly made points about intention and the ministry of the proposed new Church which were to be in the forefront of later debates. This was made even more clear in the revised form of his amendments which Kirk sent to the Archbishop on January 8th.

SOUTH INDIA REUNION
DRAFT REPLY TO THE METROPOLITAN OF CALCUTTA

Proposed Amendments

I. For answer (a) substitute:—

"(a) As regards the first of the two questions to which we are asked to reply, our answer is simple; our answer, as at present advised, is 'no'. Such a rupture of fraternal relations as the question envisages could only be brought about, on our side, by an Act of Convocation passed in the most formal manner possible by both of our Houses. There is not the remotest indication that any member of either House would, in the event of the consummation of the Scheme of Church Union in South India, put forward a proposal for such a rupture; or that were he to do so, he would have the slightest hope of obtaining any support for it.

"But it would be disingenuous to say this without drawing attention to the limiting clause 'as at present advised'. Not one of us in England but hopes most earnestly that the new United Church of South India, if or when it comes into existence, may prove in every respect as loyal to the Scriptural and Apostolic truths of Christian faith and order as the Church of England has always striven to be. But if, in the years following the inauguration of the Scheme, evidence should accumulate that these hopes were unlikely (for whatever reason) to be realized, it might well be that our Province would feel the need to redefine its attitude. We cannot believe that, in such a dire emergency, the Church of India, Burma and Ceylon would not find itself in agreement with whatever steps this Province felt bound to take; but we must recognise that there is at least the possibility of disagreement here; and unite in prayer to God that His Providence will safeguard us all from such a disaster."

2. *To subclause (b) of answer (b) append:*—

"Note:—After the Act of Inauguration has taken place, it will of course be the duty of Churches and Provinces desiring to define their relationship to the newly United Church of South India to consider such a question as the validity of the Orders conferred in it, with reference not only to the Matter & Form employed in their administration, but also to the Intention with which they were administered."

In acknowledging the receipt of this document Temple wrote:

You are quite at liberty to say, when introducing them, that you had consulted me in advance and that I had told you that if the Bishops approved them, I should see no objection in principle to incorporating them.

I think some Bishops will feel that there is a balance to be struck between claims of adequate caution and a desire to appear cordial in our attitude to the scheme, and there may be other arguments about the expediency of introducing either point; but there is certainly nothing that I should regard as in principle at all contrary to the purpose of the reply as drafted.

I think it likely that the Lower House will follow its own Committee in asking us to insert something to declare our view with regard to members of our Province who might find themselves in that part of India, and we could meet this by inserting certain words from the Lambeth Conference Report, to the effect that "no censure should attach to any Anglican, clerical or lay, who should communicate with or officiate in the Church of South India if it is established." If this were inserted as well as your two amendments, it could be held that they balanced each other in the matter of favour towards the scheme, your own expressing a little more anxiety than our draft did, the other tending to a more positive attitude—and therefore the original balance would not have been disturbed if both were adopted, though if the second were to be inserted along with yours, some words might need to be added, such as "provided that this Province is satisfied that the scheme is being carried out in such a manner and with such intention as to justify the maintenance of the relationship to the United Church now proposed". (I have not tried to draft that properly but will try to have something ready.)

The Lower House may also ask that we should insert in the reply some words making it quite clear that we have not thought it our duty either to approve or to refuse approval to the scheme itself, but to consider it only so far as was needed to qualify us for answering the Metropolitan's questions. I think it would be a gain to have that made perfectly explicit.

If we adopt our reply in anything like the form in which it now stands, I shall probably make a statement at the close of the discussion, after the decision is reached, in which I shall try to set that decision in its context as I understand it. In doing so, I shall refer to the question of intention, saying that provided the Scheme is worked in what I believe to be the spirit of its framers and the spirit which seems to me to be expressed in the scheme itself, I do not think there need be anxiety on that point, but that it is one concerning which there should be vigilance. I take it you would not feel that this was in any way contrary to your own concern in the matter.

In reply Kirk said that he fully agreed with the additional sentences which the Archbishop had it in mind to add to the letter. He had now seen the Lower House Report and thought that if it came up unaltered his own amendments might meet several of its points.

The Convocation met on January 19th, 1944, but the Upper House took the unusual course of sitting in Committee on the Wednesday and Thursday while the Lower House debated the Report of their Committee on South India. On the Friday Kirk was allowed to introduce his amendments in the Upper House. In fact he spoke fully on only the first of them as the debate was interrupted by the arrival of the Report of the decisions of the Lower House and thereafter took a somewhat different course. Kirk emphasized that he was speaking without any consultation with any member of the Lower House, but he reminded the bishops that there were large numbers of loyal and devoted Church people of whom it could be said that they were very anxious about the implications of any action taken at the present time, and that it was therefore of the utmost importance that there should be no ambiguity whatever in anything which was said, and that there should be shown the maximum amount of frankness which was compatible with friendliness. He held that in the draft answer to the first of the Metropolitan's two questions there were ambiguities which might give rise to serious misapprehension. Firstly, the Metropolitan's question was absolutely categorical. It asked whether in certain circumstances the Province of Canterbury would break off communion with the Church of India, Burma and Ceylon. To that question the draft answer gave an absolutely categorical reply, but the Archbishop had more than once stated that a decision of such importance as to involve a breach of communion would require the most solemn act on the part of both Convocations. No such action had hitherto been taken or was proposed, but the draft reply was so worded that a reader might easily conclude that it was itself a synodical decision not to break off communion. Kirk wished it to be made quite clear that if the Metropolitan's question was to be answered categorically it could only be answered by the two Convocations, and that as there had been no action on the part of the whole province, the reply was therefore to that extent informal and not formal or categorical.

The second misapprehension was that the draft answer implied that in no circumstances whatsoever, arising out of the consummation of the Scheme of Union in South India, would the Province of Canterbury break communion with the Church of India, Burma and Ceylon. There was, of course, no proposal for rupture with the Church of North India, but there might be tragic circumstances in which the situation would be altered, and the Province of Canterbury could not be committed to a certain attitude for all time. The third misapprehension which might arise was due to certain expressions in the draft reply which said that the Church of India, Burma and Ceylon was "competent to decide" certain things, and that in this matter it exercised its responsibility "in a matter within its competence". These expressions seemed to refer to moral and canonical competence and at once raised the question of how far any one Church could enter upon an experiment and at the same time expect other Churches to remain unmoved. He would prefer to leave the question of competence, which was a question of principle for theologians and canonists to discuss, entirely on one side, and fall back upon the fact that so far as could be seen no one at present in either House was going to propose that communion with the Church of North India should be broken after the act of inauguration took place.

The Bishop of Ely (Dr. Wynn) seconded the amendment, and after some discussion of the last point the Bishop of Chichester (Dr. Bell) spoke on the subject as a whole. He complained that none of the bishops knew that it was the intention of one of their number to produce amendments to the draft reply. As Kirk had been in correspondence with the Archbishop about the matter for five or six weeks before the meeting and had, in fact, sent in his amendments on December 16th, and the revised form of them on January 8th, ten days before Convocation met, he could hardly be blamed because Temple had not had them circulated earlier. Dr. Bell went on to dismiss Kirk's three points as being of little substance, but at the same time suggested that the first amendment was so substantial as to introduce into the draft reply an atmosphere of depression rather than of hope. The Bishop of London (Dr. Fisher), however, had a certain sympathy with Kirk's point of view. He agreed that the phrases about 'competence' seemed to give entire freedom to any Province to decide upon its own action, even though that action were heretical, and to imply that even in such a case the Province of Canterbury would not break off communion with it. He also agreed that there was something too absolute in saying simply that the answer to the first of the Metropolitan's questions was 'No'. That did not take into account sufficiently that future possibilities must be borne in mind. Dr. Fisher was, indeed, almost the only supporter of the South India Scheme to understand that what was being discussed was a document which though in a sense informal nevertheless would be of great importance for the future and could not properly be regarded as merely a message of good will. The Bishop of Bristol (Dr. Woodward) went so far as to say that there was a danger of the reply becoming an official document and not an expression of faith and hope. Dr. Fisher, more realistically and more accurately said that they were considering what was in fact if not in name a formal document and that it was right to see that such a document was as securely based as possible and did not give ground for any misunderstanding in the future. He made certain suggestions with which Kirk was able to agree.

The arrival of the Report containing the decisions of the Lower House interrupted the discussion, and attention was turned to a consideration of those points. Some of them covered ground similar to that of Kirk's first amendment. One of them, however, raised the point of his second amendment and, in view of its later importance, deserves some explanation here.

In his draft reply the Archbishop had written: "An episcopally ordained minister of the united Church would be qualified to receive the Licence or Permission of a Bishop to officiate, subject, when they apply, to the provisions of the Colonial Clergy Act, and to such rules and customs as are accepted in respect of all ministers in the Province." The Lower House wished to substitute for the first eight words the following: "A minister of the United Church whose ordination as deacon or priest or whose consecration as bishop is accepted in this Province." Here was clearly the point that Kirk had been pressing on Temple in his earlier correspondence. It should have been obvious that in the Church of South India after the Union there would be two sorts of episcopally ordained ministry, one consisting of the former Anglicans and the other of those who had been ordained after the Union and according to the rites of the Church of South India, rites which were not yet in existence. Whether or not other people wished to raise questions about the validity of South Indian ordinations on theological grounds, the existence of the Colonial Clergy Act laid a legal obligation upon the Archbishop of Canterbury to satisfy himself as to the validity of the orders of any person ordained overseas, who wished to minister in the Church of England. Any decision in this matter necessarily affected the whole province and it was quite right that attention should be called to it at this stage. The following extract from the *Chronicle of Convocation* shows the way in which it was discussed.

The Bishop of Oxford said that he thought the point raised by the Lower House was identical in principle with his own amendment (2), only his amendment made explicit what he presumed was implicit in what the Lower House had brought forward. There was a danger that at some stage the question of intention would be raised as it had not been raised hitherto, and that danger should be recognized and faced. The United Church ought also in the same way to be prepared to face it, so that if any future crisis of this kind did arise it could not be said that it had been allowed to develop through sheer lack of foresight. That was all he had in mind in putting forward that amendment. He did not much mind whether the Lower House's suggestion or his own was adopted, but he thought that a definite reference to the question of intention would present the issue in its clearest form.

The Bishop of Lichfield said that he appreciated deeply the spirit in which the Bishop of Oxford had brought forward this amendment, but he felt that it would be the height of unwisdom to attempt to make a forecast at this time. The issue should not be forced, and room should be left for inevitable divergence of form. Their successors would, of course, pass the situation in review, and it would be for them to do what they thought right when the time arrived. But to insert anything of this kind at the present moment was highly dangerous and even misleading.

The Bishop of Derby hoped that this would go forward in the form suggested by the Lower House. It would be less difficult than the form of the Bishop of

Oxford's note. The latter brought in an explicit reference to a theological question, the validity of Orders and the intention with which they were administered. They were not being called upon to discuss the theology of the Scheme, and he hoped the House would not think it necessary to do anything beyond accepting what the Lower House had proposed, which was, he thought, harmless.

The Bishop of Oxford said that his only desire was to make the inference perfectly clear. But he would be content if the form adopted by the Lower House were adopted by the Upper House too.

The Bishop of Chichester hoped the House would not adopt the Lower House form. Clearly there would be two grades of episcopally ordained ministry, and the effect of the proposal of the Lower House would be, unless special action was taken by the Convocations, that those belonging to the old Anglican Communion would be admitted to the ordinary functions of bishops, priests and deacons customary in the Church of England while those who had had this other form of episcopal ordination were not assured of that reception. The effect of such a distinction at this stage would be most disastrous.

The Bishop of Oxford said that it was quite clear that in this country that distinction would be made, and that there were very large numbers of clergy who would hesitate very much until the Province had declared its acceptance of what had been described as "second grade".

The Bishop of Chichester moved:

"That the reply in this respect should stand as it was first drafted, and that the Lower House be so informed."

The House Agreed.

The history of South India at the Lambeth Conference in 1948, and the Convocation of 1950 shows that it was Kirk and not the majority of the Upper House who was right on this point. It may be that Dr. Temple appreciated more of Kirk's foresight than he showed in the debate, for in his formal address at the end of the discussion, an address which was later published separately and a copy of which was sent to the Metropolitan, he included a paragraph which discussed the question of intention, although he said that it did not seem to him to be likely to be a source of difficulty.

At the end of the debate it was agreed that the Archbishop should re-draft the reply to the Metropolitan, first obtaining the counsel of the Bishops of London, Winchester, and Oxford on what he had written, and then making his own final decision concerning the text to be sent. On January 24th, he wrote to Kirk enclosing a copy of the Reply and of the covering letter as he had re-drafted them, and added:

We have not specifically said we should receive the South Indian Bishops as Bishops, though we quote that expression from the Encyclical Letter of the Lambeth Conference. Bishop Palmer would like this put in, but even if I had brought it up in Convocation I should have counselled against it. It is really implicit and I think is best left out.

Kirk's reply was as follows:

My Lord Archbishop,

South India

Thank you for sending me the redraft of the official Reply to the Metropolitan of India, Burma and Ceylon, together with the draft covering letter. If I may say so, they seem to me to cover the ground very fully, and I have little to suggest by way of comment except the following:—

(1) The Lower House (if I remember rightly) was very anxious that nothing in the Reply should suggest that a decision of the Province as a whole was involved. According to the rough notes which I made when their answer was read out, the kind of decision they had in mind was only one of "approval or disapproval of the Scheme, or a decisive judgment on the Scheme." This, I think, is fully guarded against in the Reply. But I also carried away the impression (perhaps mistakenly) that the Lower House wished it to be clear that the Reply, within its own proper sphere, was not a formal Act of Convocation. Nothing in the language actually suggests this, but there is no doubt that it may often be quoted as though it were such an Act. I wonder, therefore, whether it might not be wise to insert words which would guard the Reply against any such interpretation. It would meet any hesitation entirely if after the words "liable to review" at the end of the last line but six of the first page of the Reply were added "either by the Diocesan Bishops or by Convocation as such." I do not remember that anything was said in the Upper House which would preclude such an addition.

(2) If I remember rightly, the question of "intention" was touched on in your Grace's Address, of which a copy is accompanying the letters to the Metropolitan. As the general opinion of the Bishops was opposed to the inclusion of any reference to this subject in the Reply, I am most grateful that you have adopted this alternative method of allaying my scruples.

(3) This encourages me to raise another matter which was not definitely before us in Convocation, though it was implicit in the whole discussion of "intention". I am still very alarmed at the regrettable confusion,—possibly legal (in so far as the terminology of the Colonial Clergy Act is involved) and certainly canonical,—which will be produced in England by the substitution in the Scheme of the word "presbyter" for the word "priest" in the enumeration of the traditional threefold ministry of the Church. Without going into details, it seems inevitable that in some dioceses, and in very many parishes, in this

country, visiting "presbyters" from South India will not be allowed to minister the sacraments, on the ground that their ordination as "priests" is in doubt. If by any chance one of them were presented by a patron to a benefice, the matter might quite possibly come into the Civil Courts. Thus, as things stand, there is bound to be much heart-burning and perhaps some scandal. It may be suggested (as in the case of "bishops") that a study of the duties assigned to "presbyters" in the Scheme should remove all anxiety. My own feeling, however, is that the two cases are by no means parallel, and that as far as "presbyters" are concerned this argument would carry little weight.

I believe, however, that the distressing results I have mentioned could be avoided by the United Church without any sacrifice either of principle or of expediency. They will very soon discover that the "words accompanying" the laying on of hands (if no other part of the Ordination rite) must be identical for all dioceses; and if these "words" always named the person ordained as "priest" (whatever he were called thereafter) many doubts would be resolved. Incidentally, such a plan would be identical with that of the Scottish Episcopal Prayer-Book of 1929 (and earlier books I believe as well), where the minister is ordained (by the English formula) as "priest" but throughout the service of Holy Communion is spoken of as "presbyter".

Again, Letters of Orders will have to be identical throughout the United Church. If these spoke of the ordained person as "priest", or even "presbyter or priest", the situation would be greatly eased.

Another method would be for the United Church to publish a declaration (e.g.) that, in ordaining men as presbyters, it intended to convey to them (or did not intend to convey to them less than) the full spiritual status and office appertaining to priests in the Episcopal and to fully ordained ministers in the non-Episcopal Uniting Churches.

Any of these expedients would help matters considerably; together they should reconcile all but the most stubborn critics of the use of "presbyters" proposed in South India. In any case, it seems only reasonable and courteous that the Uniting Churches should explain to the Universal Church, of which when united they will claim to form a Province, why they should adopt a title for the second order of the ministry which is not in current use (at all events for the ordained ministry) amongst any of them—nor, I suppose, amongst any other English speaking body of Christians. It is, in fact, as necessary in principle to explain the relation of the new "presbyters" to non-Episcopal "ministers" as it is to explain their relation to Episcopal "priests", though no doubt the problem will not press upon non-Episcopal Churches in any degree so severely as it will with us.

It is evident that this matter is not one which the Bishops desired to be mentioned either in the Reply or even in the Covering letter. But I venture to hope that perhaps in some other letter to the Metropolitan (or to some other prominently engaged in negotiating the Union) your Grace will think fit to draw attention to it.

So ended that stage of the affair. Looking back the whole proceedings seem even more peculiar now than they did then. Here was a matter of the first importance involving the departure of four dioceses from the Anglican Communion and the inauguration of a wholly novel scheme of reunion which was already being regarded as a model for elsewhere, not excluding England. A letter was received from the Metropolitan of India asking what action the Province of Canterbury would take in certain respects if the Scheme went through, questions which could not be properly answered without an examination of the Scheme itself. The reply to the Metropolitan's letter was bound to be regarded in India as expressing the official attitude of the Province of Canterbury towards the Scheme. In spite of all this the reply was treated almost as if it were a matter of personal correspondence between Dr. Temple and the Metropolitan. It is true that the Upper and Lower Houses of Convocations were consulted, but the reply was in no sense a synodical act, although anyone not well acquainted with the procedure of Convocation might easily assume it to be so. Further, the little time allowed by the Archbishop for consideration of his reply prevented any thorough and synodical examination of the Scheme. In fact the Convocations had no opportunity of formally considering the Scheme itself until 1950, when they were faced with a *fait accompli* in the existence of the United Church and a near *fait accompli* in Temple's reply to the Metropolitan. This story may explain some of the suspicion with which Temple was regarded by many people in these matters, and some of the resentment and bitterness which the name of South India still arouses among sections of Churchpeople. If the proposal for a Commission made by Kirk in his letter of October 12th had been accepted, and a real synodical examination of the Scheme allowed, much of this later bitterness might have been avoided.

By the beginning of 1947 it had become plain that the inauguration of the new Church of South India would take place before the end of the year, and various bodies in England had to determine what would be their attitude towards it. One of these was the Society for the Propagation of the Gospel. As we have already seen, a warning had been given as long ago as 1933 that the S.P.G. might not be able to continue its support of work in a Church formed on the basis of the South India Scheme, and this warning, unheeded at the time, became unhappy fact in 1947. A special group appointed by the S.P.G. to advise came to the conclusion that the Society was precluded by its Charters from allocating block grants to dioceses not in communion with the Church of England. This left open the question whether it could support individual workers within the Church of South India and a special meeting of the Standing Committee of the S.P.G. was held on May 8th to decide this matter. It was decided by sixty-eight votes to thirty-four that for the period January 1st to December 31st, 1948, an honorarium equal to one year's emoluments be paid to individual European missionaries who, having been sent out under the auspices of the Society, elected to join the South India Church, and that thereafter the Society's responsibility in respect of them should determine; and that Indian workers previously dependent for their salaries on S.P.G. block grants should be given an honorarium based on the amount of the emoluments they would have received during the same period, in order that the cutting off of block grants might avoid financial embarrassment to the workers concerned.

This decision was felt by some members of the Society to be excessively hard and unfair and on June 4th the Archbishop of Canterbury (Dr. Fisher) wrote as President of the Society to suggest that there should be opened a special fund to which S.P.G. subscribers might contribute for the support of those S.P.G. workers who joined the South India Church. This suggestion had been made in one of the documents which was before the meeting of May 8th, and it appeared to the Archbishop that neither in the majority nor in the minority report then presented was the possibility of such a step ruled out. The proposal, however, seemed to some an attempt to reverse the decisions of the previous meeting, and suspicion was increased by the short notice allowed for its consideration. The following extract from a letter to Kirk by a very reasonable and pacific correspondent gives some indication of the atmosphere:

On June 5th a telegram reached me at breakfast time to tell me there was to be an ordinary meeting of the Standing Committee that day at which an effort would be made to side-track the decision arrived at on May 8th. I had not been summoned to the meeting, but I went as a Vice-President. On arrival we found the long letter from the Archbishop, dated June 4th, a copy of which I believe you have now received.

This letter was read from the Chair, and a resolution was moved then and there by the Chairman that we should thank the Archbp. for his letter & agree to his proposal. It was added that the Archbp. was ready to respond to a telephone call to come at once & commend his proposal in person, so that we might agree to it at once. But we refused to be stampeded, and we demanded time for consideration, and declared that in view of the decision on May 8th, the question ought to be dealt with only by another special meeting. This meeting has been called for June 26th, but there is no formal motion, only the Archbp.'s letter. I understand he is to move a resolution from the Chair.

A number of appeals, including letters from three retired missionary bishops, were made to Kirk asking that he should attend the special meeting on June 26th and lead the opposition to the Archbishop's proposals. An old friend who was connected with the S.P.G. wrote:

The opposition badly needs a strong lead which can help them to face the heavy guns which are being brought into action, and I do not think there is anyone but yourself that can do the job. I am afraid that the big majority which carried out the Minority Report at the last meeting cannot be relied on unless they have the backing of somebody like yourself. I think, too, that the proposers will be strongly reinforced specially by dignitaries . . .

There is much anxiety amongst us of the small fry, and of course we have no voice in the matter. I do not know what Bishop Roberts wants but I know what practically all the rest of the Staff want. It is frightening to see letter after letter from Bishops and such like who are all out for the plan, and then to read the many letters from those who have no vote and who want to oppose it. We of the staff mainly see the position very simply, perhaps too simply; we do not see how the resources and the machinery of the Society can be used to collect money for those who are supporting a body not in communion with the Anglican Churches. We also see that the agents of the Society will be placed in a very difficult position.

Personally, I am 'agin' the whole thing because it appears to me that a magical and superstitious conception of episcopacy is involved; that is unless it is a mere bit of machinery, and if this is what it is it is utterly useless and altogether to be damned. Please come if you can.

To this appeal Kirk replied:

Many thanks for your letter. I could not get to the meeting next Thursday without producing chaos in diocesan things here: it is a day full of urgent deliberations in which a great many people are concerned.

I did what I could in the matter when I was up for the Church Assembly last week. I am whole-heartedly with you in your condemnation of the scheme; and I think you have got nearer to the real objection to it than anyone I know. But I cannot help feeling that S.P.G. cannot divest itself of a certain paternal interest in those who have served it in the past, and who (in most cases through no fault of their own) suddenly find themselves severed from the Church of England and faced with economic dangers of the gravest kind.

If, as I hope, a plan could be evolved by which a special fund should bear practical witness to this paternal interest without implying any kind of condonation of the South India scheme, it would be well worth while exploring its possibilities. I earnestly trust that that is the way in which the meeting may go on Thursday.

To one of his episcopal correspondents he wrote outlining various possibilities by which the suggestions contained in this last paragraph might be carried out, and he urged that they should not get involved in what would appear a sordid financial squabble. He added that he could not clash with the Archbishop except on a clear issue of first principle. In the event the meeting of June 26th agreed that the Society should accept subscriptions for the maintenance of the former S.P.G. work in South India in a 'South India Separate Account' and forward any such subscriptions to India.

While these discussions were taking place a problem arose within the Oxford Diocese. A Committee representing the various Missionary Societies, Anglican and non-Anglican, concerned in the South India Church Union had arranged a joint Intercession Service at St. Martin's in-the-Fields at which the Archbishop of Canterbury was to preach and the heads of other churches had been invited to take part. This service was to be held in September at the time of the Inauguration of the Union. The C.M.S. Association in the Oxford Diocese was anxious to hold a similar service in an Anglican Church in Oxford and in May Kirk was approached for his consent to this proposal. He was in an awkward position as he had throughout his episcopate fairly consistently refused permission for interdenominational services in Anglican churches, believing them to be productive rather of disunity than of unity. However he was ready to suggest a solution as the following three paragraphs from his letter to the Secretary show:

My difficulty is a very simple one. What are called "United services" in Parish Churches invariably arouse controversy, and a bishop who has given permission for them is the principal sufferer—he has to answer all the letters of protest, and deal with critics. I do not think that you or any other member of the Association would wish to put me in this position; but it will inevitably arise if I were to sanction such a service. And in addition, the occasion provided by union in South India would do a disservice to the cause of reunion at home.

These objections could be met if I took the whole service myself, and I do not think Non-conformists who were willing to come to an Anglican building, could very well object to the service being taken by the Bishop of the Diocese.

You must not infer from anything I have said that I deprecate the idea of the service as such. The developments in South India, whether one feels anxious or confident about them, are obviously an occasion for heartfelt prayer.

M

The following is the outline of an address which Kirk gave at St. Peter's Hall, Oxford, at the time of the Inauguration of the Union.

A. (1) Met to pray that God's never-failing Providence will (thro' H.S.) guide and bless in its second stage a venture which began 30 yrs. ago.

(2) Representatives of 4 Anglican dioceses met representatives of non-episcopal bodies to discuss how best to consolidate forces of Xtianity against surrounding evils of paganism.

(3) Terms of union drafted & redrafted—advice sought in many quarters—scheme formulated—has come into being—first stage ended—second stage begun.

B. (1) How begun? Four dioceses have left Anglican Communion, resolved in new Church to maintain and promote essential principles of Anglican Ch.—"fulness of Catholic faith & Order" (Abp.) Have entered into unity on this basis, wh. others have accepted; & in new Church consecrated new bishops.

(2) Has not happened without heartsearching. Great sacrifices on every side; many points still uncertain.

(3) Much anxiety: surrounding paganism, rising tide of nationalism, seeds of disunion & controversy may spread, & cause of Xt. be hindered. All this in minds of those who have negotiated & now have to administer the union.

C. (1) Our duty clear: shall thank God that during past century the truth as it is in Jesus has taken deep root in S. India; that he has set it in hearts of pious men to undertake so brave an experiment, so high a venture, that their efforts have already reached such measure of agreement. More particularly commend this new approach towards Christian unity to His fatherly care; asking that the dangers alluded to (of wh. all in S. India are more conscious even than ourselves) may be averted; & that results exceeding even the highest hopes that any one has cherished may accrue.

(2) Fortified by liturgy (aspirations of Psalmist; message of prophets; canticles of those who were nearest to our Saviour at the time of His Incarnation; words of evangelists & apostles; creed of our fathers) shall with confidence lift up our hearts in prayer.

(3) Need not doubt that in ways perhaps hitherto undreamt of those prayers will be answered, & that all will be turned in God's mercy to His greater glory.

The next year, 1948, was to be the year of the Lambeth Conference, the first since 1930, and it was obvious that South India would be a major item. In an address to the Oxford Diocesan Conference in May, 1948[1] Kirk attempted to survey the problem. He gave a brief account of the history of the Scheme and outlined some of the points for and against it. Then he turned to the questions which it would raise for

[1] Oxford Diocesan Magazine, June and July, 1948, reprinted with other articles under the title *Lambeth Reunion and South India*.

consideration at Lambeth. On two points he thought that no question would be raised. First as to the degree of relationship between the Anglican Communion and the new Church he pointed out that there was no possibility of full intercommunion (meaning thereby that every minister or member of the one Church may, if in good standing there, be received as a minister or member of the other without further question) as long as the Church of South India numbered among its presbyters and deacons men who had not been episcopally ordained, or among its communicant laity persons who had not been baptized. Such a state of things, he thought, would continue for a considerable time. Secondly, there was the question of bishops and clergy episcopally ordained in the Church of England and at present serving in the new Church who might desire to return to England and take up ministerial office here. Statements already made clearly meant that, as far as England was concerned, no bishop would be entitled to refuse to employ any returning missionary priest *merely* on the ground that he had served in the new Church, although if any bishop had reason to be anxious lest long experience in the new Church had unfitted the candidate for work in England under English ecclesiastical laws and customs, he would be entitled to satisfy himself on the matter before accepting the candidate as one of his diocesan clergy.

Two other points, however, were likely to cause discussion. First was the position of a presbyter ordained in the Church of South India who desired to exercise his ministry in some Church of the Anglican communion.

He would have been ordained by a bishop himself duly consecrated in apostolic succession, and by rites which in word and action were technically valid. But as the present Archbishop has said, 'The fact of episcopal ordination does not by itself necessarily suffice.' I take this to mean that there would have to be some assurance that the ordaining bishop intended to do what the Church has always done; and it would open the question whether this could be said of any bishop who was required by his position in the new Church to treat non-episcopally ordained ministers as in all respects the equals of those episcopally ordained. It may not be necessary to settle this question at the present Lambeth Conference, but sooner or later it will become a very live issue indeed. Indeed, successive Conferences may have to take it under review, as the temper of the new Church varies in one direction or another on the doctrine of the ministry from time to time.

The other point arose from the fact that the South India Scheme was the first practical attempt of its kind towards reunion and as such was likely to be taken as a model by other areas. The Conference would almost certainly desire to guide these other areas and help them to avoid such pitfalls as may have exhibited themselves in South India.

In my opinion, discussion should be primarily addressed to the problems raised by the fact that the South India Church starts its journey with what may be called a 'dual ministry'—half its clergy having been episcopally ordained, the other half not. If what I have said is true, the main difficulties which have been raised about the Scheme are all focussed upon this fact, and there is widespread agreement that if it could be eliminated the path to reunion would be infinitely simplified. Can Lambeth then devise a satisfactory method of eliminating it from future negotiations of the same kind? The problem is one of extreme difficulty, but I cannot believe that the Holy Spirit will fail to assist the Conference to a wise and practicable solution.

The discussions at the Lambeth Conferences are confidential and only the reports of committees and the Resolutions are published. It is, however, no secret that at the 1948 Conference Kirk was a dominating figure in the discussions of South India, and that the expression of what came to be known as the Lambeth minority view was his work. On the second of the two questions raised in his Diocesan Conference Address Lambeth went a considerable way to meet the problem. It expressed a decided preference for schemes of reunion which did not involve a dual ministry, even for an interim period, and it said that "the integral connexion between the Church and the ministry should be safeguarded in all proposals for the achievement of intercommunion through the creation of a mutually recognized ministry."

On the question of the bishops, presbyters and deacons ordained in the Church of South India, however, the Lambeth Conference had to record disagreement. There were those who were ready immediately to recognize such ministers as true bishops, priests and deacons in the Church of God, but there were others, including Kirk, who held that it was much too early to reach a decision on a subject of such importance. The two views were, therefore, included in the Resolutions, the first being stated as held by a majority, the second as held by a substantial minority. Figures of voting were not given, but in February, 1949, the Bishop of Southern Ohio, who had been Secretary of the Sub-Committee on South India, stated that the majority consisted of 135, and the minority of 94. As the total number of bishops attending the Conference was 329 it would seem that about 100 bishops did not vote. The 'substantial minority' is known to have included the Archbishop of York, Dr. Garbett.

It needs to be emphasized that the minority did not desire to condemn outright or declare invalid the episcopally consecrated and ordained ministry of the Church of South India. In the Report of the relevant Sub-Committee their view was expressed as follows:

The Church of South India is very young. Less than a year has passed since its inauguration. Although it has been possible to study its basis of union and its constitution, and to receive some information about its life since the inauguration, there has not yet been time in their judgement for the fruits of the union to be fully experienced and for the character of the Church of South India in its new corporate life to become apparent. They are of the opinion that time must be allowed for that Church to grow into fuller unity and to manifest its stability and its validity as a living part of the body of Christ.

In an article in the Diocesan Magazine for January, 1949, Kirk paraphrased the minority view as follows:

The actions of the Church of South India do not square with its professions in this matter. It professes to aim at a ministry fully and exclusively organised on a Catholic and apostolic basis. In fact, however, it admits, and proposes for at least thirty years (if not for an indefinite period) to continue to admit non-episcopally ordained ministers to the full exercise of the responsibilities of the priesthood. For the moment, therefore, there is a serious contradiction between the words and the action of the Church; and this puts its real intention in doubt. In due course, we hope,—perhaps long before the thirty years' period is over,—this contradiction will be resolved by some amendment of Constitution or change of practice in South India. Till then, however, the most we can say is that "it is not yet possible to pass any definite judgment" on the validity of the ordinations in question.

He added a further point which he raised more than once in later discussions:

It is a universal principle of Church order that where the validity of the sacraments is in question the benefit of the doubt may not be taken. It would, for example, be wholly wrong for anyone to pronounce the divine absolution upon sinners if there were a doubt whether he had received 'power and commandment' from his Master to do so. Or again, it would be wrongful for a bishop to authorise anyone to celebrate the Eucharist so long as the validity of his ordination to the priesthood could be reasonably challenged. Thus anyone who shares the doubts of the minority in the Conference must recognise the compelling nature of their refusal to recommend the acceptance of the ministers of whom we are thinking as bishops, priests or deacons. No other course was possible.

In the same article he was also concerned to defend the Committee on Unity against the charge of having abandoned the Augustinian view of validity.

It is quite certain that there has at times been a widespread tendency in the Church to make the validity of the ministry dependent in part upon the general orthodoxy of the ordaining body, and therefore to reordain persons ordained in a heretical community, even by validly consecrated bishops, if they desire to enter the Catholic fold and exercise their ministry there. This was the general teaching and practice of the early Eastern Church, of St. Cyprian, and of the Donatists. But in the West, on the basis of the outspoken arguments of St. Augustine, strongly reinforced centuries later by St. Thomas Aquinas, 'an ordination (with laying on of hands, prayer, and the general intention of making a man what the Church intends) conferred by a bishop who has himself been so ordained, even if he is a heretic, is valid and cannot be reiterated without sacrilege'. The vacillations of many Popes and prelates in this matter throughout the mediaeval period do not refute this principle.

And obviously, even on grounds of expediency alone, the Augustinian view must be accepted. If we were ever to find ourselves under the necessity of defining what degree of error in the faith and life of a Church must invalidate an otherwise valid ministry, debate would be endless, and practice in all probability chaotic. I cannot for a moment believe that the Committee desired to open the door to such confusion. I have no doubt, therefore, that in its references to the 'faith and life' of a Church in this connection it had in view nothing but the problem of intention.

Stated shortly it may be said that the presence in the Church of South India of numbers of ministers performing the full office of the priesthood without having received episcopal ordination and the expectation that as the area of union widened these numbers would be increased raised in Kirk's mind a doubt as to whether the Church of South India in its ordinations intended 'to do what the Church does', and consequently about the validity of their ordinations. This point, which he made clear in conversation was, unfortunately, not always made equally clear in writing.

It was obvious that the Resolutions of the Lambeth Conference on South India would have to be considered by the two English Convocations and, in January, 1949, Kirk seconded a motion proposed by the Bishop of Chichester asking for the appointment of a Joint Committee to do so. Kirk was himself appointed a member of the Joint Committee. He was the only Bishop of his way of thinking on the Canterbury Joint Committee, but the Chairman of the corresponding York Committee, the Bishop of Newcastle, Dr. Hudson, was of like mind, and they were ably supported by Lower House Representatives who included Dom Gregory Dix and the Dean of Chichester, the Very Rev. A. S. Duncan-Jones. The Joint Committees held a number of meetings in 1949 and the first quarter of 1950 which Kirk found very tiring and trying. There were certain members of the Joint Committees who were ardent and emotional supporters of the Church of South India and it was a hard struggle to obtain such a compromise as was likely to win wide acceptance. In March, 1950, he had one of his bad winter colds and it seemed unlikely that he would be well enough to attend the final residential session of the Joint Committees in April. This produced a cry from Dom Gregory:

Monseigneur!

Alas! What a business! But you *must* come to Birmingham. It will be "Macbeth" without Lady M. if you don't turn up. I have been slowly making up my mind that the thing to recommend is the *Interim Policy* continued—as a tribute to Wm. Temple! I can think of lots of arguments. That amounts to the "Standstill". I think a coalition of "Moderates" ("Hurray! We *still* needn't make up our minds") & Catholics with some diplomats could carry that in the Upper House. And if the election doesn't go against us—in the L.H. —but the Evangelicals are making strenuous efforts everywhere— & not mentioning South India in their addresses at all! But John D. will be violent against it. He is thinking—as I am—of the *English* Scheme—which will have to be published within 12 months.[1]

On April 1st. Kirk wrote to Dom Gregory:

Dear Gregory,

I am slowly getting better, but there seems no chance of my getting out of doors at present until the weather really alters . . .

I suppose you have had George Bell's draft Report? It is ever so much better than I feared; comparing it with the letters I have had from him, he really has behaved in a very Christian way. I have got a number of secondary points that I am putting in a letter, of which I will send you a copy as soon as possible. But two vital ones that occur to me are these:—

Page 12, seven lines from the bottom. He must expand what he means by "do not desire to avail themselves" i.e. that Hollis will desire to celebrate in the Cathedral on one Sunday, and in Mansfield College the next. You will see that he is not going to suggest that any such people should be allowed to celebrate in our Churches at all (that is point (2) on page 13).

Page 14, clause (6). This is the thing he is keenest on now, and he will fight hard. At present I am inclined to accept it, provided that (a) the words "as

[1] The reference here is to the Committee which produced the Report on Church Relations in England.

Visitors from Overseas" go in after "welcomed" in the second line; and "at the discretion of the Bishop" after "England" in the third.

The first of these amendments would prevent any analogy being drawn from our relation with C.S.I. to John Derby's idea of opening the doors to thousands of English Baptists and Congregationalists. The second would give us a real check if Hollis proposed to behave as suggested above; because the Bishop's discretion would come into play.

I shall also point out that the *caveat* in the case of a bishop unwilling to take the majority view must also be duplicated for the far more likely case of the bishop unlikely to take the minority view.

I do hope that subject to these and similar amendments, you will be able to accept the thing. If you can, I believe we should carry it in both Houses, and so get peace for five years at least. I am going to suggest to George that "not more than ten" would be better than "five".

Eventually Kirk was able to attend the meeting, and after it Dom Gregory wrote to him:

Monseigneur,

I think that I ought to send you a little line to say that on reflection I am quite sure that you brought us out of the business last week better than could have been hoped. (I put it that way because I think that is how the credit lies. Certainly not with me. I was tired & far from well & could not weigh things at all justly. I am going away to-morrow to sleep till the end of the week!) It has the 2 advantages we sought, I think—No mixed bathing, & no decision between "maj." & "min." And it leaves us quite untrammeled to fight Jacky's Scheme when it appears in Oct. Nov. (And it at last gets the words "South India" off the agenda for a bit.) Nevertheless, the whole issue of *principle* will come up on the English Scheme. But on that I think we shall fight on stronger ground.

Anyway, I think we all owe you a good many thanks & congratulations, & though there were mutterings among the Cath. proctors, I know they did admire your handling of it all.

I do hope you are better. This foul weather has completely got me down.

In May, 1950, it was possible for the Joint Committee to present a unanimous report to Convocation and for that report to be accepted after a short debate. It was widely recognized that a reasonable compromise had been reached, and also recognized, as the Archbishop of Canterbury said in a letter to Kirk, that the two men decisively responsible for it were the Bishops of Chichester and Oxford. Kirk did, himself, in his speech in the Upper House on May 24th repudiate the word 'compromise'. It was rather, he said, an attempt, and not a wholly unsuccessful attempt, to bring together, so far as they could at present be brought together, the principles of two groups whose outlook on the problems of reunion was in many respects very divergent. He regarded it as a victory for sanity, patience, charity and faith in God's over-ruling power, over the forces of narrow partisanship on all sides. This speech made a deep impression. It was not as Kirk had intended to make it for, as he explained in a letter to the Archbishop, he became aware almost at the last moment that unfortunate impressions had in some quarters been made, both by the Dean of Chichester's speech seconding the report in Full Synod, and by a speech by the Bishop of Derby in the Upper House. He therefore set himself to do what he could to mitigate the immediate situation and altered his prepared speech accordingly.

It is necessary to say a further word about finance. Kirk had in his Diocesan Magazine in March and again in December, 1949 appealed for subscriptions to the Special account which the S.P.G. had opened for South India. After the Convocation decisions of May, 1950, there was a move to get the S.P.G. to reconsider the position, and the Bishop of Chichester asked Kirk's support for an episcopal appeal to the S.P.G. In his reply Kirk said:

This perpetual "nagging at" S.P.G. (if you will forgive the expression) is only embittering the whole situation, and making it more difficult for us to bring folk together in quiet talk and prayer about it. I have strong and incontestable evidence to this effect. As a matter of expediency alone, I believe it to be a wholly false trail.

But I find it wrong in principle too. It is in danger of looking something like an organized attempt to bully Christians as conscientious as any others into betraying their convictions. As such it could easily be regarded as a complete abandonment of the policy of the Conclusion of our Report. We had a great deal of trouble reaching an agreed formula in that Conclusion; we don't want to run the risk of having it said that one side has torn up one of the most important sections of the Report.

A much more difficult question arose at the end of November, when the Bishops of Winchester, Chichester and Bristol sent a circular letter to the other members of the Bench, asking for their signatures to an appeal for financial help for the Church of South India. The division of opinion about the theological soundness of the South India Scheme necessarily carried with it a difference as to the nature and extent of financial and other support that could rightly be given to the new Church. Half a dozen carefully worded sentences in the Conclusion to the 1950 Report had put the two points of view. The proposed letter was an appeal to those who held one point of view, and it seemed, both to Kirk and to some other bishops, to overthrow the balance so carefully achieved. Kirk wrote to the Bishop of Chichester:

My dear Bishop,

The document you have drafted for publication in the "Times", though not going beyond the strict letter of the Joint Report and the Convocation debates, seems to me to be wholly discordant with the spirit which animated them. The Report took its final shape under the influence of a unanimous conviction that nothing must be done which would exacerbate the existing tension on this and allied subjects in the Church of England. Under that influence we suggested (1) a five-year moratorium in the theological debate and (2) an interim policy of mutual toleration as between diocese and diocese for the same period in regard to the status to be accorded in England to C.S.I. ministers episcopally consecrated or ordained at or since the Union. We also recorded (3), in objective and highly non-committal terms, two opposed conscientious views as regards the financial help that might fairly be expected to be extended to C.S.I. by Anglicans, and refrained from any attempt to discriminate between these views in respect of their legitimacy, reasonableness, or theological justification. Implicitly, here as in the two other matters, we called for a period of tolerance, quiet discussion, thought and prayer; in the hope that during that period the two sides would gradually come together without bitterness, and an agreed solution be found.

My own conviction is that if, during the standstill period, anyone reopens any of these three allied questions by pressing for decision or action in one sense or another, it will imperil all our hopes of resuming the discussion in five years' time in a more conciliatory and constructive spirit than hitherto, and may give rise to even greater tension than we have known so far. Your document urges those who hold one of the two opposed conscientious views I have mentioned to act upon it to the fullest extent and in one sentence at least it suggests that the view which you yourself hold has more claim on conscience than any others. This goes beyond anything suggested in the Report or decided by Convocation; and it will inevitably tempt those who hold the other view to assert it with equal vigour and publicity, and to lay full emphasis upon the fact that the Church at least has refused at present to adjudicate in any way between the two. If anyone succumbs to this temptation, it will reopen immediate discussion of all three points as to which our Report pleaded for postponement; and the responsibility for provoking this result must lie with the signatories of your letter. I foresee nothing but such an aggravation of whatever bitterness underlies the situation with regard to C.S.I. that no agreed solution will be possible—the Church of England will be irrevocably divided into two hostile camps, and no one can tell what the end of that will be. At all events the whole policy embodied in our Report and accepted by the Convocations will lie in ruins.

I plead most earnestly therefore that you do not proceed to make your document public. Its consequences will be disastrous to our joint hopes that five years' peaceful consideration will lead to a common mind in the matter. There is nothing from which I shrink more than the possibility that I may be forced to become a party to public controversy on the C.S.I. question; but if your letter is published I foresee that I may not be able to avoid being drawn in. So it is with a very heavy heart that I feel obliged to reserve the right to make public what I have here written to you. In certain circumstances I must be able to prove that I at least have pleaded for restraint and peace.

A fortnight later Kirk wrote again in answer to a reply from Dr. Bell which suggested that he had misunderstood the document and disclaimed any desire to question the interim policy of mutual toleration.

Dear George,

Many thanks for your letter of December 19th. I never for one moment questioned the good intention of the document you sent me. I was merely perturbed (as I still am) as to the increased divisive effect that it seems to me certain to have on the Church of England. That, I think, has been the trouble with the South India scheme from the beginning. As long ago as 1933 I was present at a meeting at which Bishop Palmer was told quite definitely that the Scheme as it then stood must jeopardise the supply of funds from S.P.G. to South India: his enthusiasm, I suppose, led him to ignore the warning.

In the same way, I cannot help feeling that many of us don't realise the degree of cleavage which has been caused in the Church of England by what has happened in South India, and the things that have been said about it on either side. That is why I plead for five years without public advocacy of questions in regard to problems either of principle or practice. But I won't cavil any more, at all events until I see your document in the final form in which it is printed.

Other bishops felt as Kirk did in this matter, and when the letter eventually appeared in *The Times* it lacked the signatures of the Bishops of London, Oxford, Ely, Exeter, Guildford, Truro, Blackburn, Bradford and Newcastle. The wording had, however, been distinctly altered from that originally sent to Kirk and he did not think it necessary to take any further public action.

In 1953 discussion of the theological issues raised by South India began again. Unofficial committees were set up by the Prolocutors of the two Lower Houses of the Convocations in order that there might be calm private discussion well in advance of the public reopening of the subject in 1955. The Bishop of Malmesbury made a special visit to South India and brought back to the committees a record of personal observation. Kirk was acquainted with much of this and from time to time took part in private discussion by groups of the clergy, but when early in 1954 new Joint Committees were set up to reconsider the

1950 decisions he asked to be excused from serving again, saying that he thought that fresh minds should be brought to bear on the problem. He was generally understood to have meant that at least one other episcopal member of the 1950 Joint Committees should similarly have declined to serve, or rather should not have been asked. It is not possible to say what attitude he would have taken if he had survived to be a member of the Convocation which met in July, 1955. It must be said, however, that at the time of his death in June, 1954, he had not moved far from the position of the Lambeth minority on the subject of the South Indian Orders.

The present writer had the privilege of fairly frequent conversations with Dom Gregory Dix and others involved in the South Indian controversy from 1942 onwards, and he was a member of the Canterbury Convocation in 1950 and 1955. He has no doubt that the policy of mutual toleration which Kirk secured in 1950 was the only one that offered any prospect of peace in the Church, and although the decisions taken in 1955 caused much distress in some quarters they were immeasurably better received than any similar decisions would have been in 1950. To that extent history has already justified Kirk's position. It can also be said that the pro-South India party consistently underestimated the disquiet which the scheme caused and the extent to which controversy about it soured and damaged the life of the Church of England. Those who prevented a full discussion of the Scheme in 1943 must bear much of the blame for this. Kirk could be a most irritating critic. He would wrap up major questions in apparently finicky points of language, and what appeared to be legalistic quibbles, but if his advice had been followed from 1943 onwards not only would there have been less bitterness and distress in England, but also much misunderstanding and consequent resentment would have been avoided in India.

IX

RELIGIOUS COMMUNITIES AND
THE WOODARD SCHOOLS

I

TRINITY SUNDAY, 1841, the day on which Marian Rebecca Hughes entered formally upon a life of consecration to God by taking the three vows of poverty, chastity and obedience, is generally reckoned as the date of the restoration of the Religious Life in the Church of England. Some fifty years later, at the Lambeth Conference of 1897, the revival received generous recognition from high ecclesiastical authority. It was now obvious that some *modus vivendi* between the Communities and the episcopate must be worked out, and various discussions led up to the outline of a formal scheme by the Lambeth Conference of 1930 and the suggestion that an Advisory Council should be established to deal with technical matters and to encourage incipient Communities. After further debate in the two English Convocations the *Advisory Council on Religious Communities* was set up in 1935 and held its first meeting on November 21st of that year. It consisted of six priests elected by the Communities together with six members appointed by the bishops, being "expert in questions connected with Community life". Kirk was one of the bishops' representatives from the start, though illness and other impediments prevented him from attending any meeting until February 10th, 1938, when, as Bishop of Oxford, he took the chair in the absence of the Chairman of the Council the Bishop of Wakefield. On Bishop Seaton's death later that year Kirk succeeded him as Chairman and from 1938 to his death in 1954 he attended all meetings, except on three occasions when he was prevented by illness, a striking testimony to the importance which he came to attach to the Council.

Kirk has himself described the early years of the Council's work:

I came to the Council originally with some little academic understanding of the principles of the Religious Life, but only the barest contact with the embodiment of those principles in the daily life and administration of modern Communities. My first reactions to its discussions, therefore, were that, although we were all using the same traditional terminology, there was a good deal of variety in the meanings we attached to words, and that (even when we were more or less agreed upon meanings) the circumstances of to-day gave many of the words concerned a very different connotation from that which they must have had a few centuries ago. In these respects it seemed clear that our difficulties were not without their parallels even in the Latin communion, in which of course the organization of the Religious Life is far more fully developed than in the Church of England.

Little by little we discovered that we were all groping in this same fog in the hope of finding solid meanings on which we could agree. The realization of this fact introduced a new feature into our work. We became more analytic in our approach to the problems submitted to us. These problems were of two kinds. In the former, we were called upon to advise in particular cases of difficulty, usually concerned with the interpretation and obligation of vows. In the latter, we were asked to review, if not even to advise upon, existing constitutions and statues with a view to their possible revision or expansion at some later date; or to help with their drafting of constitutions for Communities as yet in the experimental stage.

At first it seemed that what was needed was a glossary of the principal terms of the Religious Life, but it quickly became apparent that something more was required and so Kirk set the Council to work on a more ambitious project which issued in 1943 in the publication of *A Directory of the Religious Life*, a kind of guide book for the use of those concerned with the administration of the Religious Life in the Church of England. This work had no canonical authority, but it proved of the greatest importance in guiding the development of Communities new and old. Within ten years it had gone out of print, and the increased experience of the Council in that period also contributed to make a new edition necessary. In 1951 Kirk persuaded the Council to undertake this task. The new *Directory* was published in 1957, three years after his death, but he had seen and discussed in detail a major part of it. Of the first edition the late Dean of Wells, F. P. Harton, has written:

The work of drafting was, naturally, carried out by a committee of experts but Dr. Kirk took the chief part in its revision. No point was too small for his consideration, every sentence, almost every comma, was subject to his careful scrutiny, no less than seven complete drafts were made before he was satisfied and there is no section of the book which has not been improved by his hand.

In the years following 1938 Kirk very quickly added to his theoretical knowledge of the Religious Life a practical acquaintance with the problems of Communities. Of the eight Communities for men in the Church of England two are in the Oxford Diocese: one is the oldest of all, the Society of St. John the Evangelist at Cowley, the other is the Benedictine Community at Nashdom Abbey. During most of his episcopate there were also twelve or thirteen Communities for women, including one of the largest of all Anglican Communities the Community of St. Mary the Virgin at Wantage. In addition to his duties as diocesan Kirk was Visitor of the Society of St. John the Evangelist, of ten of the Communities for women in the diocese and of two outside it. The late Dean of Wells, who was for many years closely associated with him both as his Commissary for Religious Communities and as Secretary of the Advisory Council, has written:

One had only to assist him at a Visitation or the Installation of a Superior to realise how unusual was his understanding of the Religious Life and his wisdom in guiding it.

Kirk's own annual retreats were nearly always made in some Community House, for several years at Nashdom, and his piety and devotion always impressed those with whom he stayed. Sometimes he was able himself to take a Retreat for a Community, and the one which he gave at Nashdom in 1947 on the messages to the Seven Churches has left enduring memories. Of the address on Rev. ii. 10, the Abbot of Nashdom writes:

The reward, he said, of tribulation endured and responsibility exercised is greater responsibility. And, à propos of the gift of the crown, he went on to quote Henry V's speech "Upon the king!" in Act IV, scene 1. I think that in this passage Shakespeare must have spoken very meaningfully to the Bishop himself concerning the exercise of his own responsibilities. The address did not however convey the sense of the burdensomeness of responsibility (though that was there), but rather of the invigorating challenge it issues to the man who is charged with it.

These close personal contacts made the Communities feel that in the Chairman of the Advisory Council they had a bishop who really understood the problems of the Religious Life, and this made them all the more ready for the establishment of orderly relations between them and the episcopate. On the other side Kirk was able to give useful help to other bishops in problems arising in connexion with Communities in their dioceses. He was trusted although he could on occasion write sharply when a bishop was in his view troubling a Community unreasonably, as the following passage from a letter to another diocesan shows:

I frankly regret that you have not seen your way to deal with the matter by private administrative action. To raise an official controversy fraught with many dangerous possibilities at a time when the Church is already over burdened both with problems and with opportunities seems to me less than statesmanlike. What is at stake is the breakdown of the harmonious relations which have been developing between the bishops and the communities over the last generation.

In the nature of things much of Kirk's work for particular Communities cannot be told, at least in this generation, but the last word may be left to one who knew more of it than any one else:

As the theologian, teacher and bishop Kenneth Kirk has his place in the select company of the great, but in his work for the Communities he is unique. He was dealing with a new problem, the integration of the Religious Life in the Church of England, a task in which he had no predecessors and for which he alone possessed the necessary qualifications. The time is not yet ripe for an adequate appraisal of his success, but it is certain that all future administration will be built thankfully on the foundation he has so surely laid.[1]

2

The circumstances in which Kirk first became connected with the Woodard Schools do not appear to be known. He was admitted a Fellow of the Western Division on July 24th, 1924, but it seems unlikely that he took a very active part in things until some six or seven years after that. The affairs of the Western Division were, at that period, very much in the hands of the Provost, who was an elderly man of considerable means, and another of the Fellows who was a wealthy layman. Substantial expense was incurred in the erection of new buildings at a particular school, the only guarantee being promises of financial help from the layman who, unfortunately died suddenly without having made provision for this in his will. The Division faced bankruptcy and had to appeal to the whole Woodard Corporation. In 1932 a Western Administrative Committee was formed consisting of representatives of each of the Divisions with Kirk as chairman and there followed a period of very hard work and bargaining which

[1] Oxford Diocesan Magazine, August, 1954.

resulted in the complete overhaul of the finances of the Division and the administration of one of the schools, until eventually matters were placed on a sound footing. Those who survive of that committee are full of praise for the ability, shrewdness and firmness with which Kirk handled this very difficult situation. Most of his colleagues were laymen, and some of them men of long experience in business and administration, but all acknowledged their chairman's mastery. No doubt they were impressed by tricks such as his ability to write with both hands at the same time, or to follow the course of a discussion while drafting a memorandum on some other subject, but they recognized that there was also a real man of business capable of meeting any of them on his own ground.

Towards the end of 1936 Bishop Southwell announced that in the following year he would resign the office of Provost of Lancing which he had held for thirty years. The Woodard Corporation is organised in four Divisions, and at that time the Provostship of Lancing (head of the Southern Division) carried with it the Presidency of the whole Corporation. The choice of Bishop Southwell's successor was, therefore, a matter of more than usual importance, and it was, no doubt, the remarkable impression made by his work as Chairman of the Western Administrative Committee that caused Kirk to be chosen for this office. He was first elected a Fellow and Vice-Provost of the Southern Division with the intention that he should succeed to the Provostship when the Bishop's resignation took effect. In March, 1937, however, Bishop Southwell suddenly died, and Kirk had at once to assume the full duties of the office. On October 6th, he was formally installed by the Bishop of Chichester, as Visitor of the Society of St. Mary and St. Nicholas, at an impressive ceremony in Lancing Chapel attended by the Bishops of Lewes, Stafford, Pontefract and Taunton, and by representatives of all the sixteen Woodard Schools. In the same month there was published the first edition of his book *The Story of the Woodard Schools*.

Between March and October, however, Kirk had been nominated for election to the see of Oxford, and there were those who wondered how long the new Provost of Lancing would be able to continue in his office. In the end it proved to be for seven years, and they were years of extraordinary difficulty and strain. As Provost of Lancing he was Chairman of the Councils of the five schools of the Southern Division, and those were the ones most seriously affected by the war. Mr. R. C. Freeman, Clerk to the Woodard Corporation, has written of Kirk at that time:

How does a man, through seven years of slump and war, handle—I gather that is the word—a sprawling diocese and 'chair' the government of five public schools, none of them in Oxford and two of them forced to evacuate? He did so, attending most of their meetings and concerned that he could not more often visit the schools for more personal contact with staffs and pupils. What those years contained of strain to schools and those in them, alike, cannot be written here; it must suffice that when one could tell a School that the Provost would be at a Council meeting, one had told it that its own 'Winnie' was back in its London from somewhere or other. When it was necessary, at one school, to seek the personal indulgence in emergency of each of twenty masters separately, he said 'Of course, I must do that'. When I must have his guidance within my sphere of things, more than once after dinner, I, in a chair, had it from him, in his bed, to which his doctors had ordered him.

In 1944 Kirk felt that he must give up the Provostship of Lancing. He remained a Fellow of the Western Division and a member of the Corporation but no longer had direct responsibility for any of the Schools. On the appointment of his successor a somewhat difficult situation arose as the Provosts of the other Divisions were very senior persons and it seemed invidious that a new and junior Provost should take precedence over them as head of the whole Corporation. This matter was considered during the next two years when the statutes of the Corporation were being revised, and a change was made to allow the Presidency of the Corporation to be held by someone who was not a Divisional Provost. In 1946 Kirk was elected to be the first holder of this new office of President, and he held it until his death. Of this period Mr. Freeman writes:

Though he then had no direct contact with the Schools, his office was indeed no sinecure; for he seemed always to know up to date about all sixteen of them, and I think that Statute was well used which reads 'it shall be his special duty to advise every Provost upon all matters concerning his Division which the Provost shall refer to him.' Corporate Chapters increased both in stature and in humanity, for, great though his mind was, he properly enjoyed the good things of earth—good friendship, good company, good fare and a good story.

In 1952 he revised and brought up to date his *The Story of the Woodard Schools*, which Mr. Freeman describes as "the only really well-written book on that Foundation of a hundred years, and on every separate School within it".

As President Kirk drew the whole Corporation together and gave it a sense of its own prestige. In that office and earlier as Provost of Lancing his methods of chairmanship could be described at times as 'ruthless', but they were accepted because he was so often right, and because people realized his shrewdness and his complete dependability. His speeches and his sermons made a lasting impression on the boys and girls of these Schools as they did everywhere, and for the Woodard Corporation he was above all the right man in the time of need.

X

THE END

THE difficulties caused by the South India Scheme took up a great deal of Kirk's time in the years after the war, and he often longed, as many other Anglicans do, that the Church of England could be given a period of peace from this kind of controversy so that it might be free to devote more attention to the urgent tasks facing it in the fields of evangelism and reconstruction at home. In the years immediately following the 1950 decisions he began to consider changes that would have to be made in the diocese. His three suffragans were all older than himself. First the Bishop of Dorchester and then the Bishop of Reading had to resign on account of ill-health. Kirk began to surround himself with younger men, plans for church extension in the new housing areas around Oxford and in other parts of the diocese were brought to maturity, and there was much discussion about ways and means of making the Church more effective in the industrial south-eastern parts of the diocese. In 1953 he received an invitation to pay a second visit to the United States, an earlier visit in 1949 having been a great success and a welcome change. Since Lambeth 1948 he was being increasingly looked to by Catholic minded Anglicans all over the world.

Kirk was aware also of the approaching need for change in his own domestic arrangements. Most of his children had now left home and the house on Boar's Hill was much bigger than his needs. The retirement of Miss Harden in 1941 had been followed after an interval by the arrival of Miss N. F. Carter who remained with Kirk until his death. What he owed to her is difficult to express. To the duties of housekeeper at Sandridge and nurse in his frequent illnesses she added the functions of secretary and chauffeur. No-one who lived in the Oxford diocese in Kirk's last twelve years could think of the bishop without thinking of Miss Carter. Sandridge was, however, becoming increasingly difficult for her to manage, and in the summer of 1953, after several months' search, a move was made to No. 7 Rawlinson Road in North Oxford. Kirk began to speak in terms of another seven years of episcopate before retirement.

On Whit Sunday, 1954, the bishop celebrated pontifically in the

Cathedral at 11 a.m. as usual, and seemed in good health. On the next morning he carried out his customary Whit Monday Visitation of St. Stephen's House, bidding farewell to those of the students who were leaving to be ordained at Trinity. In the afternoon he did a little gardening at home but came in complaining of a pain in the stomach. It did not seem serious but he retired to bed and spent a restless and painful night. In the morning the bishop being still in pain Miss Carter sent for the doctor who, after an examination, decided to call in a specialist. At about 11 a.m. Miss Carter took up a hot drink and found the bishop out of bed sitting by the window. He tried to stand up but appeared to be seized by a violent spasm of pain and collapsed unconscious on the floor. An ambulance was summoned and he was taken to the hospital but he was probably dead before he left the house. It was Tuesday, June 8th. A post-mortem showed that the cause of death was the rupture of an aneurism in the aorta.

Shortly after his wife's death Kirk had drawn up detailed directions for his own funeral which was to resemble hers as nearly as possible. In 1943 he added a note to say that he had not at that time contemplated that a Sung Requiem might be desired in his own case, but that as this possibility had now arisen he placed on record that it would be in accord with his own wishes and that he would like it to follow as nearly as possible the form of the Solemn Requiem which he had himself sung at Christ Church on the occasion of the funeral of Dr. N. P. Williams. It was characteristic of him that, to these last details, all his affairs were in perfect order.

Accordingly his body, which had rested in the hospital chapel, was taken to the Cathedral at 9 p.m. on Thursday, June 10th, a continuous watch being kept by never less than ten people. At 11.30 a.m. next day a Solemn Requiem was sung by the Bishop of Exeter, Dr. Mortimer, and at 2.30 p.m. the Funeral Service was conducted by the Dean of Christ Church, the hymns being 'The King of love my Shepherd is' and 'Praise, my soul, the King of heaven' which Kirk had chosen on the occasion of his wife's funeral. The Cathedral was packed by over a thousand people for the service. At the end the clergy of the diocese, who were present, three hundred in number, left the building first and lined the whole south side of Tom Quad from the Cathedral doors to the College Gate. Outside hundreds of people stood on the pavements of St. Aldate's from Christ Church up to Carfax. It was a scene which none who were present are ever likely to forget, and an impressive testimony to the affection with which Kirk was regarded by the clergy and people of the diocese. He was buried next to his wife in the Christ Church portion of Osney Cemetery.

In some respects Kirk was a sad figure in his last years. His ill-health and the depressions resulting from it have been mentioned more than once, and the letters printed at the end of this volume giving a touching insight into his feelings during the last period of his episcopate. From the time of his wife's death he was a lonely man. His children could not supply what he had lost in her, and indeed their absence at boarding-school combined with his own ill-health and exceptionally busy life made it difficult to maintain the same intimate understanding which had existed in earlier days. The following letter written to one of his grandchildren shows at once the lighter side of him, but also a certain underlying sadness.

My darling Christopher,

There was once an elderly Bishop who had five sons and daughters, a son-in-law and a daughter-in-law. He went away from home; and they all came and stayed in his house—except one daughter, who was away in Africa. Now believe me or believe me not, he was away ten days or rather more, and NOT ONE OF THEM WROTE TO HIM. It's no good saying that they didn't know how to write, because he had paid a lot of money to have them taught; though between you and I (as your aunt Patricia will teach you to say), they still have a good deal to learn about grammar and spelling. If it hadn't been for kind Nanky's letters (and Joan has written from Africa) he wouldn't have heard anything about them—or about you and Richard either. So he founded a Quite Forgotten Association, and made himself President of it, and took a coat of arms which shewed an Absolute Blank rampant in a Total Void.

Ask your Mummy if she remembers an elderly grey-haired clergyman with a nice face who married her to your Daddy a few years ago. If she does, give her my love. She has seen me once or twice since then, but I daresay she has been too busy to notice me. Tell her I'm well and getting very fat, and say I hope you're all having a very happy time. So lots of love from Granpy. (President and Founder, Q.F.A.)

At Christmas and other similar occasions the family was drawn closer together, but gradually the children grew up and left home for work and for marriage. The advent of grandchildren, as the above letter shows, to some extent brought out again his great gifts for talking and writing to small children. The following extracts from a letter to one of his daughters on her engagement shows how he had to exercise the responsibilities of both father and mother:

My own darling,

As you will imagine, I have been thinking about you and M. a lot since Tuesday, and now I've got a minute or two to spare I'm going to put down on paper a few things that occur to me. They're all quite nice, so don't get alarmed.

(1) You're changing your career now; so there's no point in thinking of finishing at Oxford any more. Take your war-degree of course; but with that and what you know already you'll be equipped for school teaching on a modest scale if at any time you have to earn money once more. You can't ride two horses at once.

(2) I can't imagine any career more arduous than that of a parson's wife. So you've got to equip yourself for it as fully and as quickly as you can—and before you marry. That means not only cooking, dress-making, house management and so on; but also doing all in your power to be alert, business-like and effective. You're doing this last part already, keep on with it, and don't be afraid of self-discipline. How and when you're going to become expert in the first part I can't think; but it is frightfully important to get well ahead with it before the wedding. You mustn't treat M. as something to be experimented on: you've got to join up with him as a competent and trained mistress of his house.

(3) Take the utmost care of your own dress, complexion, hair and so on. There's nothing braces a man more than having a lady in tow on whose looks and appearance he can pride himself. You've got to keep yourself neat and tidy even when you are at work or alone, in order that you may get the habit firmly fixed . . . an attractive vicar's wife does a lot to keep a congregation happy, loyal and active.

(4) You may have a great deal to do in the way of advising M., making suggestions, and at times bullying him and taking decisions for him. (Remember that men like being bullied by their women folk, provided that it's done kindly and with a kiss at the end). Don't shrink from this. You'll never be a termagent or anything like it, thank God: but you've got to be a real companion and partner, pulling your full weight, and not just a housekeeper.

I'm not such a fool as to imagine that you haven't thought out all this for yourself; of course you have. But you might like to know that I've thought about it too; and if you can live up to it you'll only be doing for M., according to his needs, as your dear Mummy did for me according to mine. And it may help you to feel how happy I am about the whole affair, and how willing to give advice or answer questions whenever you think I can be of use that way. It's a very heroic thing to say that you will marry a man; I'm proud that you should have done it, and certain that you'll make a good job of it. But if ever you need it, remember that I'm standing by; and that anyone whose married life has been as happy as mine was has got a reserve of experience and a wealth of memories which may be of use to his children if they care to draw upon them.

And indeed they did draw upon him constantly when they needed his advice and help, and not they alone but also their friends. One of the most endearing of Kirk's traits was the real interest that he showed in the people whom he met. School-friends of his children who came on visits to Sandridge were always impressed by this, and some of them later wrote to him or came from long distances to see him and ask his

advice, because at their first meeting they had been made to feel his
interest in them. Nobody who visited Sandridge could fail to be
attracted by his kindness and quiet humour.

Kirk had many friends upon whom he relied greatly. There were
those with whom he had to do in the ways of theology and of Church
business, such as the present Bishop of Exeter, Dr. Mortimer, the Rev.
A. H. Couratin, Principal of St. Stephen's House, and the Rev. D. F.
Horsefield. There were also laymen such as Colonel Leslie-Melville,
Mr. R. F. Pawsey, with whom he went on several summer holidays,
Sir William and Lady Fitzherbert, and the husband and wife to whom
the letters printed on pp. 203-211 were written. There was also, down
to 1952, Dom Gregory Dix, whom Kirk himself described as "my
oldest and closest friend", and about whom Bishop Graham wrote the
following lines in 1948:

> How happy are the Oxford flocks!
> How free from heretics!
> Their priests securely orthodox,
> Their Bishop orthoDix.

Lines which might easily have been written by Kirk himself. We have,
however, already seen that he by no means always agreed with
Dom Gregory, and in the opinion of some who knew them both his
influence upon Gregory was as great as Gregory's upon him. Each in
his own way could be a delightful and amusing companion.

Nevertheless there were reserves which very few of Kirk's friends
penetrated. They were conscious of his loneliness and physical handi-
caps as well as of the irritating sides of him which occasionally
appeared. But among those who knew him best as well as among a
much wider group who only met him in the ordinary course of things,
the predominant impression was one of immense strength of character,
reliability and breadth of outlook. Men and women felt, and have said
so to the present writer more than once, that as long as Kirk was there
things could not go very badly wrong.

This was so in a wider sphere than the purely ecclesiastical, but it
was perhaps most obvious in the practical controversies that arise
from time to time in the life of the Church, and it is all the more
remarkable in that Kirk not infrequently disappointed those who
looked to him for leadership in debate in the assemblies of the Church.

The same oblique approach to problems which had characterized
him as a don persisted in some of his work as a bishop, and it weakened
his influence in such bodies as the Church Assembly, Convocation and

Bishops' meetings. One of his colleagues said to the present writer: "The bishops are for the most part simple pastoral men and they often could not follow the workings of Kirk's mind. He was always listened to with attention, but his method of approach often failed to carry his hearers with him." The story of the South India debates told in an earlier chapter of this book is an illustration of that weakness. In the matter of the reply to the Metropolitan's questions Kirk had important points to make, but they were wrapped up in what seemed to some to be verbal quibbles, and some who would have supported his main points were left confused. The Bishop of Ely, Dr. Wynn, complained that he and other bishops who thought like him and who looked to Kirk for leadership were more than once left in the dark as to what he wanted them to do.

Kirk was, in fact, always a man of independent mind and a widely catholic outlook. He was a convinced believer in the Catholicity of the Church of England as a whole and he wished to be a bishop of and to speak to the Church of England as a whole rather than to one section of it. He believed himself to be standing, in regard to the various reunion schemes as in other matters, for the maintenance of Catholic faith and order (he would not have separated the two) and he was most reluctant to take any action which might imply that he represented merely a group in the Church. He was a member of a London club in which he saw a number of the evangelical bishops meeting regularly to discuss common policy on some of the issues before the Church, and he was determined never to let himself be pushed, either by supporters or opponents into the position of being the leader of any such clique. He once said to a friend: "I am not going to let them (meaning the other bishops) put me in a corner as they did Michael Furse". He was frequently consulted by others but he would not lobby himself. In the course of one Convocation debate a bishop referred to "the Bishop of Oxford and his friends". Kirk immediately replied: "I have no friends". One of those who heard it remarked how pathetic it sounded, but in fact it represented Kirk's integrity and independence of mind. In the councils of the Church he spoke as the Bishop of Oxford, not as a party member or leader.

Yet in spite of this independence, this lack of party leadership, no English diocesan before or since has been trusted and looked to by high churchmen of all shades of opinion as Kirk was. The explanation is probably to be found in the fact that the heart of Anglo-Catholicism, in all its varieties, is a profound belief in what is sometimes called 'sacramentalism', or 'the sacramental system', as the divinely appointed means for the restoration of mankind to its lost union with God. The belief, that is, that the sacraments are the means whereby the effects of the saving work of Christ are applied to the individual soul, and the life of the Church is sustained. About Kirk's firm convictions in this matter there could never be a moment's doubt. His work in moral theology and ascetic theology with its special application to the sacrament of Penance, his teaching on the primacy of worship, and above all of Eucharistic worship, his defence of the Apostolic Ministry, his teaching about the sacrament of Holy Matrimony all bore witness to it. And it was realized that his convictions were based upon a knowledge and a power of mind which few could approach. There was about him a strength and a sureness upon which men came to know that they could rely, a strength supported by a supreme competence in all forms of ecclesiastical business.

When one surveys Kirk's thought and work as a whole there is most obviously plain a remarkable consistency not often found in human affairs. This consistency flowed from that belief to the examination of which he devoted his greatest book, the belief that 'the life of man is the vision of God', with its practical application in the primacy of worship. In worship he found the solution to the problem of self-centredness, and the central point of Christian moral theology. He believed that the primary purpose of the Church was to lead and train men to worship God. This belief, as has been shown in earlier chapters, was the basis of his criticism of the 1944 Report on Training for the Ministry, and it was also plain in a dozen other addresses, and in his recovery of the primitive conception of the bishop as a leader in worship. From at least one of his writings[1] it can be seen that it was the danger to the liturgical, God-centred worship of Catholic Christendom which prompted much of his criticism of certain schemes of reunion. It was largely through his understanding of the primacy of worship that he became the champion of those schools where education could be carried on in the atmosphere of Church worship, and that he was looked to as father, guide and protector by the Religious Communities whose life is based upon the call to be with God in constant prayer. The last paragraph of *The Vision of God* so clearly sums up this belief and its implications, and is in many phrases so near a commentary on Kirk's own life, that with it this biography may fittingly conclude.

But if any man presses the question, *What* should I renounce? or, *How* am I to deny myself? he must expect no other reply than to be directed to that life of prayer which consists in seeing God—in meditating upon the person of

[1] *Beauty and Bands.* pp. 138ff.

Jesus. Sympathetic understanding—always partial, but always progressive—of *His* renunciations and self-denials will help the Christian to know what he too must renounce, and wherein he too must exercise self-denial. The exigencies of life—ill-health, misfortune, claims beyond the ordinary upon his time, patience, initiative or endurance,—will appear to him no longer as burdens to be borne with resignation, but as providential calls for the heroic renunciation of joys and liberties which would otherwise be legitimate enough. He will not often have to look further afield. The light of divine knowledge vouchsafed to him in the life of meditation will throw into high relief these opportunities for other-worldliness which God sets in his daily path. The excellency of the knowledge of Christ Jesus the Lord will be for him a gaining Christ, a seeing God; and thereby he will attain a righteousness not of his own, not of an arbitrary law, but of God through faith. Through the power of the Risen Christ he will come to that fellowship in His sufferings and conformity to His death, in which the highest Christian self-renunciation must always consist. The spirit of worship will carry him forward along the *via crucis* so revealed to him, until through a spiritual death gladly accepted he attains, with the saints of God, to the resurrection from the dead.[1]

[1] *The Vision of God.* pp. 471ff.

SOME LETTERS

THE letters printed here were written during the last three years of the Bishop's life, but his friendship with John Henry and Dorothy, the husband and wife to whom they are addressed, went back to the latter half of the Second World War, when they were living in the Oxford diocese and met him when he came to consecrate the chapel at a Naval Establishment in the diocese. After the war they moved to a farm in Devon and there both the Bishop and some of his children often visited them. Dorothy had been partially paralysed for several years and later became incurably ill with cancer, the disease which is referred to more than once in the letters.

(September 25th, 1951.)

My dear John Henry,

Please forgive a type-written letter in answer to yours. I should be quite delighted to receive you as a candidate for confirmation.

As things stand one of my Assistant Bishops is taking pretty well all the West Berkshire confirmations this autumn, though I might manage to exchange with him so as to take a confirmation at Hungerford on the afternoon of Sunday, December 2nd at 3 o'clock. Or, again, I have a big one at Reading at 3 p.m. on November 24th, and another at Abingdon at 6 o'clock on November 25th.

On the other hand would it not be much better for you and Dorothy to come here for a night or two? Then we could have a quiet confirmation in my chapel in the early morning, followed by a Communion service at which you could make your first communion. I could arrange this almost any day, and, as the children have all gone back to school etc: there is plenty of room in the house and I am sure we could make you both comfortable. I think myself this might be much the best way, because we could cancel or alter the date at short notice, as suited you best. Of course there are a good many days on which I am running about a good deal, but not at 8 o'clock in the morning. What do you think about all this?

(October 10th, 1951).

My dear John Henry,

I'm delighted you & Dorothy will come Nov. 7th to 10th. So we'll consider that fixed.

Like a fool I have lost the letter in which you told me what books you have read. Do you know Gore's "Reconstruction of Belief"? I still think it's the best book I know for educated folk. His "Religion of the Church" is older, &

simpler, but very good; unfortunately I don't know whether it's still in print. I will try & think up some more. Edwyn Bevan's "Christianity" in the Home University Library is very good on first principles.

(February 20th, 1952.)

Dear Dorothy and John Henry,

I am so distressed at your grievous news, & do hope that you will get some reassurance from the doctors. You've been through so much, & been so brave about it, that it's dreadfully hard that you should have still more to bear. But I know that you *will* bear it with all your tried courage, & that the great love you have for each other & your clear faith in God will carry you through. I have you constantly in my thoughts and prayers, & so have Joan & Nancy Carter—the only two at home at the moment. God bless & keep you both in this troubling time, & give you happier days to come.

Please let me have any news as you get it; but don't make a burden of it.

(February 26th, 1952.)

My dear Dorothy,

Thank-you so much for your little note. We are praying for you earnestly— all in the house, & Pat & Joan send their dearest love. I can guess how you dread pain, & I do hope you may be spared any more. Will it help you a little if I ask you, even when you are suffering, to pray for three other friends of mine, who are also struggling very hard against great odds?

The first you know—that nice & loyal little man the *Bishop of Dorchester*. He has got chronic water on the lung, which gives him dreadful spasms every now & then, and (in strict confidence, for we are keeping it a dead secret at the moment) will have to give up work & live an invalid's life in a few months' time. He is completely broken by it, & very unhappy; & when we make the news public I shall ask you to send him a line of comfort.

The second is my closest & oldest friend, & the most brilliant man in the Church of England,—*Gregory Dix*. He had a major internal operation last year, & for a while everything seemed most hopeful (he stayed here with me for a week in November & was so bright & happy); now something—they don't quite know what—has gone wrong & there is a prospect of a series of more operations, all of them difficult & dangerous. He is being wonderfully brave, but is very weak & tired.

Then there is a very good parish priest of this diocese called *Harold Fallows*. He is down with bad blood pressure, & the doctors don't think he can live long; but if he comes out of hospital it will only be as a permanent invalid. He has a wife (no children); she is in a dreadfully unhappy way about it all & finds it very difficult to be bright & cheerful with him. He had just started in a new parish, & was doing brilliantly, with, as one hoped, many years of useful work before him.

Yes: & then there is the *Dean of Christ Church*—who was Vice-Chancellor till September, & then went on a Commonwealth Commission to visit Universities in India & Pakistan. He has had to break off his Indian tour, & has just got home—suffering from 'thrombosis of the brain' they say. I don't know much about it, as I've been rather tied down at home & haven't been able to see him & the doctors aren't saying much. A very capable, likeable man, not more than fifty—it will be dreadful if he has to resign, but I suppose it might well come to that.

I thought that, sad tho' this letter is, you might like to know about some of the people with whom I have you in my prayers. And it may help you a little when you are downhearted to pray for them too. They haven't had anything like your long years of suffering & courage; but they are all being very brave & are in need of all the help of prayer.

God bless you & John Henry; I'm anxiously waiting for more news. Unless you tell me not to, I'm keeping my promise to accept your invitation to visit you after Easter. How nice of you to repeat it in your letter.

(March 3rd, 1952.)

Dear Dorothy and John Henry,

You will imagine how your last distressing news affected me, I can just a little guess how terrible a blow it has been for you both. So I won't say anything more about it—for anything I said might make things more difficult. Let me tell you a little about my own experience. It's almost eighteen years since my Beatrice died—she had some mysterious poison in her system which didn't worry us much, tho' in what proved to be her last few months it made her very tired & listless, & I couldn't understand—nor could she—what was the matter. But the end came with a sudden attack of pneumonia—once more a mystery, for it was a lovely warm May day when she fell ill. She fought it for 3 weeks, & then her heart quietly failed early one Sunday morning. What I want to tell you most is that in all these years since then I have never thought of her as far away; she is very near, and very happy, & her happiness spreads back into this world & helps me constantly & wonderfully when the bad patches come. I've never felt anything like this in the case of friends who have died—they are like people who have gone to other jobs, so to speak; but Beatrice & I are sharing our married life as much now as ever. Of course it's been dreadfully lonely sometimes; but the lonely stretches only make the joy of her nearness more rich & inspiring every time when it comes back—as it always does.

It *is* good of you not to put me off coming to you after Easter, & I have it all booked up. But of course if it interferes with your plans at all you must let me know; anyhow I mean to come and see you, if only for a short time. Joan & Pat send their warmest love, so does Nancy. We think of you both continually.

Do forgive this rambling letter. But I saw a chance of writing this morning (the last week has been very heavy going), and thought any letter would be better than none at all. Please don't feel bound to answer—drop me a line from time to time to say how things are with you both.

(May 6th, 1952.)

My dear Dorothy and John Henry,

It's almost silly to say 'Thank you'. I just want to say that I loved every minute of it, & shall have it as a vivid memory till, I hope, the end of my life. I didn't feel myself a 'guest', or think of you as 'my hosts', at all—it was just friendship flowing all around one—around *us*, I hope you'll let me say. But 'Thank-you' all the same for all the happiness of the weekend. You have given the house an incomparable atmosphere. I cannot think it will ever lose it.

Here at Teignmouth there are little boys everywhere, delightful little animals—they snored & kicked & tossed & talked in their sleep all night in the dormitory next to my room. Nancy & I go over to see my old aunt at Torquay this afternoon. I expect we shall have to drift back to Oxford on Thursday as things seem to be piling up at home, & there are one or two storm clouds gathering. But nothing that can't be dealt with, so far.

God bless you both, my very dear friends. I have been thinking that we might have talked more about the Holy Spirit. It is a wonderful truth that He is within us, a living creative Person; & that, however much we limit & confine Him, He is ready to take full possession of us when we call on Him—"Come, Holy Ghost, our souls inspire, and lighten with celestial fire" is a lovely prayer; and when one finds it most difficult to realize God's presence & love, it seems to get an immediate answer every time it is raised. I wish I knew more about this mystery; I am sure it is very full of strength & comfort. I am trying to write something about it, but it is very hard.

You know all my hopes and prayers for you both. May you give as much help & happiness to everyone who comes to L. as you have done to Nancy & me.

(May 27th, 1952.)

My dear Dorothy and John Henry,

It was so nice to get your letter. Gregory's death is a sad blow to many of us; but he had a happy and wonderful end. In the last few hours there was no pain; he knew he was about to die; but he saw quite a number of friends (alas, I did not get there till an hour after he died); he helped at least two people with much needed spiritual advice; & he even interviewed his publisher. I met quite a number of those who had been with him during those hours; it was clear that he had made them even happier at the end than during his lifetime—and he had always spread happiness. He was one of the saintliest people I have ever known, & though he died young the mark he left on the Church of England will live for a long time.

I am so happy you have had such a good report from the doctor; it must be a great joy to you both. I have had a very busy time since I last wrote— very few days with less than twelve hours work and travel. But the weather has been a great joy, though we have had some very hot days . . .

I have got a new Bishop of Dorchester, & now there are all the wearisome formalities to go through with the Archbishop & the Crown before any announcement can be made. He is only in the forties, but quite distinguished; I have worked with him a good deal in the past, and like him very much. He's very much what I want.

I'm afraid the present Bishop is really very poorly. The slightest exertion is in danger of upsetting him, & I shall really be relieved when he gets into his new house at Cheltenham. It's a tragic business for him, & he's feeling it very much.

I must stop now & go to bed. My very best love. I was ever so much better for the holiday, & look back on it with the greatest pleasure.

(August 6th, 1952—written from Tissington.)

Dear Dorothy and John Henry,

I'm really on my holiday now—800 feet above sea level, in a beautiful Tudor house; lots of food (my host & hostess have a small home farm) flowers everywhere, and an adorable little Norman church. I've told you about the friends I am staying with, I think—he is 78 & she not much younger, & they just live for their garden. So when the weather is steady, I get good walking on the hills; & when it's unsettled (as it is at present) I weed & dig between showers. I'm beginning to feel a few muscles coming back, but I get stiff all over by nightfall. It's a wonderfully friendly house—as friendly as yours— Indeed H. L. & Tissington are the most welcoming places I know.

I think of you both constantly, and pray that God is keeping you in all peace and love. You must find life hard at times, but your splendid faith gives you the strength you need. God bless you both, now and always.

I have been thinking a good deal lately about the nearness of God. I fancy we don't quite realize how differently people speak about it, all meaning the same thing—"I've found a friend in Jesus", "The heavenly Father leadeth me", "I am filled with the Spirit"—all these mean the same thing, that we know God is as near as anyone can be. It's mainly a matter of upbringing, aesthetic preference in use of language, temperamental difference (emotionalism versus intellectualism) & so on—as in musical or artistic matters of choice. In every case, the ultimate vindication of the nearness of God is in Revelation & the Gospel; & this would be said even by those who speak in terms of immediate experience if they were challenged to exonerate themselves from the charge of self-hypnotism or hallucination. The essential fact is that God *is* near, and whether we think of this as a matter of experience or of faith makes little difference—it is in fact based upon both. But as long as one teaches oneself to remember it constantly, & not simply to strain after it in time of need, all will be well . . .

(October 15th, 1952—written from London.)

Dear Dorothy,

Nancy has sent me on John Henry's letter. I am so happy that you are feeling stronger—I hope the mouth is better too.

o

This is just to say how nice it is to know that you will have us again—
I shall look forward to it very much, as I've been rather full of throat trouble
lately. I will of course gladly anoint you again & I hope it will make for
happiness, strength & peace. I will bring the oil with me, & also the book about
the Reformation that I promised. I'm having a weary time with meetings in
London, & it's a pleasant break to have got a minute or two in which to write
to you . . .

(February, 6th, 1953.)

My dear Dorothy and John Henry,

I have been meaning day after day to write to you, but have continually
put it off. Three weeks ago I went down with influenza & a temperature, &
though I only had a few days in bed, I've had a poorish time since, with one of
those coughs that won't go. Luckily, I've had very few engagements of the
Committee & interview kind, & not many services; but this has had its bad
side too, for though it has spared my voice, it means that I have seen very few
people, & with the children all away (or at best only home from late at night to
early morning) it has been pretty lonely. I get out for a short stroll in the sun
each morning when there is any sun, but that's about all. So I haven't been
able to go shopping & see about that three-volume Bible & other books that
you might like. Next week I have to be in London—I'm not looking forward
to it much, but it can't be helped.

Dear both of you, it's been such a comfort to know that your prayers are
with me; & even when I've been pretty off colour it's always helped to spend
a few minutes praying for you.—Nancy has been wonderful. There were three
days when she was worse than I was, but she carried on as somehow I can't;
& though she's dreadfully tired & has a bad cold, she gives her whole life to
her many jobs: including nursing me. She spares herself nothing.

How selfish it is of me to take up time just writing about my own little
physical troubles. But you mustn't think I mind them very much; what
worries me is the possibility that I may not be able to do what's expected of
me on any occasion. And of course to worry about that is just to give way to
faithlessness. So I'm trying very hard to keep cheerful & resist anxiety.

I do hope all goes well with you both. I came across a new anecdote that
I hadn't read before the other day. Someone said to one of Drake's sailors that
he didn't seem to have profited much by all his sea-faring; & he answered
"No, but I have served the finest Captain who ever sailed the seas!" I think
that's a nice spiritual tonic at times when one is depressed.

Lots of love to you both, & my ever-constant thoughts. Nancy sends all
love too.

(April 1st, 1953.)

Dear Dorothy and John Henry,

So many thanks for your letter. I started to write to you for Easter last
Sunday, & then something happened (I forget what) & that was that. However,

I have a little time now, & hope to get this letter finished without interruption. What wonderful weather you have been having!—we have had a lot of sun, but I have only been able to sit out in the garden once— & then for a short time only. This last week-end the weather has broken; we have been having cold gales, with a good many rainstorms . . .

I'm ashamed to write about myself, so I'll just say that I haven't quite managed to throw off either the physical or the spiritual lassitude which set in after the influenza. But I really hope & believe it's going away slowly, & in the meantime I have put in as heavy a couple of months' work as I can remember. I have been praying for you both every day, & I was very glad to get first-hand news of Dorothy from C. R. when I met her at confirmation the other day. But I'm sorry to hear the migraines have reappeared, & that the mouth is still sore; & the other disability about which you write is annoying & painful but I hope it's really better now. God bless you both & increase the wonderful peace & courage you show in all things.

I'm most interested in your friend from Buckfast & shall look forward to meeting him. I know no one more helpful than a really good monk—Roman or Anglican—they have such a wonderful background of an organized devotional life, & their reading always amazes me. How they find time to cultivate their refined, peaceful, & deep lives is a miracle beyond my understanding.

I have been re-reading the "Pilgrim's Progress" with great profit & interest lately, & am getting more & more puzzled by the difference of the two parts. The story of the first is so dramatic, that of the second (as it seems to me) so dreary; the characters of the first are astonishingly real & vivid, though ob-viously mere personifications of virtues & vices; those of the second are real people, drawn on the large scale, & in the end more satisfying, though you have to dig deep into them to get to know them. My point is that Talkative & Worldly Wiseman are diverting caricatures, but Greatheart, Standfast & Valiant-for-Truth are genuine flesh & blood. What happened to Bunyan between his writing the first & second parts? . . .[1]

(June 8th, 1953—written from Westcote, Gloucestershire.)

My dear Dorothy and John Henry,

Here I am (& have been since the Coronation) at my little Convent in the Cotswolds. It has been delightfully restful so far, & though I have to go back for a day or two (I have the Diocesan Conference on Wednesday, & also want to see how furniture & books are fitting into the new house) I hope to relax again before the end of the week. Nancy, I imagine (for I have not heard from her) has been hard at the move since 8.30 last Thursday morning; I only hope that she hasn't tired herself out.

Well, I got to the Coronation, & wonderful it was. I had the luck to be offered a bedroom in a very hospitable Almshouse in Rochester Row, & that

[1] Cf. Oxford Diocesan Magazine, 1953. pp. 121-123, 137-140, 153-156.

made a lot of difference. We allowed four or five hours for the journey up, having heard terrible tales about traffic blocks, but in fact there was much less on the roads than usual, & whatever may have been the condition in the processional area, south of Victoria Street everything was sub-normal. This was equally so on Tuesday—within five minutes of leaving the Abbey on the south side I saw three taxis gently cruising unoccupied, looking for passengers. My host, the Warden of the Almshouses, was hospitality itself—he is one of the principal Stewards in the Abbey, & was on duty from 4.30 a.m.—so I got up at 6, was given an admirable breakfast at 7.0, & was comfortably in my place by 8 a.m. The Abbey was beautiful beyond words—they had blocked off all the aisles (making passages & rest-rooms of them) by partitioning up the arcades as high as the top of the choir screen; above the partitions & over the aisles were the tiers of seats for the thousands who couldn't be accommodated on the ground floor. All the partitions were hung with blue & gold tapestry (damask? brocade?), & the blocking of the aisles concealed all the dreadfully second-rate eighteenth & nineteenth century monuments to nonentities which are usually such an eyesore. So the Abbey looked as it may have looked in the greatest days of medieval splendour.

I won't tell you about the service, for you have read all about it. The stage-management of the ceremonial could have been tightened up a bit without any loss of dignity or solemnity, especially during the homage—but there was not the slightest noticeable hitch or uncertainty. The queen was every inch a queen, & went through it all with astonishing grace. The weight (& heat) of her golden robes & St. Edward's crown must have been overwhelming (high power arc-lights were beating down on her from every angle) & for much of the time she was encumbered with sceptre & rod as well, but she showed no sign whatever of fatigue. I was within 8 feet of her all the time she was in St. Edward's chair, & not more than a cricket pitch from the throne itself, so no one could have been better placed. In fact, in the foreground of pictures of her in the Chair you will have noticed an admirable close up of my bald head, together with the bald heads of several other elderly bishops.

The only thing I hadn't bargained for was that the amount of standing (in court shoes) during the ceremony might be too much for my phlebitic legs, ankles, & feet. It nearly was, & I was definitely tottering at the end. However they let the bishops out tolerably early (I was back at the Almshouses by the time the Queen left the Abbey), & I made for the refreshment room in the Church house, where I took my shoes off (as did other bishops) & had three small whisky & sodas in quick succession at her Majesty's expense. After a pleasant little buffet lunch I walked the half-mile to my night's lodging, rang up Nancy, & we could have started home by 4.30. In fact we had tea with my host & his housekeeper, & started at 5.30. The roads were as empty as ever (no lorries & very few buses) & we were easily home by 8.0. p.m.—to spend our last night at Sandridge. I would not have missed it for the world, even though I have had to keep my legs up for most of the last four days.

All this is very superficial, but it was time I reported again. The treatment is certainly doing me good (though not quite so quickly as the doctors had led me to expect), and I am quite equable in mind. I do hope all goes well with you, & that you are getting the upper hand over your migraines. God bless you both, & give you every happiness until we see each other again.

SELECT BIBLIOGRAPHY

THIS list does not profess to include all the articles and reviews that Kirk wrote. A complete bibliography is being prepared by the Rev. Francis Frost in connexion with his study of Kirk's Moral Theology, and it is to be hoped that it will eventually find a publisher.

1909: *Indian Students in England: Another Point of view.* In *The Nineteenth Century* for October.

1911: *The Christian Practice of Prayer.* S.C.M. Press.

1917: *When the Priests Come Home.* Chapter XVI of *The Church in the Furnace,* edited by F. B. Macnutt. Macmillan & Co., Ltd.

1918: *A Study of Silent Minds.* S.C.M. Press.

1920: *The Way of Understanding.* S.P.C.K.
Some Principles of Moral Theology and their application. Longmans, Green & Co., Ltd.
Moral Theology, no. VI of Annotated Lists of Books on Religion and Theology, edited by F. Underhill. A. R. Mowbray & Co., Ltd.

1921: *Moral Theology, Some lessons of the Past. Theology,* January, pp. 3-13; February pp. 58-67.
Review of O. D. Watkins, *A History of Penance. Theology,* July, pp. 47-49.

1923: *God made Man.* In *The Report of the Anglo-Catholic Congress of 1923.* Society of SS. Peter and Paul.
The Christian Moral Ideal. Congress Books no. 20. Society of SS. Peter and Paul.

1924: Review of *Moral Theology* by F. J. Hall and F. H. Hallock, in *Theology,* May, pp. 285-289.

1925: *Ignorance, Faith and Conformity.* Longmans, Green & Co., Ltd.
Review of *A Handbook of Moral Theology* by A. Knock and A. Preuss, in *Theology,* January, pp. 53-55.
Four Cases of Conscience. Theology, July, pp. 24-31; August, pp. 76-85.
Magic and Sacraments. Theology, December, pp. 319-338.

1926: *The Atonement.* In *Essays Catholic and Critical.* S.P.C.K.

1927: *Conscience and its Problems.* Longmans, Green & Co., Ltd.
On Calvary. In *The Report of the Anglo-Catholic Congress of July, 1927.* Society of SS. Peter and Paul.

1928: *The Evolution of the Doctrine of the Trinity.* In *Essays on the Trinity and the Incarnation.* Longmans, Green & Co., Ltd.
The proposed New Rubric on Fasting Communion. Theology, July, pp. 10-17.

1931: *The Vision of God.* Longmans, Green & Co., Ltd.
Sermon preached in Bristol Cathedral before the University of Bristol at the Commemoration of the Founder.

1932: *Foreword* and *The Challenge to Morals.* In *The Report of the Second Anglo-Catholic Priests Convention.* The Catholic Literature Association.

1933: *Marriage and Divorce.* Centenary Press.
The Threshold of Ethics. Skeffington & Sons, Ltd.
The Fundamental Problems of Moral Theology.
Truth. In *The Report of the Oxford Movement Centenary Congress.* The Catholic Literature Association.
Conscience and its Problems, 2nd edition. Longmans, Green & Co., Ltd.
Review of *Christian Marriage,* by G. H. Joyce, in *Theology,* October, pp. 225-229.

1934: *The Vision of God.* Abridged edition. Longmans, Green & Co., Ltd.
Personal Ethics (edited). Clarendon Press.
Loyalty to the Church. In *The Church of God* edited by E. L. Mascall. S.P.C.K.

1935: *The Fourth River and Other Sermons from the Bible.* Skeffington & Sons, Ltd.
St. Paul's Parable of the Missing Heir. In the *Church Times,* January 4th.
The Church and Marriage. In the *Church Times,* September.

1936: *The Crisis of Christian Rationalism.* Longmans, Green & Co., Ltd.
Conscience and its Problems, 3rd edition. Longmans, Green & Co., Ltd.

1937: *The Epistle to the Romans.* Clarendon Press.
The Story of the Woodard Schools. Hodder & Stoughton, Ltd.

From December, 1937 to October, 1954 with only one or two exceptions the Oxford Diocesan Magazine contained an article of importance by Kirk. Some of them were later issued as pamphlets and those alone are listed here.

1938: *The Virgin Birth of Our Lord*. A. T. Broome & Son.

1939: *The Study of Theology*. Edited by Kirk and containing an Introduction and a chapter on *Moral Theology* by him. Hodder & Stoughton, Ltd.

1940: *The Menace to Faith*. Oxford University Press.

1941: *The Atonement and the War*. A. T. Broome & Son.

1943: *A Directory of the Religious Life* (edited). S.P.C.K.

1946: *The Ministry of Absolution*. Dacre Press.
  Church Dedications of the Oxford Diocese. Clarendon Press.
  The Apostolic Ministry, edited by Kirk and containing an Introduction and a chapter on *The Apostolic Ministry* by him. Hodder & Stoughton, Ltd.

1947: *Marriage Discipline in the Church of England*. A. T. Broome & Son.

1948: *Conscience and its Problems*, 4th edition. Longmans, Green & Co., Ltd.
  Marriage and Divorce, 2nd edition. Hodder & Stoughton, Ltd.

1949: *Lambeth, Reunion and South India*. A. T. Broome & Son.

1950: *The Coherence of Christian Doctrine*. S.P.C.K.

1952: *The Story of the Woodard Schools*, 2nd edition. Abingdon, The Abbey Press.

1955: *Beauty and Bands and Other Papers*, prepared by E. W. Kemp, and containing a number of articles extracted from the Oxford Diocesan Magazine. Hodder & Stoughton, Ltd.

INDEX